The Parisian Sans-Culottes
and the French Revolution
1793-4

The Parisian Sans-Culottes
and the
French Revolution
1793-4

BY

ALBERT SOBOUL

CLARENDON PRESS · OXFORD
1964

Oxford University Press, Amen House, London E.C.4

GLASGOW   NEW YORK   TORONTO   MELBOURNE   WELLINGTON
BOMBAY   CALCUTTA   MADRAS   KARACHI   LAHORE   DACCA
CAPE TOWN   SALISBURY   NAIROBI   IBADAN   ACCRA
KUALA LUMPUR   HONG KONG

English translation by
GWYNNE LEWIS

Printed in Great Britain by
The Camelot Press Ltd., London and Southampton

CONTENTS

ABBREVIATIONS

A.D.S.   *Archives du département de la Seine*

A.N.   *Archives nationales*

A.P.P.   *Archives de la Préfecture de police*

B.H.V.P.   *Bibliothèque historique de la Ville de Paris*

B.N.   *Bibliothèque nationale*

B.V.C.   *Bibliothèque Victor Cousin*

INTRODUCTION

BOURGEOIS REVOLUTION AND POPULAR MOVEMENT

The Problem

THE French Revolution, together with the English revolutions of the seventeenth century, marks the culmination of a long economic and social evolution which brought the bourgeoisie to power.

This fact, which today might appear commonplace, had been recognized as early as the nineteenth century by historians particularly conscious of the role of the bourgeoisie in France. Guizot, seeking to justify the Charter through history, thought that the advent, rise, and ultimate triumph of the bourgeoisie was one of the most distinctive features of French society. Between the lower classes and the aristocracy, they had slowly constructed the framework and outlined the ideas of a new society consecrated in the Revolution of 1789: 'Everyone is aware of the important part which the Third Estate has played in France,' wrote Guizot; 'it has been the most active and the most decisive element in French civilization, that which, in the final analysis, has determined its direction and character. Considered from the social standpoint, and in its relationship with the various classes which co-existed in our land, what has been called the Third Estate has progressively expanded and elevated itself, and, at first, powerfully modified, then overcome, and finally absorbed, or very nearly absorbed, all the others.'[1] Guizot, then, identifies the Third Estate with the bourgeoisie. After Guizot, Toqueville emphasized the gradual increase in power of the bourgeoisie, speaking with 'a kind of religious terror . . . of this irresistible revolution which, striding for so many centuries across every obstacle, is advancing today into the middle of the destruction which it has wrought'.[2] Taine has

[1] *Histoire de la civilisation en France depuis la chute de l'Empire romain* (1828–30), 4 vols. in-8⁰, 46th essay, p. 592 of the 1839 edition, 1 vol. in-8⁰.

[2] *De la démocratie en Amérique* (1836–9), complete works, t. I, 1951, Introduction, p. 4.

also outlined this slow ascent of the bourgeoisie up the social ladder, at the top of which inequality becomes intolerable: 'Since the nobility, having lost a particular capacity, and the Third Estate, having acquired a general capacity, find themselves on equal terms as far as education and aptitudes are concerned, the inequality which separates them has become offensive in becoming useless.'[3] But, convinced that the origin and advancement of the bourgeoisie could be attributed primarily to the emergence and subsequent development of personal wealth, followed by the growth of commercial, then industrial ventures, these historians hardly bothered to make an exact study of the economic causes of the Revolution, or of the social classes responsible for its direction.

As early as the revolution period, however, Barnave had studied the question more closely. Having lived in the Dauphiné when, according to the *Inspecteur des manufactures* Roland writing in 1785, the number and variety of its industrial enterprises had made it one of the most important provinces in the kingdom, Barnave came to realize that 'industrial' property might provide the key to the problem of succeeding to the political inheritance of a class intent upon retaining power itself. In his *Introduction à la Révolution française*,[4] having laid down the principle that property 'exerts an influence' upon the creation of institutions, Barnave concluded that those institutions created by, and for, the landed aristocracy retarded the dawning of a new era: 'As soon as the lower classes of society begin to take an interest in Art and Trade, creating a new medium of wealth within the range of the ordinary man, a revolution begins to operate in the political laws; a new distribution of wealth leads to a new distribution of power. Just as the possession of land elevated the aristocracy, so industrial and personal property elevates the power of the people' (meaning the bourgeoisie).[5] Barnave clearly explained the antagonism between landed property and personal property, emphasizing the conflict between the classes founded upon these two forms of ownership. These ideas were taken a stage further during the first half of the nineteenth century by socialist utopians, and forcibly underlined

[3] *Les origines de la France contemporaine. L'Ancien régime* (1876), book IV, Ch. III, p. 412.
[4] *L'Introduction à la Révolution française* was published in 1843 in tome I of Barnave's *Œuvres* edited by Bérenger de la Drôme. Jean Jaurès emphasized the importance of this work in his *Histoire socialiste*, Vol. I, p. 98.
[5] *L'Introduction à la Révolution française*. 1st part. Ch. III, p. 13.

by Marx and Engels in the *Communist Party Manifesto* of 1847, which explained that at the end of the eighteenth century the feudal system of land tenure and the methods of agricultural and industrial production no longer corresponded to the rapidly expanding forces of society, but were, in fact, just so many obstacles to economic development: 'It was necessary to break these chains,' wrote the authors of the *Manifesto*. 'They were broken.'[6] Jean Jaurès, influenced to a certain extent by historical materialism ('to a certain extent' only, since he had written in his General Introduction that his interpretation of history would be 'materialistic with Marx, but at the same time, mystical with Michelet'), recreated, on one huge canvas, the economic and social substructure of the history of the Revolution—his *Histoire socialiste* is still an eloquent and valid testimony to this achievement.[7] 'Involved in the feverish struggles of assemblies and political parties,' Jaurès was well qualified, as Albert Mathiez suggests in his preface to the 1922 edition of the *Histoire socialiste*, 'to bring to life the emotions, the concise or obscure thought of the revolutionaries'. 'We know', wrote Jaurès, 'that economic conditions, the mode of production and the form of ownership constitute the very foundations of history.' But perhaps Jaurès's work errs on the side of oversimplification: the Revolution appears to unfold too smoothly—its origins lie in the economic and intellectual power of the bourgeoisie who have reached maturity; its outcome is the consecration of this power in the law. But this interpretation does not explain why the Revolution should have taken place when it did, nor why it should have been so violent in character, making it one of the most dramatic struggles in the history of the bourgeoisie.

Albert Mathiez, taking Jaurès's work a stage further, made a detailed study of a subject which had already attracted the attention of Phillipe Sagnac—the problem of the aristocratic reaction in the eighteenth century reaching its climax in the years 1787–8, to which Mathiez has given the rather ambiguous title: *révolte nobiliaire*. The expression is used to describe the stubborn opposition of the nobility to every attempt at reform and—of even greater importance—the monopolization of all the offices of the State by a privileged minority: in fact, the obstinate refusal of the aristocracy

---

[6] See, in particular, the first part of the *Manifesto*, 'Bourgeois et prolétaires'.
[7] *Histoire socialiste*, 4 vols. in-8°, n.d. (1901–4).

to share its pre-eminence with the upper bourgeoisie.[8] This opposition on the part of the aristocracy largely explains the violent character of the Revolution, and why the accession of the bourgeoisie to power was not the result of a progressive evolution, but of a sudden and fundamental change.

The dramatic upheavals of the Revolution cannot be explained, however, by the resistance of the aristocracy alone. The question of the rapid disintegration of the Third Estate has to be considered, a point upon which Jaurès and particularly Mathiez have quite rightly insisted. The conflicts which emerge between the different strata of the bourgeoisie, as between the bourgeoisie and the craftsman and shopkeeper element of the sans-culotterie, illustrate the complexity of revolutionary history. Albert Mathiez succeeded in distinguishing four successive revolutions—the last, on 2 June 1793, aiming at the establishment of social democracy. Without going into the details of these four divisions (the Revolution is, after all, a single historical event and remains essentially bourgeois for all its sudden changes of fortune), we must, however, emphasize the importance of Mathiez's work in so far as it concerns our immediate study.

Georges Lefebvre turned from Paris and the big cities, which had hitherto monopolized the attention of historians, and concentrated on the peasantry—an important and neglected aspect of revolutionary history, particularly when we consider that at the end of the eighteenth century France was essentially a peasant country. Until Lefebvre, peasant activity had been regarded as a repercussion of movements originating in the cities, directed mainly—with the sanction of the bourgeoisie—against feudalism and royal power: in this way the revolution of the Third Estate retained both its homogeneity and its majestic continuity. Beginning with detailed social analyses, Lefebvre showed that within the framework of the bourgeois revolution a separate revolutionary current had developed which was specifically peasant in its origins and evolution.[9] Apart from his own significant contribution to

[8] Albert Mathiez, *La Révolution française* (1922), t. I, Ch. I—'La crise de l'Ancien Régime'; and Ch. II—'La révolte nobiliaire'.

[9] It will be sufficient for us to refer to the abstract of the results of his research which Lefebvre published in 1933: 'La Révolution française et les paysans' (*Cahiers de la Révolution française*, No. I, p. 6; *Annales historiques*, 1933, p. 97. This text was reprinted in *Etudes sur la Révolution française*, 1954, p. 246).

revolutionary studies, Lefebvre followed methods of research which set an example for all subsequent historians. However, Lefebvre's contribution does not quite complete the picture. One social group of *ancien régime* and revolutionary France has not been given its true place. This group was referred to by contemporaries as the *sans-culottes*.

Every historian of the Revolution has insisted upon the part played by the popular classes in the towns, particularly in Paris: the Revolution is largely their work. From the spring of 1789 to the spring of 1795, from 14 July to the *journées* of Prairial Year III, they devoted all their energies to it, placed all their hopes in it, lived and suffered for it. No historian has ignored this extremely important contribution.

The people are the principal actors in Michelet's *Histoire de la Révolution française*.[1] Not the sans-culottes, but *le Peuple*, a word which is neither defined nor analysed: it is as if the nation in its entirety had been moulded into one mythical person. But whether the part played by the 'people' of Paris in the fluctuating course of the Revolution has been fully appreciated is still open to question. Have historians truly assessed it? Or have they usually assumed that it was the bourgeoisie who determined the activities of the people; activities directed mainly against the aristocracy, feudalism, royal power, and the *ancien régime*? The general consensus of historical opinion would seem to be that the sans-culottes, particularly the Parisian sans-culottes, always acted in complete and perfect harmony with the revolutionary bourgeoisie.

Certain aspects of this problem have indeed been studied. Thiers, for example, occasionally emphasizes the role of the Parisian Sections, and refers to the autonomous character of their activity. On the question of food supplies, he compares the demand for price-fixing by the Sections with the attitude of the Jacobins who, 'condemned the fixing of prices as a threat to the freedom of trade'.[2] But this appears as a hasty addition to the text. The theme remains essentially political: the economic factors and social conflicts which provide the backcloth to the popular revolution are ignored. The sources of information used by Thiers were

[1] *Histoire de la Révolution française* (1847–53), 4 vols. in-8º.
[2] *Histoire de la Révolution française* (1823–27), 7th edition (1838), t. VIII, Ch. VI, p. 310.

the official documents and personal memoirs of the period. The huge deposit of papers of the Parisian Sections which were available at the time, Thiers completely ignored. Michelet went a stage further. In his 1868 preface, he tells us that his book could not have been written without the documents which he discovered in the various archives: 'For the great tragedies of revolutionary Paris, the collection of documents at the *Hôtel de Ville* introduced me to the registers of the Commune; and at the *Préfecture de Police*, I found a comprehensive and varied set of papers in the minutes of the forty-eight Sections.' Michelet not only studied the work of the municipality—the elected representatives of the people—but he also looked at the people themselves in their Sections. He informs us that in order to understand the events of 31 May he read and 'religiously' copied the registers of the forty-eight Sections; and for 9 Thermidor he followed, 'step by step' the thirty-one official reports of the Sections which were still in existence. However, if we look at the results of his labour a little more closely, we find that he has hardly bothered to study anything but the *grandes tragédies du Paris révolutionnaire*, when the sans-culottes make their sudden entrance upon the political scene. Having introduced the people to history, he has spared himself the task of studying their daily life. What were their anxieties, their hopes, their needs and the motives which caused them to act as they did? And what did the word 'people' convey to Michelet? Were the sans-culottes a homogeneous social unit? Were the interests of the *compagnon* and the property-owning craftsman the same? And what exactly were these Sections, committees, and popular societies which suddenly appear in the tumult of the revolutionary *journées*, only to fade almost immediately into obscurity? Having sifted through the documents, and acquired a living knowledge of the Revolution through eyewitness accounts, Michelet was able to express the innermost thoughts of the people who had participated in it, to describe their enthusiasm and their disappointment. He wrote of the sense of expectancy in 1789, the popular anger which lay beneath the 'aristocratic plot', the patriotic fervour of 1792. Living amongst the people in those districts where memories of Marat, Jacques Roux, and the *Père Duchesne* were still vividly recollected, he conceived a sympathy for Hébert and the *enragés* and understood the widespread feeling of disillusionment amongst the people in the spring of 1794. But does he really understand the full implications of the political and social aspirations of the Parisian sans-culotterie when he describes Jacques Roux as one of the first socialists? 'In the very heart of Paris, in the dark and dismal streets where the working population of the capital lived (les Arcis, Saint-Martin),' he wrote in his preface of 1868, 'socialism was fermenting: a revolution beneath a revolution.' In such passages, Michelet appears to transpose his concern with man in the nineteenth century to the end of the eighteenth century—perhaps to assist him in his controversy with Louis Blanc over Robespierre.

Mortimer-Ternaux adopted quite a different attitude in his study of the papers dealing with the Parisian Sections: whereas Michelet had at least brought sympathy and human understanding to the task, Mortimer-Ternaux took advantage of every opportunity to discredit them. In order to write his *Histoire de la Terreur*, he searched tirelessly in the Minutes of the Sections for anything which might support his political prejudice and prove that they were actually 'forty-eight hot-beds of continual agitation'.[3] But at least Mortimer-Ternaux served posterity well by transcribing many documents, the originals of which have now disappeared.

Taine, in his *Origins de la France contemporaine*, frequently without consulting the original sources, also collected every hostile piece of evidence he could find in the work of his predecessors, particularly Mortimer-Ternaux, in order to support his own preconceived ideas. His picture of the Parisian populace—'a beast wallowing on a blood-red carpet'[4]—can only be regarded as a caricature. But it must be admitted that Taine's work opened up avenues of research which provided new opportunities for the historian. He spotlighted the social aspect of the bid for power by the Sections, and pointed out how it threatened the interests of the bourgeoisie; and although his attitude to popular movements was a mixture of contempt and fear, he did underline their complexity, showing the overlap of social forces, personal interests, and collective passions. For these reasons he remains a pioneer.

[3] *Histoire de la Terreur: 1792–1794* (1862–9), 3rd edition (1868), Introduction, Vol. I, p. 27.
[4] *Les origines de la France contemporaine: La Révolution*, t. III. *Le Gouvernement Révolutionnaire* (1885), Preface, p. 1. Taine writes: 'This volume, like those which preceded it, has only been written for connoisseurs of moral Zoology.' The entire preface should be quoted!

The positive aspect of this research, from which Taine had been diverted by class prejudice, was taken up in a modest way by a man whose work, if it does not bear comparison with that of his illustrious predecessors, had at last the merit of indicating what might be achieved. In 1898, Ernest Mellié published his *Sections de Paris pendant la Révolution française*. His work is concerned, above all, with the organization of the Sections and the way in which they functioned; he was anxious to rediscover the people, not during the important *journées*, or at the bar of the Assembly, 'but in their own homes, in their daily meetings, and in the midst of their different occupations'. Observed in their assemblies, committees and popular societies, the activity of the people would no longer appear to be irregular or confined to the political field alone, but something coherent, continuous, reflecting the needs and anxieties of their day-to-day existence. In this way, the social foundations would be restored to the history of their political activity. It was an ambitious programme which, if it had been realized, would have given us a complete picture of popular life in revolutionary Paris. In fact, Mellié satisfied himself mainly with a study of institutions. What laws governed the Sections once they had been created? How did they organize themselves? How did they arrange their business? And how did their jurisdiction gradually widen until simple electoral organisms transformed themselves into autonomous municipalities capable of compelling recognition from the Parisian authorities and the National Assemblies? Mellié examined every different aspect of life in the Sections; he set their wheels in motion, re-created the whole complex machinery of their existence. But, unfortunately, he did not go on to study those aspects of the revolutionary activity which belonged specifically to the popular movement, for which the Sections provided the framework. 'To write the history of the Sections', says Mellié, 'would be almost the same as relating the history of the Revolution.' But to say this is to imply that the popular movement only developed in conjunction with the bourgeoisie, and that it had no specific identity and no degree of autonomy. If it is true that the Parisian Sections exercised an influence on the course of the Revolution, not only during the revolutionary *journées*, but during the debates in the national and municipal assemblies where they intervened daily, and that as a result of this their history is often confused with that of the

Revolution itself, it is none the less true that they conducted an active and strenuous life of their own. To write the history of the Sections of Paris is not to retell the story of the Revolution; it is to write, at least from 1792, the history of the Parisian sans-culotterie. This history of the Sections, which Mellié had only just begun, was successfully completed by F. Braesch for the period June–December 1792. His thesis on *La Commune du dix août* is also concerned with the wider study of the history of Paris: 'It seems to me', wrote Braesch, 'that the most important historical figure in the French Revolution . . . this figure with a hundred heads and a thousand arms which we call Paris, deserves to be placed at the very heart of the Terror.'[5] Braesch pointed out that the real explanation of municipal policy, which, in many cases, influenced general policy, is to be found more often in the Sections than in the central organism of the Commune. He also set himself the task of 'following carefully the intricate game of politics played by the Sections', of writing their history and, in so doing, making an original contribution to the study of the Revolution. However, the work was not without its limitations. Although a considerable portion of the book is devoted to economic and religious matters, the author still contrives to consider them purely from a political angle. To borrow one of Michelet's phrases, Braesch regards the economic question as 'an outcome, a significant widening of the concept of liberty'—liberty is always the 'first consideration'. As far as Braesch is concerned, this is a matter of principle derived from a false analogy with the problems of the twentieth century which often leads to an error of perspective, such as his conclusion that: 'The struggle then was the same as it is today—a struggle between wage-earners and the propertied bourgeoisie.' This overlooks the fact that as far as the sans-culottes were concerned the real enemy was still the artistocrat. It fails to distinguish between the workshop *compagnon* and the factory-worker. This is not 'simply a matter of degree'—the difference is fundamental.

Albert Mathiez gets to the root of the problem in *La vie chère et la mouvement social sous la Terreur*, in which he points out that the issue at stake between the sans-culottes and the *possédants* was the economic question of price-controls or freedom of trade, and shows how the *enragés* rejected the right of ownership in favour of

---

[5] *La Commune du dix août 1792, Etude sur l'histoire de Paris du juin au 2 décembre 1792* (1911), Introduction, p. 11.

the right of every citizen to receive at least the basic necessities of life (*le droit à l'existence*). But were there not many Montagnards who made the same distinction? Concentrating mainly on the question of food supplies, and quite rightly emphasizing the 'profound and violent antagonism' between the plan for the General Maximum—the 'economic terror' desired by the sans-culotterie—and 'the aspirations of a social group passionately concerned with liberty'[6] (it would be more accurate to say the interests of the bourgeoisie), Mathiez tended to overlook the political incompatibility between sans-culotte democracy and the Revolutionary Government, as he overestimated the part played by Robespierre in the latter.

In contrast to Mathiez, Daniel Guérin in his *La lutte des classes sous la première République*, depicted Robespierre as the harbinger of the Thermidorean reaction. Guérin regarded the Parisian sansculotterie as an *avant garde*, and its achievements in the Year II as the embryonic form of the proletarian revolution. This supported the theory of 'the continuous revolution', according to which the outlines of the proletarian revolution of the twentieth century could already be discovered in the bourgeois revolution of 1793, when the latter 'was superimposed upon the embryo of the proletarian revolution'.[7] Guérin has transposed the problems of our times to the eighteenth century; he has made the craftsman and shopkeeper sans-culotterie a factory proletariat; he has taken as a proletarian *avant-garde* what was often nothing more than an *arrière-garde* defending the traditional economy. In fact, Guérin deprived the popular movement during the Revolution of its most distinctive characteristics.

Some historians, as we have seen, have looked at the popular movement through the eyes of the bourgeoisie as being directed essentially against the aristocracy and the *ancien régime*, becoming perfectly integrated as a result in the bourgeois revolution. Others have seen it as a movement which foreshadowed the social struggles of the nineteenth and twentieth centuries. But most historians, with different degrees of emphasis which could probably

---

[6] *La vie chère et le mouvement social sous la Terreur* (1927), Conc., p. 611.

[7] *La lutte de classes sous la première République. Bourgeois et 'bras nus': 1793–1795* (1946), 2 vols., Vol. I, p. 8. Elsewhere, the author speaks of the 'coexistence of a bourgeois revolution and the embryonic form of a proletarian revolution' (Vol. I, p. 2).

be explained by their temperament, their social background and the times in which they lived, have tended to underestimate the original and specific character of the popular revolution.

The 14 July, Valmy, and their patriotic enthusiasm as volunteers in the revolutionary armies, undoubtedly prove that the first task, as far as the sans-culottes were concerned, was to overthrow the aristocracy and royal absolutism. They supplied the revolutionary bourgeoisie with the human striking-force necessary for the destruction of the *ancien régime* and the defeat of the foreign coalition. But this does not mean that they were in complete agreement with all the policies of the revolutionary bourgeoisie. They could not deviate the general direction of the Revolution, but they could, and did, pursue their own aims, often in alliance with the bourgeoisie, sometimes in opposition. The sans-culotterie, like the peasantry, looked beyond the defeat of the aristocracy towards objectives which were not exactly those of the ruling revolutionary class. In the same way as there was an autonomous peasant movement within the framework of the Revolution, so there developed a movement which was specifically 'sans-culotte'.

We must look for its origins in the position of the shopkeeper and the craftsman within *ancien régime* society; in the crisis of the French economy upon which the works of C. E. Labrousse have thrown a new light; and in the decline of living standards experienced by the popular classes in Paris long before 1789. The shortage of food supplies played at least as significant a part in rousing the sans-culotterie to action as the belief in the 'aristocratic plot'. Not only were the origins of this popular movement peculiar to the sans-culotterie, but its behaviour and political organizations— general assemblies of the Parisian Sections, dominated by the sans-culotterie in the Year II, and particularly the *sociétés sectionnaires* founded in the autumn of 1793. There was a very marked difference between the latter and the popular societies of the censitary period, as there was between a *société sectionnaire* and the Jacobin club, even in the Year II. Lastly, the crises which distinguish this popular movement were peculiar to the sans-culotterie: the crisis of the summer of 1793 which led to the *journées* of 4 and 5 September, which Mathiez calls the 'Hébertist drive', and Daniel Guèrin 'a specifically working-class' manifestation, but which were, in fact, simply sans-culotte *journées*, followed rather than directed by Hébert, Chaumette, and the Paris Commune. These *journées* have no clearly defined link with the general course of the Revolution: the sans-culottes demanded fixed prices and controls on trade, and it was only the sanction of force which finally compelled the jacobin bourgeoisie to adopt such measures.

It is this last point which finally emphasizes the specific character of the sans-culotte movement. Tied to a system of controls and fixed prices which was typical of the old methods of production and exchange, the sans-culottes generally remained hostile to the programme advocated by the bourgeoisie who filled the assemblies and the administrative posts, and who worked tirelessly to install the type of government which would favour their own interests. Fundamentally, the outlook of the Parisian sans-culotte was identical with that of the peasant, eager to preserve rural communities and collective rights which defended him against the inroads of capitalist agriculture and agrarian individualism. Apart from the conflict between the Third Estate and the feudal aristocracy, two social groups in France appeared to be in opposition: that of the craftsmen and *compagnons*, shopkeepers and the smaller peasantry; and that of the farmers, prominent tradesmen and the heads of commercial and industrial concerns.

Political differences increased the bitterness of social conflicts. The popular movement after 1789 aimed at decentralization and local autonomy—an old deep-rooted desire which a strong monarchy had repressed for centuries, but which was released again during the Revolution. Toqueville's work, which pays very little attention to popular mentality, reveals nothing of this. It did not fit in with the essential theme of his book which traces the whole course of the *ancien régime* towards centralization. War brought a renewed demand for centralization. In the spring of 1793, the logic of national defence reunited the disparate elements which remained of the revolutionary Third Estate as the only means of safeguarding the interests of the State. The people imposed a Revolutionary Government, the *levée en masse* and a controlled economy geared to the task of feeding the cities and towns, as well as providing for the armies. As for the bourgeoisie, who had directed the course of the Revolution from the beginning, they were firmly resolved that, through the Montagnards, they, should continue to control its destiny. Would the sans-culottes be content with the passive role of obedience? The Revolutionary Government had been created to wage war against the Allied coalition on the frontiers, and complete the downfall of the aristocracy within the nation; but, having installed it in power, would the sans-culottes continue to support the weight of a strong and centralized government? It was clear that the conflict between the sans-culotterie and the bourgeoisie would be intensified by their different outlook and political behaviour. Did they both share the same ideas of democracy and revolutionary dictatorship?

Thus, social and political struggles become increasingly complicated. The evolution of history cannot be reduced to a mechanical scheme: it is a dialectical movement. Those who interest themselves in its study, if they do not wish to misrepresent or oversimplify the issues involved, must take into account the complexity which is its richness, and the contradictions which confer upon it its dramatic character.

Although the source material for the history of the popular movement in Paris, which, from the spring of 1789 to the spring of 1795, animated and frequently provided the impetus for the Revolution, has suffered irreparable loss and can now only be studied in incomplete series or disparate collections, it is still quite rich and appears to have been little used.

It is chiefly composed of the papers of the Paris Sections which survived the fire at the *Archives de la Prefécture de police* in May 1871. The forty-eight Sections of Paris, created by the municipal law of 21 May–27 June 1790, finally disappeared on 19 Vendémiaire in the Year IV. These Sections had taken the place of the sixty districts created by the royal decree of 13 April 1789. The Sections added an important collection of their own to the papers which they received from the districts—the registers of the deliberations of the general assemblies; minutes of the meetings of the *comités civils, comités révolutionnaires* and other committees in the Sections; correspondence between the forty-eight Sections and various administrative authorities (the Commune, Department, and Committees of the National Assemblies): enrolment registers, identity cards, passports and the papers of the numerous popular societies which were gathered together after their disappearance in the spring of the Year II or in the Year III. This entire collection of documents was then transferred in the Year IV by the supressed Sections to the twelve municipalities which replaced them, and many of them were then catalogued. One year before the *comités révolutionnaires* of the Sections had handed over their papers in the same way to the twelve *comités de surveillance d'arrondissement* created by the law of 7 Fructidor Year III. However, the archives from the *comités révolutionnaires* and the Sections had not been transferred to the new administrative bodies without serious loss. When, after the execution of Hébert, and particularly after Thermidor, the Revolution, which had been momentarily deviated by the popular movement, again assumed the character which had been stamped upon it by the 'men of '89', the sans-culotte personnel of the Sections and various committees thought it wise to take a few precautions. Evidence of this can be found in the documents of Prairial Year III, when proceedings were being taken against former terrorists for the purpose of disarming or throwing them into prison. The Commissions of Inquiry which were created expressly for this purpose hastened to demand all the papers and registers of the Year II so that they could unearth sufficient evidence to justify the repression: often these registers had been burnt or compromising pages torn out. But despite the extent of the damage carried out after Thermidor, the Sections and *comités révolutionnaires* still transferred a considerable mass of documents, papers, and registers to the administrative bodies which replaced them.

What became of this unique collection of documents? It is difficult to trace the exact history of the archives of the forty-eight Parisian Sections. We do not know when, or following what principles, these documents, at first regrouped in the twelve municipalities set up in Vendémiaire Year IV, were transferred either to the *Archives nationales*, where a fairly important collection of registers is to be found, or to the *Archives de la Préfecture de police* where, although we would expect to find, almost intact, the series dealing with the minutes of the *commissaires de police* in the Sections, it is rather strange to find the registers of the general assemblies. One thing only is certain. It was at the *Archives de la Préfecture de police*, which used to possess 'more than 300 registers of the Sections', that Barthélémy Saint-Hilaire carried out the singular spoliation from September to November 1834 which has preserved for us a few precious documents. It was these records which gave Michelet 'the divergent variety' of their accounts of the 'great tragedies of revolutionary Paris'. And it was there also that Mortimer-Ternaux consulted the papers of the Sections for his *Histoire de la Terreur* and verified the absence of the registers of three Sections. Some of these registers had lain untouched in the municipal archives where they had been deposited in the Year IV—those of the Section des Postes for example, discovered in the *mairie* of the 2nd *arrondissement* and deposited in the *Archives de la Seine* in 1891. An important number of documents belonging to the Sections were destroyed in the fire of May 1871 at the *Archives de la Préfecture de police*: the only papers to escape the disaster were the minutes of the *commissaires de police*, and the pages which Barthélémy Saint-Hilaire had cut out of the registers with scissors in order to escape the tedious work of transcribing them. They are mainly to be found in the collection of his papers at the *Bibliothèque Victor-Cousin*. The loss incurred in May 1871, however, was still an extremely serious one despite the survival of this collection.

Nevertheless the fortuitous distribution amongst the various archives of the documents belonging to the Sections, the lack of scruple shown by Barthélémy Saint-Hilaire, and the existence of an important collection of papers at the *Bibliothèque national*, still make it possible for us to draw upon an imposing mass of documents indispensable for the historian of the Parisian sansculottes. In addition to this, numerous other papers taken from the Sections are scattered amongst the different series of Revolution documents at the *Archives nationales* which must be searched carefully if one is not to overlook items which occasionally prove to be of vital importance. For instance, in the dossiers of the Revolutionary Assemblies which make up the series C—motions, addresses and petitions of the general assemblies and popular societies; a smaller collection of these documents can also be found amongst the papers of the *Comité de legislation de la Convention*. The series F7, and particularly the papers of the Committee of General Security with its inexhaustible alphabetical series, present us with a mass of documents of the greatest importance, especially if we wish to study the revolutionary personnel of the Parisian Sections. Finally, we must not overlook the dossiers of the Revolutionary Tribunal and the Military Commissions of the Year III grouped in the series W. The whole collection of revolutionary archives from 1790 to the Year IV seems to provide the necessary complement to the various papers belonging to the Sections—a wide field where the joy of discovery often rewards the patience of the searcher.

However damaged the collection of papers which the Parisian Sections and their different committees left on their disappearance to bear witness to their remarkable activity and vital contribution to the Revolution appear today, we still have at our disposal, after we have added the personal collections and many small items which have been scattered around the different archives, a numerous and varied mass of documents. Their study is bound to point to a new departure in the history of the Revolution and provide us with the opportunity of marking the true place of the Parisian sans-culottes without whose co-operation the bourgeoisie could never have achieved their victory.

Our aim in this study will be to re-create their contribution to the course of the Revolution from 2 June 1793—a date which, as a result of their efforts, marks the fall of the Girondins and the collapse of the liberal Republic—to 9 Thermidor, when their dream of an egalitarian Republic faded with the execution of Robespierre. We intend to add to the study of the Convention, its Committees, and the Paris Commune, which has chiefly attracted the attention of historians to the present, a study of the Parisian people in their general assemblies and *sociétés sectionnaires*: by altering the focus of our attention, new aspects will emerge which will add to our existing knowledge. The history of the 'great tragedies of revolutionary Paris', to borrow Michelet's expression, must be viewed from different levels: from that of the Convention and its Committees, as well as from that of the Commune, and of the Sections themselves—we need to distinguish the general course of the Revolution from that taken by the popular movement. Between these different levels certain factors intermingle and overlap, posing two sets of questions in 1793 and the Year II. A question of political order: how to reconcile the outlook and behaviour peculiar to the sans-culotterie with the urgent problems facing a revolutionary dictatorship—in other words, how could the problem of the relationship between popular democracy and the Revolutionary Government be resolved? Then a question of social order: how to reconcile the aspirations and economic demands of the sans-culotterie with those of the bourgeoisie who continued to determine the general character of the Revolution—in other words, how to resolve the problem of the relationship between the popular classes and the property-owning classes? We shall endeavour to prove that, within the framework of Paris and the chronological limits which we have fixed, the sans-culotte movement possessed its own autonomy and particular identity, and that an important place in the history of the Revolution must be reserved for it. In the first place so that our knowledge of the period can be enriched, but also so that we can fit it more precisely into the perspective of the origins of contemporary France, and in so doing, help to emphasize the original characteristics of our national history.

I

THE MENTALITY AND SOCIAL COMPOSITION OF THE SANS-CULOTTES

FROM June 1793 to February 1794, the Parisian sans-culotte movement played a major role in the political struggle leading to the consolidation of the Revolutionary Government and the organization of the Committee of Public Safety. During the same period, it imposed economic measures upon a reluctant Assembly intended to improve the living standards of the masses. If we wish to study the motives which explain the attitude of the people at this time, some kind of social definition of the Parisian sans-culotterie, some assessment of its composition is required.

This is not an easy task, for the economic or fiscal documents which could provide us with detailed analyses are missing, and what little statistical evidence we have is both vague and misleading. It is mainly through the political documents that we can explore the social characteristics of the sans-culotterie, particularly the dossiers dealing with the anti-terrorist repression of the Year III. The true image, the mentality and behaviour of the Parisian sans-culotte, only emerges by comparing the attitudes of two social groups. Not particularly conscious of class distinctions, the sans-culotte reveals himself most clearly in relation to his social enemies. This absence of class-consciousness is reflected in the social composition of the Parisian population—in so far as it is possible to analyse it—and even more strikingly in the social composition of the political personnel of the Sections.

If we attempt to delimit the social contours of the sans-culotterie, we should, first of all, discover how the sans-culotte defined himself. There are enough relevant documents available for us to make, at least, an approximate definition.

The sans-culotte was outwardly recognizable by his dress, which served to distinguish him from the more elevated classes of society. Trousers were the distinctive mark of the popular classes; breeches of the aristocracy, and generally speaking, of the higher ranks of the old Third Estate. Robespierre used to contrast the *culottes dorées* with the *sans-culottes*—those who wore fancy or embroidered breeches with those who simply wore trousers. The sans-culottes themselves made the same distinction. The police-agent Rousseville, listing the intrigues which had undermined the *comité de surveillance de Sceaux* in his report of 25 Messidor Year II, emphasized the hostility which existed between the *bas-de-soie* and the *sans-culottes*.[1] Dress also distinguished the latter from the *muscadins*. Fontaine, a gunner in the Section de la Réunion, was arrested on 5 Prairial for repeating that he wished to revenge himself on the *muscadins*, defining the latter as 'those (citizens) in the National Guard who appeared to be better dressed than him-self'.

With the dress went a certain social comportment. Here again, it is in his opposition to accepted social behaviour that the sans-culotte asserts himself. The manners of the *ancien régime* were no longer fashionable in the Year II; the sans-culottes no longer accepted a subordinate position in society. Jean-Baptist Gentil, a building-contractor and timber-merchant, arrested on 5 Pluviôse Year II for having failed to fulfil his obligations towards the Republic, was criticized by the *comité révolutionnaire* of the Section des Quinze-Vingts for his manners: 'People had to take their hats off before they could approach him. The expression "Monsieur" was still used in his house, and he always affected an air of importance.' As a result, he had never been regarded as a good citizen.[2]

The sans-culottes readily judged a person's character from his appearance; his character then decided what his political opinions would be. Everyone who offended their sense of equality and fraternity was suspected of being an aristocrat. It was difficult for a former noble to find favour in their eyes, even when no definite accusation could be levelled against him, 'because such men can-not rise to the heights of our Revolution. Their hearts are always full of pride, and we will never forget the air of superiority which they used to assume, nor the domination which they exercised over us.' It was for these reasons that the *comité révolutionnaire* of the

---

[1] *A.N.*, F⁷ 4708. Concerning the origin of the word *sans-culotte*, and how its usage spread, see Ferdinand Brunot, *Histoire de la langue fran-çaise*, ix, 715.
[2] *A.N.*, F⁷ 4721.

Section de la République arrested the duc de Brancas-Céreste on 16 October 1793, pointing out that he still enjoyed a yearly income of 89,980 *livres*.[3] The sans-culottes could not endure pride or disdain, since these feelings were thought to be typically aristocratic and contrary to the spirit of fraternity which should reign amongst citizens equal in rights: they obviously implied a political attitude hostile to the kind of democracy which the sans-culottes practised in their general assemblies and popular societies. For this reason, such personal defects are frequently mentioned in the reports justifying the arrest of suspects.

On 17 September 1793, the committee of the Section Révolutionnaire decided to arrest Etienne Gide, a wholesale merchant in watches and clocks, because he had given his allegiance to the Brissotin party, but also because he was of a 'haughty and proud' disposition, and had often been heard to speak 'ironically'. On 28 Brumaire, the committee of the Section des Marchés arrested a music-dealer named Bayeux. It was alleged that he had said in a meeting of the general assembly that 'it was disgusting to see a cobbler acting as president, particularly a cobbler who was so badly dressed'. In the Section du Contrat-Social, the crime of the watchmaker Brasseur, who was arrested on 23 Floréal, was his remark 'that it was very disagreeable for a man like himself to be in a guard-room with the sort of people whom, in the old days, one had nothing to do with'. In extreme cases, a mere attitude of indifference towards a sans-culotte was enough for a person to be charged with harbouring 'aristocratic feelings'. Explaining the arrest of a former banker, Girardot-Marigny, on 12 Brumaire, the committee of the Section de Guillaume-Tell simply observed that it was a case of 'one of these rich citizens who would not deign to fraternize with Republicans'.[4]

Even more incriminating in the eyes of the sans-culottes than an attitude of pride, contempt, or plain indifference, was an insinuation of their social inferiority. In its report of 9 Frimaire upon Louis-Claude Cezeron, arrested as a suspect, the committee of the Section Poissonnière referred in particular to some remarks he had made at a meeting of the general assembly in the preceding May, 'that the poor depended upon the rich, and that the sans-culottes had never been anything but the lowest class of society'. Bergeron,

---

[3] *A.N.*, F⁷ 4615, d. 3.
[4] *A.N.*, F⁷ 4584, pl. 5; 4615, pl. 4; 4726.

a dealer in skins from the Section des Lombards, 'when he saw the sans-culottes fulfilling their obligations as citizens . . . said that it would be better if they got on with their own affairs instead of meddling in politics': he was arrested as a suspect on 18 Pluviôse. The sans-culottes also had no time for the type of person who took advantage of his social position, wealth, or even his education, to impress or influence those beneath him. Truchon, a lawyer from the Section de Gravilliers, who had been denounced on several occasions by Jacques Roux in his *Publiciste*, was finally arrested on 9 Prairial in the Year II: the *comité révolutionnaire* accused him of having influenced citizens of 'little discernment', and of expressing the opinion that 'positions of authority should be filled by enlightened men with private means, since they alone had the time to spare'.[5]

It is true that the sans-culottes had an egalitarian conception of social relationships. But beneath the general theory, there were more clearly defined factors which help to explain their behaviour, and it is interesting to consider to what extent they themselves were conscious of, and able to express, this deeper motivation.

Above all, the sans-culottes were conscious of the social antagonism which divided them from the aristocracy. The aristocracy had been the real enemy from 14 July 1789 to 10 August 1792, and it was against the aristocracy that they continued to struggle. The address of the *société des Sans-Culottes de Beaucaire* to the Convention on 8 September 1793 is significant in this respect: 'We are sans-culottes . . . poor and virtuous, we have formed a society of manual workers and peasants . . . we know our friends—those who have delivered us from the clergy, the nobility, feudalism, the *dîme*, royalty and all the evils which accompany it. They are the same people who are called anarchists, trouble-makers and followers of Marat by the aristocrats.'[6] The idea of a class struggle emerges more clearly in the address of the *société populaire de Dijon* on 27 Nivôse Year II which stated that 'in future, we must be a united people, not two nations in opposition.' To achieve this the society advocated the death penalty 'for everyone, without exception, who is known to be an aristocrat'.[7]

The aristocrat was such a figure of hatred to the sans-culotterie

[5] *A.N.*, F⁷ 4775³⁵.   [6] *A.N.*, C 271, pl. 666, p. 37.
[7] *A.N.*, C 289, pl. 394, p. 9.

that it was not long before the expression was being used to describe all their enemies, irrespective of whether they belonged to the former nobility or to the higher ranks of what had been the Third Estate. This failure to distinguish between the real aristocrat and a member of the upper bourgeoisie—which was peculiarly sans-culotte—helps to underline the separate and distinct character of their contribution to the Revolution.

On 25 July 1792, in an address demanding the dethronement of the king, the Section du Louvre denounced along with the landed aristocracy, 'the ministerial, financial and bourgeois aristocracy, and, above all, the aristocracy of the refractory priests'.[8] By broadening its original meaning, the term 'aristocrat' came to be used in the Year II to encompass every social group against which the sans-culottes were struggling. Hence the significant expression *aristocratie bourgeoise* which recurs so frequently in the texts, and the specifically popular definition given to it by an anonymous petitioner in the Year II, in which social and political considerations were intermingled. The 'aristocrat' was the type of person who regretted the passing of the *ancien régime* and disapproved of the Revolution, did nothing to support it, and had not taken the civic oath, nor enlisted in the National Guard. He was the type of citizen who refused to buy National Lands, even though he had the opportunity and the means of doing so; he did not cultivate his lands, but refused to sell them at a reasonable price, or farm them out, or lease them on a system of *métayage*. The 'aristocrat' did not find employment for labourers or journeymen, although he was very well able to do so; he did not contribute 'at a rate relative to the cost of living' to the collections made for volunteers to the armies, and had done nothing to improve the conditions of poor and patriotic citizens. The 'true patriot' was his opposite in every respect. The word 'aristocrat', therefore, was used to describe all the enemies of the sans-culotterie—bourgeois as well as noble—who constituted 'the class of citizens from whom we should levy the forced loan which must be raised throughout the Republic'.[9] Extreme sans-culottes no longer used the word 'aristocrat' to designate the former nobility, but the bourgeoisie. On 21 May 1793, a popular orator from the Section du Mail stated that 'aristocrats are the rich, wealthy merchants, monopolists,

[8] *A.P.P.*, AA/266, p. 297.
[9] *A.N.*, D XL 23, d. 77.

middlemen, bankers, trading clerks, quibbling lawyers and citizens who own anything'.[1]

The economic crisis helped to sharpen these social conflicts, and as the crisis developed and the *patriote* party of 1789 began to disintegrate, differences of opinion between the sans-culottes and the upper classes of the old Third Estate were added to the fundamental sans-culotte-aristocrat antagonism. A note intended for the Committee of General Security in Pluviôse Year II referred to the existence of two parties in the Section de Brutus: one representing the people—*sans-culottisme*—and the other composed of 'bankers, stock-brokers and moneyed-people'. An address to the Convention on 27 Ventôse contrasts with the 'brave sans-culottes', not only the clergy, the nobility and the sovereign heads of Europe, but also solicitors, barristers, notaries, and particularly 'well-to-do farmers, selfish citizens and all these fat, wealthy merchants. They are fighting against us instead of our oppressors'.[2] Is this simply a struggle between citizens who owned property, and those who did not, a struggle between *possédants* and *non-possédants*? One cannot really say that it is, for we find crafts-men and shopkeepers amongst the sans-culotterie who were themselves property-owners. It is rather a conflict between those who favoured the idea of restricted and limited ownership, and those who believed in the absolute right of property as proclaimed in 1789; and even more clearly, a conflict between the defenders of a system of controls and fixed prices, and those who preferred an economic policy of *laissez-faire*—in general terms, a struggle between consumers and producers.

The sources enable us to probe fairly deeply into the social antipathies and preoccupations of the sans-culotterie. They denounced *honnêtes gens*—those citizens who, if not rich, enjoyed at least a comfortable and cultured life, and also those who were conscious, if not necessarily proud, of being better dressed and better educated than themselves. They denounced *rentiers*—citizens who lived off unearned incomes. And finally they denounced 'the rich'; not just property-owners or *possédants*, but the *gros* as opposed to the *petits*—the wealthy, big business-men as compared with those of their own kind who possessed but limited means. The sans-culottes were not hostile towards pro-perty so long as it was limited; they accepted property of the kind

[1] *A.N.*, C 335, pl. 1864, p. 44.   [2] *A.N.*, C 295, pl. 994, p. 27.

which artisans and shopkeepers already owned, and which many *compagnons* dreamed of owning themselves in the future.

The expression *honnêtes gens* appeared after 2 June 1793: when the sans-culottes and the moderates found themselves in opposition politically and socially. It was used, at first, to describe those members of the bourgeoisie who refused to accept the principle of equality, but it finally assumed a meaning as broad as that of the word 'aristocrat', embracing all the enemies of the sans-culotterie. But if the latter ironically referred to their adversaries as *honnêtes gens*, the latter did not hesitate to brand the sans-culottes as the 'rabble'—the *canaille* of the Revolution. These two expressions emphasized the social cleavage which separated one class from the other. On 25 September, a carpenter named Bertout was arrested by order of the Section de la République because he had expressed the desire for 'another government which would crush the *canaille*, for *honnêtes gens* were finished'.[3] In the documents of the Year III, we sometimes find the expressions *honnêtes gens et meneurs* contrasted—*meneurs* referring to the sans-culotte militants in the Year II. The vocabulary does not usually go so far as to underline the social aspect of the contending factions; however, on 16 Pluviôse Year III the *comité de surveillance* of the 6th *arrondissement* mentioned that stormy scenes had taken place in the general assembly of the Section des Lombards between *hommes aux quarante sols* and *honnêtes citoyens*. Such phraseology bears witness to the underlying hostility between the sans-culottes who were paid forty *sous* for attending each meeting of the general assembly, and those who could afford to attend without any such compensation: a social conflict between the leisured class and those who worked with their hands.

This conflict is also revealed in the hatred which the sans-culottes felt for the *rentiers*, becoming increasingly marked during the autumn of 1793 when the economic crisis and the difficulties of day-to-day existence aggravated the class conflict. The mere fact that someone belonged to the *rentier* class came to be accepted as sufficient grounds for suspicion. On 18 September 1793, the *comité révolutionnaire* of the Section de Mutius-Scaevola ordered the arrest of the chief secretary of the Paris police, Duval, on two charges: showing contempt for the assemblies of the Section, and for enjoying a private income of 2,000 *livres* a year.[4] An extreme

[3] *A.N.*, F⁷ 4596, pl. 11, p. 3.   [4] *A.N.*, F⁷ 4699.

case was that of Pierre Bequerel of the Section de Guillaume-Tell who was arrested on 19 Ventôse during a police raid in the gardens of the Palais-Royal simply 'for having said that he was living off his private income'.[5] On the preceding 2 Frimaire, the *société populaire Lepeletier* had accepted a petition which sought to exclude from all administrative posts, not only the former nobility, sons of ministers of the Crown, stock-brokers and jobbers, but also every person who was known to have enjoyed a private income of over 3,000 *livres* a year: the positions left vacant after implementation of such a law would be reserved for the sans-culottes.[6] The sans-culottes, therefore, did not condemn *rentiers* indiscriminately, but only those in the higher income group—the *gros rentier*. Numerous small *rentiers*, retired craftsmen and shopkeepers figure amongst the political personnel of the Sections in the Year II. Potin, a stationer and *commissaire de police* in the Section du Contrat-Social stated in May 1793 that 'the *loi agraire* would have to be enforced against persons enjoying an income of over 4–5,000 *livres* a year'[7]—a social ideal to suit the pockets of street-stall and shop-owners.

The conflict between the sans-culottes and the wealthy *rentier* is only one aspect of the former's instinctive hostility towards the rich. Extreme sans-culottes, such as Babeuf in the Year IV, went so far as to state that the Revolution was a war 'between the rich and the poor'. This attitude largely conditioned the terrorist mentality of the sans-culotterie. On 5 May 1793, a woman named Saunier was arrested near Saint Germain-l'Auxerrois 'for having shouted at the top of her voice that it was about time they had another "10 August" so that they could murder and cut the throats of the rich'. In the Year III, the same opinions constituted grounds for arrest, even if they had been voiced in the preceding year. Viguier, a wig-maker from the Section Poissonnière, arrested on 5 Prairial, was alleged to have stated 'that we will never be happy until we have cut the throats of the rich and the *muscadins*'.[8] Full of animosity and hatred for the rich, the sans-culottes always pursued a discriminatory policy against them once they had gained power in the Sections. Wealth was often an object of suspicion; and although it was rarely used as the sole grounds for arrest, it

[5] *A.N.*, F⁷ 4592, pl. 4, p. 58.
[6] *B.N.*, MSS. new acq. fr. 2662, f. 56–57.
[7] *A.N.*, F⁷ 4774⁸⁰.   [8] *A.N.*, F⁷ 4775⁴⁶.

was frequently introduced to confirm, or add substance, to some vague political accusation.

From certain statements which led to the imprisonment of Jean-Baptiste Mallais, a shoemaker and *commissaire révolutionnaire* in the Section du Temple, on 13 Ventôse Year II, it would appear that Mallais had conducted a personal campaign against wealthy citizens. He informed one that 'he had not been arrested because he thought of him as one of the sans-culottes, but that he had arrested his employer because he always put the rich in jail'. He had also told one woman that 'if her husband had about 20,000 *livres*, he would be guillotined, but as he had nothing, he regarded him as a sans-culotte'.[9] Allowing for an element of provocation in these remarks, they are none the less indicative of terrorist mentality. In August 1793, a citizen from the Section des Droits-de-l'Homme was refused a *certificat de civisme* simply because 'he had money'. A haberdasher named Godefroy in the Section des Lombards was arrested on 26 Ventôse for having created disturbances in the general assemblies on several occasions. Above all, it was his social position which had increased the suspicion against him—he was the owner of a cotton-mill at Vernon in the department of the Eure which employed 120 women, elderly men and children. His profits amounted to 16,122 *livres* a year.[1]

Thus, the instinctive reaction of the humblest citizen gradually became a systematic attitude of mind and, finally, a rule of political conduct amongst the more militant supporters of the Revolution. At the end of July 1793, when it looked as if the *possédants* were favouring the move towards federalism and forming the nucleus of the moderate party, a petition from the Section des Sans-Culottes demanded that the 'aristocracy' be stripped of its wealth and reduced to beggary.[2] A petition presented to the Convention by the Commune on 5 Frimaire called for the return of every wealthy citizen who had left Paris for the countryside, and denounced wealth as 'a gangrene which corrupts everything which comes into contact with it, and everything which depends upon it'.[3] On 9 Ventôse, a member of the *commission des salpêtres* in the Section Chalier, discussing a report by the police-agent Charmont, assured his hearers 'that he had never seen anything quite so grasping as the rich citizens of this Section'. Whilst the poor were

[9] *A.N.*, F⁷ 4774³².
[2] *A.D.S.*, 4 AZ 698, n.d.

[1] *A.N.*, F⁷ 4727.
[3] *A.N.*, D III, 251–2, d. 1.

sacrificing more than they could afford, the rich thought twice about giving anything at all: 'you have to hammer on the doors of these egoists who have no conception of what is meant by one's native-land'.[4]

This innate tendency amongst the sans-culotterie to attack the rich was encouraged in the Year II by leading political figures. Michel Lepeletier had written in his scheme of national education, which Robespierre read to the Convention on 13 and 29 July 1793: 'This is the revolution of the poor.' Saint-Just also announced on 8 Ventôse 'The poor are the masters of the earth: they have the right to speak with authority to governments who ignore their interests.' The actual social ideas of the Mountain and the Jacobins, their conception of class relationships, need not concern us here, nor do we need to question the sincerity of the Robespierrists; but it should be understood that this policy was only adopted as a tactical necessity, sometimes as a pretentious afterthought. The crisis from the spring to the autumn of 1793 made the popular alliance necessary: the sans-culottes represented the force which enabled the small section of the politically-conscious bourgeoisie to crush the aristocracy and its allies. 'Internal dangers', wrote Robespierre in his notebook during the insurrection of 2 June, 'come from the bourgeoisie. In order to overcome the bourgeoisie we have to rally the people.' Some *représentants en mission*, such as Fouché in the department of the Nièvre, took stock of these necessities and resolutely carried out a social policy favourable to the popular classes.

The theme of hostility between the rich and the sans-culottes was obviously exploited for political reasons by those who did not share in the responsibilities of government—Jacques Roux at first, then Hébert composed several variations on it. The sans-culottes represented an important striking-force through which pressure could be brought to bear upon the various governmental committees, and there can be no doubt that Hébert and his colleagues were prepared to exploit it in order to attain their own particular objectives. Jacques Roux had already placed an epigraph to his *Publiciste de la République française par Ombre de Marat—Ut redeat miseris, abeat fortuna superbis*. In its vulgar style, the *Père Duchesne* inveighed against the rich and exalted the poor: the expressions 'the selfish rich', 'the idle rich' and 'the

---

[4] *A.N.*, W 112.

useless rich' are all to be found in its pages. Hébert was only giving expression to a general idea which the sans-culottes already possessed; but, through his vigorous style, he imprinted it more clearly upon their imagination, giving them a better appreciation of the nature of the class struggle, in which they were engaged.

Obviously, we should not overestimate the importance of this attitude. In defining the rich, the sans-culottes did not distinguish clearly between the aristocracy and the bourgeoisie; nor did they represent a composite social unit themselves, including as they did *compagnons*, craftsmen and shopkeepers. However, a few of the sans-culottes appeared to be conscious of a policy based upon class differences. On several occasions, they petitioned for, or tried to realize the disarmament of the rich. On 20 April 1793, a number of members of the Section du Contrat-Social proposed that the rich should be forced to return their weapons. On 16 Frimaire Year II, the *comité révolutionnaire* of the Section de la Réunion decided to collect the arms of the rich so that they could be given to the sans-culottes. Others went further still. On 20 Ventôse Year III, Laugier, a former *juge de paix* in the Section de la Fontaine-de-Grenelle, was accused of having proposed to the general assembly that the rich, *rentiers*, financiers and bankers should all be despatched, since he regarded them as enemies of the Republic.[5] The same charge was levelled against Antoine Lebrun, an upholsterer and former *juge de paix* from the Section du Bonnet Rouge: 'he had roused uneducated citizens with inflammatory and bloodthirsty proposals against the rich, merchants, and decent, enlightened people'.[6] The most striking illustration of this attitude of mind was given in a petition from the Section de l'Observatoire on 29 September 1793 in which the 'nation was contrasted with the wholesale-merchant class, bankers, speculators, and the rich in general. . . . Because the sans-culottes are, after all, much more numerous, and it should be clear to everyone that the nation is "sans-culotte", and that the small number of people who dispose of its wealth cannot be the nation—they are only privileged citizens who are nearing the end of their privileges'.[7]

The more discerning members of the sans-culotterie began to realize that a privilege of wealth was taking the place of a privilege

[5] *A.N.*, F[7] 2509, f. 56.   [6] *A.N.*, F[7] 4774[8].
[7] *A.N.*, D III, 255-6[1], p. 18.

of birth. They foresaw that the bourgeoisie would succeed the fallen aristocracy as the ruling class. Fouquier-Thinville, commenting on the events which followed the flight to Varennes in his indictment of Bailly on 20 Brumaire Year II, noted this nascent social conflict when he referred to 'the people, above all those . . . who did not want to see a social group, known as the bourgeoisie, seize the inheritance of the two orders which had been abolished'. The police-agent Pourvoyeur in his report of 8 Ventôse contrasted the sans-culottes and 'a class which used to be called "bourgeois"'. However, it would be wrong to generalize about this frame of mind. It was impossible for the popular classes to gain a clear understanding of the social supremacy of the bourgeoisie until the aristocracy had finally been destroyed.

The hostile attitude of the sans-culotterie towards trade—one of the fundamental traits of popular mentality in the Year II—finally alienated sans-culotte sympathies for the rich. As urban consumers, the Parisian sans-culottes were naturally inclined to oppose those who controlled the supplies of basic commodities. As shopkeepers, they felt little affection for wholesalers. As craftsmen or *compagnons*, more rarely as workers in the real sense of the word, they remained small independent producers with no sympathy for, or understanding of, investors of commercial capital. The economic crisis and political struggles sharpened this antagonism inherent in the social position of the sans-culotterie. As food supplies grew scarce and the cost of living rose, every wholesale trader was soon suspected of being either a *monopoleur* or a hoarder. The struggle against the Girondins, then, after 31 May, against the moderates, was very often transformed into a struggle against the merchant bourgeoisie, at least in the Sections. The conflict became more acute as the sans-culottes continued to demand price fixing and controls on food supplies; as traders defended the freedom of production and distribution, so they became objects of suspicion. A new social enemy was added to that of the landed and the religious aristocracy—the 'merchant aristocracy'. When, in the Year II, political power changed hands favouring the moderates, one of the grievances which was repeatedly made against former terrorists was that of having persecuted the merchants: the purged Section des Gravilliers drafted a petition on 20 Germinal Year III stating that 'The Montagnards must bear the responsibility for ruining trade.'

In 1793 and in the Year III, sans-culotte hostility towards the merchants expressed itself during periods of acute crisis in violence and looting. It was also characterized by a constant desire for repression. According to one informer in the Year III, 'if the least disturbance arose in the assemblies of the Section des Marchés, the fault was laid at the feet of the merchants, who were threatened with the sword of the law'. The Section was largely composed of traders who were all treated as 'aristocrats': 'it was said that the greed of the grocers entitled the people to take the law into their own hands'.[8]

Once popular power had been firmly established in the Sections, merchants quickly attracted the suspicions of the various *comités révolutionnaires* simply on account of their occupation. This attitude was encouraged by the Commune which, on 19 January, listed as suspects 'those who sympathize with farmers and grasping merchants who must be made to feel the weight of the law'. Some committees had not even waited for this encouragement. On 14 September, the Section des Lombards, where hostility against traders was particularly pronounced, had already placed a citizen named Dussautoy in custody, not only because of his indifference towards the Revolution, but because he was a grocer.[9] The arrests of merchants went on until the spring of the Year II: the committee of the Section des Lombards ordered the arrest of Duthu on 18 Ventôse, and Garillaud on 1 Germinal. Apart from their indifference towards public affairs, the only charge brought against them was that the first was a merchant-grocer, and the second a merchant-haberdasher.

It was not simply a question of arresting individuals: an entire social category came under fire; and although the sans-culottes rejected the idea of eliminating it completely from political life, they were agreed that it should be subjugated until it had been rendered harmless. On 3 October 1793, the general assembly of the Section de l'Unité asked that merchants 'of whatever kind' should be excluded from the revolutionary tribunals. On 30 Nivôse Year II this same Section decided to name six *commissaires* to keep an eye on merchants 'of all kinds'. On 27 Pluviôse the *société populaire de Bonne-Nouvelle* listened to an address from citizen Jault, a member of the General Council of

---

[8] *A.N.*, F⁷ 4774⁴⁵, a declaration without date or signature.
[9] *A.N.*, F⁷ 4595, pl. 2, p. 70.

the Commune, attacking the merchant aristocracy. Such attacks on trade and tradesmen were one of the favourite themes of the *Père Duchesne*. It was only after Hébert and Chaumette had been sentenced that the arrest of merchants came to an end and the denunciations of trade ceased. The Committee of Public Safety launched a new commercial policy, and the leaders of the Commune, having decided to end a campaign which threatened to undermine the traditional structure of society, began to reinstate a profession which was now considered to be indispensable to the war effort.

At the height of the reaction of the Year III, merchants caused former terrorists to regret the cruelty which they had shown towards them. In Germinal and Prairial, innocent remarks were seized upon as providing sufficient grounds for arrest. The food crisis of this period, aggravated by the abolition of the maximum, had increased the old sans-culotte hostility towards trade even further. The records of the anti-terrorist repression make the attitude of the terrorists themselves abundantly clear: their crimes vary from a simple remark made in anger to a resolute determination to destroy an entire social category.

Davelin, a feather-merchant from the Section des Amis-de-la-Patrie, was deprived of the right of carrying arms on 5 Prairial Year III because he had stated in the previous year 'that there was no need to spare merchants or the rich'. Caillaud, a saddler in the Section de Bon-Conseil, was also arrested for having expressed the hope 'that things will get better, and that these fat rogues of merchants and *muscadins* will not always be our masters'. Some remarks give a clearer indication of social antagonisms. Barqui, a citizen from the Section de Bonne-Nouvelle, demanded in the Year II that merchants should be removed from the general assemblies and popular societies, as well as from all civil and military offices.[1]

For the militant or more extreme sans-culotte, it was a short step from hostility towards the merchants to a justification of pillage. Gillet, one of the most militant sans-culottes in the *société populaire des Quinze-Vingts*—if information deposited in the Year III can be relied upon—incited workmen at the port de la Rapée to loot the property of the merchants, describing the latter as 'swindlers and scoundrels'. 'The method he adopted to incite

---

[1] *A.N.*, F⁷ 4663; 4631; 4587, pl. 3, p. 93.

them to brigandage was to commiserate with their unfortunate lot, and to point out that they were earning too little.' On 5 Prairial Year III, in the Section des Gardes-Françaises, Chesneaux, a former president of the Cordelier club, was accused of having said in 1793 that 'pillage had a moral aim'. Debon, a carpenter from the Section des Quinze-Vingts was reproached 'for having urged the people, on several occasions, to pillage the merchants, saying that they were the worst possible enemies of the people'.[2] In a way, pillaging satisfied the deep-rooted egalitarian ideas of the sans-culottes (Chesneaux emphasizes this point when he says that pillaging had 'a moral aim'): individual acts of reprisals were justified by the inequalities in living conditions.

The profound antagonism which existed between the sans-culottes and the merchant bourgeoisie reveals itself more clearly in primitive impulses and terrorist exaltation than in the remarks made against traders or even in the encouragement given to pillaging. Many of the militant sans-culottes used the threat of the guillotine as an effective remedy against famine. In order to compel the farmers to sell their grain at a controlled price they demanded the creation of a revolutionary army, and once this had been decreed, they immediately began to ask for a mobile guillotine to accompany the army in order to make it more effective. This attitude accounts for the many scurrilous attacks on merchants in the Year II. A widow named Barbau from the Section de l'Indivisibilité, according to those who denounced her, was a woman with a furious temper who frequently expressed the opinion that 'as long as selfish merchants, nobles and people with money . . . were not guillotined or finished off *en masse*, things would never come right'—she naturally gave the merchants precedence over the nobles. A sans-culotte named Roux from the Section de l'Unité demanded the construction of guillotines 'on all the street-corners of Paris, and on the door-steps of the merchants so that goods can be bought more cheaply'.[3]

In the Year III, shortages and misery increased the hatred of the sans-culotte still further: the source material for this period reveals this bitterness to the full. Vivid recollections of the Year II convinced many of them of the necessity for a recourse to organized terror, so that the merchants would suffer the same fate as the

[2] *A.N.*, F⁷ 4645; 4664.
[3] *A.N.*, F⁷ 4585, pl. 5, p. 73; 4594, pl. 8.

aristocracy. The hatter Ferrier in the Section des Gardes-Françaises, calling to mind the rebellions of Lyons, Marseilles, and
Bordeaux in 1793 and the repression which followed, was alleged
to have said, 'we had to destroy the big *communes* which were
full of merchants and wealthy people whom it was necessary to
exterminate'. Baillieux, a tailor and member of the former *comité
révolutionnaire* of the Section du Muséum, declared that 'in the
event of a new uprising all the priests, nobles and merchants
would be butchered in their homes'. As for the Barbot sisters, who
kept a haberdashery shop in the Section des Gravilliers, they were
supposed to have said that 'if the Jacobins get the upper hand,
they will put guillotines on every street-corner so that all aristocrats, moderates and merchants could be brought to justice'.[4]

It would appear from this that in order to gain a true picture of
the sans-culotte it is necessary to depict him in opposition to the
aristocracy, wealth, and commerce. The need for so negative
an approach shows how vague the social boundaries within the
old Third Estate were, and how difficult it is to define the sans-
culotterie as a social class. The line of demarcation between the
latter and the bourgeoisie was by no means clear. A coalition of
disparate social elements, the unity of the sans-culotterie was
undermined by internal contradictions. It is these contradictions
which explain its incapacity to formulate a coherent policy and, in
the last analysis, its political defeat.

The ingrained hatred of the aristocracy was not confined to the
sans-culottes alone. It had been shared in 1789 by practically
every member of the Third Estate; although as the Revolution
became more extreme, they began to reconsider their attitude,
some sections of the bourgeoisie envisaging a compromise similar
to that made in England during the Glorious Revolution of 1688.
But in the Year II, the montagnard bourgeoisie—particularly its
jacobin wing—remained resolutely at the head of the struggle
against the aristocracy within France and on the frontiers. The
demands of this struggle determined the entire policy of the
Revolutionary Government.

Popular hostility against wealth and trade brought with it, on
the other hand, certain contradictions, in as much as the sans-
culotte shopkeeper and craftsman often owned his business

[4] *A.N.*, F⁷ 4706; 4584, pl. 5; 4586, pl. 3.

premises. Their spokesmen were always careful to explain that their anger was directed simply against property-owning on a large scale. The violent outbursts in the *Père Duchesne* arose from the fact 'that the *gros* continue to eat up the *petits*'. 'Our native-land be damned! The merchants do not know what the word means,' stormed Hébert, but then hastily added, 'Do not let it be said that I despise trade. No one has more respect than I for the honest man who lives by his toil'—meaning the craftsman and small tradesman. Hébert did not suspect that the interests of the latter were not always identical with those of the *compagnon* or wage-earner.

These contradictions, which militated against sans-culotte unity, emerge in some of the documents in which the sans-culottes endeavour to define themselves in a positive manner. These documents are all the rarer because they came from the humblest level of society; but they do underline the heterogeneous composition of the sans-culotterie.

In some of the texts, the sans-culottes are referred to as people who do not own anything—as proletarians in the traditional sense of the word. Didot, president of the *comité révolutionnaire* of the Section de la Réunion, defining the spirit of the Republic in a *Précis sur la Révolution et le caractère français*, published in Brumaire Year II, contrasts the rich with 'the true patriots who are mostly poor'. The sans-culotte protects the property of the rich, 'and every day the wealthy aristocrat violates the property of the people—its rights, its livelihood and its liberty'. In a placard dated 27 Pluviôse, Erimante Lambin of the Section Chalier, denounced lawyers, solicitors, priests and nobles, comparing them with the sans-culottes 'who have nothing'.[5] Babeuf was soon to speak of the 'propertyless' sans-culottes. Property-owners themselves were well aware that, amongst the patriots, the sans-culottes represented the bulk of 'propertyless' citizens. On 5 July 1793, Chabot addressed the Jacobins on a letter from General Ramel who had written from Toulouse, 'that only property-owners could save the State. How can your interests be entrusted to anyone else?' Ramel asked. 'Surely, your arms are not to be handed over to the sans-culottes.'[6] The clearest definition which comes from a sans-culotte source, however, is that indignantly given by Petion to the Convention on 10 April 1793: '. . . when we speak of the

[5] *A.N.*, W 191.   [7] *Journal de la Montagne*, 10 July 1793.

sans-culottes', he explained, 'we do not mean the citizens who are left after the nobles and the aristocrats have been excluded; we refer to the "have nots" as opposed to the "haves" '.[7]

Owning nothing, the sans-culotte worked in order to live, and to be more precise, he worked with his hands: in some of the sources the meaning of the word becomes even more specific. A favourite theme of Hébert's, who knew how to play upon the susceptibilities of his readers, was that the sans-culottes included the mass of the working population, representing 'the most invaluable part' of the nation. 'No one is worth more than the sans-culotte,' he wrote in the *Père Duchesne* in September 1793, 'they are the people who make the clothes in which we stand. They are the people who forge the metals and manufacture the weapons which are used to defend the Republic.' Hébert then goes on to compare 'these hardworking artisans who exhaust themselves with work', with bankers, financiers, merchants, monopolists, and lawyers, 'in fact all the leeches of the sans-culotterie'.[8] In its address to the Convention on 24 September 1793 the Section Poissonnière sets the 'selfish rich' against 'that industrious part of the population which only manages to live by its work'. Vingternier, a sans-culotte arrested on 17 Germinal Year III, when questioned about his Section replied that he belonged to no Section other 'than that of the people and the workers (*ouvriers*)'.

During the repression of the Year III, former militant sans-culottes were frequently accused of having exploited social conflicts, which property-owners had every reason to conceal, for their own political purposes. Denouncing 'the faction (which) conjured up the absurd expressions *muscadins* and *sans-culottes*', on 20 Germinal, the *honnêtes gens* of the Section de Bon-Conseil criticized it for having divided citizens into two anatagonistic classes: 'In the first (as if two classes could exist amongst Republicans), these ill-disposed persons placed lawyers, *rentiers*, men of letters, clerks, and artists. In the second . . . they put only those admirable citizens who are used to working with their hands. . . . They repeated continuously that those who were richer, better dressed or better educated than themselves were counter-revolutionaries and their enemies; and, as if patriotism could only be found in a man's profession or dress, they had founded the privileged caste of the *sans-culotterie* so exclusively that, in their

[7] *Moniteur*, xvi, 101.   [8] No. 283, n.d.

opinion, one could not find responsible citizens outside it.'[9] Even
allowing for the malice and exaggeration no doubt contained in
such a denunciation, it is clear that a small section of the sans-
culotterie tended to push the conflict between the property-
owner and the workman into the foreground, whereas the
moderates who returned to power in the Year III still persisted in
the traditional antagonism between the Third Estate and the aristocracy. The confused awareness of this conflict with the propertied-classes only hastened the disintegration of the sans-culotte
coalition, and the withdrawal of craftsmen and shopkeepers who,
although they were only small-owners, belonged none the less to
the *possédant* class.

Fully aware of the fundamental antagonisms of *ancien régime*
society, and consumed with hatred for the aristocracy—a hatred
they shared with the montagnard bourgeoisie—the sans-culotterie
were still not really 'class-conscious'. Divided into different social
categories, sometimes with conflicting aims, it was practically
impossible for them to constitute a class: their unity, in so far as
it existed, was of a negative kind. One final point emphasizes this.
According to popular mentality, a sans-culotte could not be
defined by social characteristics alone: a counter-revolutionary
workman could not be a good sans-culotte; a bourgeois patriot and
republican might very well be accepted as one. The social definition must be qualified by a political definition: they cannot be
separated. 'One can only find virtue and patriotism', announces
the *Père Duchesne*, 'amongst sans-culottes: without them, the
Revolution would be finished. The salvation of the Republic lies
in their hands.' Here the word sans-culotte is used as a synonym
for patriot and republican.

For the sans-culotte, it was not simply a question of describing
oneself as a sans-culotte, or of adopting a patronizing attitude
towards the Revolution, it was a question of political conduct.
The sans-culotte had taken part in the great revolutionary *journées*;
he had fought for the democratic Republic. In the general assembly
of the Section des Marchés on 9 Prairial Year III, Hébert, an
itinerant herbalist and a sans-culotte, defended himself against
charges of terrorism by reminding his accusers of his services to
the Republic: 'Of course I am a terrorist', he admitted, 'but the

[9] *B.N.*, L6[40] 1733.

only proof I have given of it is before the château of the tyrant Capet on 10 August, when my terrorism cost me my right arm ... I am a man of blood, but I spilt no blood on 10 August apart from my own, a loss I have only regretted because it prevented me from going to fight with my brothers on the frontiers.'[1] A still more precise definition was given by Brutus Magnier, president of a military commission to the *armées de l'Ouest* in the Year II. Having criticized 'the government which has sworn the downfall of the sans-culottes' in a letter seized by the authorities, he was asked during his interrogation on 21 Messidor Year III what he meant by the word sans-culotte. Magnier replied: 'I would say that it meant the conquerors of the Bastille, the victors of the "10 August" and the "31 May", particularly the latter who appear to have had an eternal war sworn against them. It also refers to those who had been described as terrorists and *buveurs de sang* by those cannibals who more justly deserve these titles.'[2] The sans-culotte, therefore, is defined by his political behaviour as much as by his place in society—the latter is more difficult to ascertain than the former.

A document dated May 1793 attempts to answer part of this difficulty, at least, in replying to 'the impertinent question—what is a sans-culotte?'[3] The sans-culotte '. . . is someone who goes everywhere on foot . . . and who lives quite simply with his wife and children, if he has any, on the fourth or fifth floor'. Jacques Roux also referred to the sans-culottes living in attics, and the *Père Duchesne* wrote, 'If you wish to meet the cream of the sans-culotterie, then visit the garrets of the workers (ouvriers).' The sans-culotte is useful 'because he knows how to plough a field, how to forge, to saw, to file, to cover a roof and how to make shoes. . . . And since he works, it is certain that you will not find him at the café de Chartres, nor in the dens where people gamble and plot, nor at the théatre de la Nation where they are performing *l'Ami des lois* . . .[4] In the evening, he goes to his Section, not powdered and perfumed, not elegantly dressed in the hope of catching the eye of the citizens in the galleries, but to give his unreserved support to sound resolutions. . . . Besides this, the sans-culotte always has his sword with the edge sharpened to

---

[1] *A.N.*, F⁷ 4743.   [2] *A.N.*, F⁷ 4774²⁹.   [3] *A.N.*, F⁷ 4775⁴⁸.
[4] The café de Chartres was a favourite royalist meeting-place: *l'Ami des lois* was a comedy by Jean Laya performed in 1793.

give a salutary lesson to all trouble-makers. Sometimes he carries his pike with him, and at the first beat of the drum, he will be seen leaving for the Vendée, for the *armée des Alpes* or the *armée du Nord.*'

The modest social condition of the sans-culotte is clearly of importance here; but, as we can see from the above document, a definition of the sans-culotte would not be complete without a statement of his political conduct.

If we attempt a statistical analysis of the Parisian Sections in the Year II on the basis of the texts and political documents at our disposal, we are confronted with the same difficulties when it comes to defining the sans-culotterie, and of establishing its proportion to the population of Paris as a whole.

To begin with it is impossible to say precisely what the population of Paris was at this time: it is even more difficult to estimate the proportion of the sans-culotterie in each Section. The law of 11 August 1793 ordered a census to be taken of the population of each Section, but although this began in the Year II it proceeded very slowly. Only ten Sections had been completed by Thermidor, and the census dragged on through the Year III. On 11 Fructidor, the *Comité de division* decided to draw up a list of all the holders of bread cards registered in the Sections. Its *Tableau Sommaire* of the population of Paris gives us a total of 640,504 inhabitants: a figure greater than the census taken at the time of the States General in 1789, and one which is doubtless exaggerated—the Sections being anxious to produce a list with a greater number of mouths to feed than they actually had. However, it does agree roughly with a statement of the population of Paris *relativement aux subsistances* of 13 Pluviôse Year III which appears to have escaped notice until now, and which gives a figure of 636,772 inhabitants.

However approximate these figures may be, they do throw an interesting light upon the pressure which the population in the various Sections exercised on the problem of food supplies. The Section du Panthéon-Français was the most densely populated with 24,977 inhabitants, followed very closely by the Gravilliers Section with 24,774. On the other hand, it is remarkable that the Sections in the *faubourgs* of Saint-Antoine and Saint-Marcel were not amongst the most populated zones. In the former, the

Section des Quinze-Vingts reached fifth place with 18,283 inhabitants, but Montreuil was only seventeenth (13,478), and Popincourt thirty-sixth (10,933). The Section du Finistère in the *faubourg* Saint-Marcel was listed as thirtieth with 11,775 inhabitants. Two thickly populated areas appear in the heart of Paris on either side of the Seine. On the right bank there were 180,000 people living in the twelve Sections of the centre; on the left bank, the four Sections of Unité, Bonnet-Rouge, Mutius-Scaevola, and Marat included over 70,000 inhabitants. In the Year II, these different Sections were amongst the most politically active in Paris—the shortage of food supplies being felt more acutely there than anywhere else. The name alone of Ducroquet as *commissaire aux accaparements* in the Marat Section is evidence of the pressure exerted by the popular masses upon the authorities, and the remedies which they proposed in their confusion and misery.

The distribution of the working population corresponds to these areas of population density, the majority being concentrated in the heart of the capital. The work of F. Braesch, based on the replies received from employers on the subject of the exchange of large *assignats* for smaller notes to facilitate the payment of their workmen, allows us to estimate the number of wage-earners in forty-one of the forty-eight Sections around 1791.[5] The figure Braesch gives is 62,743, and if we take an average of four people for every family, this makes a total of 250,927 inhabitants. Braesch then goes on to estimate that the working population of Paris as a whole was 293,820 persons: about half the total population of the capital. Two thickly populated zones were situated in the centre of Paris on either side of the Seine. On the left bank the Unité, Marat, Bonnet-Rouge, Mutius-Scaevola, Chalier, and Panthéon-Français Sections included more than 10,000 wage-earners. On the right bank, a compact block stretched from the Seine to the *barrières* with a total of 28,000. In contrast, the most famous *faubourgs* in revolutionary history had fewer wage-earners than the heart of the capital. The three Sections of the *faubourg* Saint-Antoine had only 4,519, only 613 in the Section du Finistère, *faubourg* Saint-Marcel, and 3,441 if we add the two neighbouring Sections of the Observatoire and Sans-Culottes.

[5] F. Braesch, 'Essai de statistique de la population ouvrière de Paris vers 1791', *La Révolution française*, t. 63, 1912, p. 288.

This concentration of the working population is equally significant if we look at it by workshop and Section. Although the average number of wage-earners to every employer stood at 16·6 for the whole of Paris, it drops to 14·9 in the *faubourg* Saint-Antoine: in the Section du Finistère it was 16·1. In the *quartiers ouvriers* in the centre of Paris the average was 15·6 on the left bank, but 19·6 on the right bank. The Section with the least number of wage-earners was the Section de la Fraternité with 305; whilst the Section des Amis-de-la-Patrie in the heart of Paris had 5,288. The concentration of labour in the Section des Marchés and the Section du Faubourg-du-Nord is clearly indicated by the fact that the average number of wage-earners to each business rises to 27·9 and 31·8 respectively: for the Section des Sans-Culottes it was 25·7. As a contrast, the small independent craftsman predominates in the Brutus, l'Homme-Armé and Révolutionnaire Sections where the average drops to 10·2, 9·9, and 8·5 respectively.

The statements for the exchange of *assignats* used by Braesch, however, do not give an accurate picture of the social structure of Parisian labour. 'The only employers who are to be found in these statements are those who were responsible for the pay of the workers. But how many small craftsmen working alone in their workshops were not included in these returns. How many *compagnons*, living under the same roof, and eating at the same table as their employer were paid mostly in kind? In fact, the calculations of Braesch do not include small artisan industry.

Proof of this is given in the reports drawn up by the authorities of the Section du Faubourg-Montmartre in June 1793 for carpentry, wheelwright, lock-making, and joinery concerns.[6] The concentration of labour appears to be considerably less than we would have expected from the documents used by Braesch. It varies according to the different professions. It is greatest for those which demand a capital outlay and a more important stock of tools—carpenters, for example, employed more men than locksmiths. In June 1793, there were nine carpentry businesses in the Section du Faubourg-Montmartre employing a total of 81 workmen, or an average of 9 to each business. However, one concern gave employment to 31 men, another to 14, and seven employed 3 to 7 workmen. The concentration is less marked amongst the wheelwrights where there were 146 men employed in twenty-three

[6] *B.N.*, MSS. new acq. fr. 2686, f. 117–22.

concerns: an average of 6·1. The largest enterprise employed 24 workmen, two of them had 14, one 12, and another 11. But two wheelwrights worked alone, two of them had only one employee each; three workshops accounted for two workmen, two employed three each. Three wheelwrights were partners in the same workshop; four others, also partners, had four employees. In the nineteen joinery concerns in the Section, the average number of *compagnons* drops to 5·2, and although one can point to four enterprises with 24, 12, 11, and 10 *compagnons* respectively, four master-joiners worked alone. One of the enterprises had only one *compagnon*, two others employed 2, and another 4: three small employers worked with 5 *compagnons* each, two with 6. The average is still lower in the lock-making business: 51 *compagnons* for twenty-five concerns, or an average of 2 *compagnons* for each workshop. One concern did employ 16 men, but ten had none at all, five had only one *compagnon* each, and three had two each. These few facts enable us to qualify Braesch's figures concerning the concentration of labour in Paris. For the Section du Faubourg-Montmartre he estimated that there was an average of 15·9 employees to every employer, but, using the reports of June 1793 which dealt with four trades, we obtain an average of 5·5. It is true that this figure does not take into account occupations in which the concentration of labour was already heavy: for example, the textile industry, cloth-making and hosiery. But it would appear to be more accurate than that given by Braesch whose calculations are falsified by the exclusion of small undertakings where the craftsman worked alone, or at the most with one or two *compagnons*. It was indeed the craftsman who left the strongest imprint on the world of Parisian labour.

On the fringe of the working population, exercising a decisive influence on the population of Paris as a whole during times of scarcity, stood thousands of wretched and starving human beings. According to a report presented to the General Council of the Commune by the hospital administrator Danjou on 14 Germinal Year II,[7] the number of destitute persons (*indigents secourus*) who had been given assistance in all the Sections of Paris reached a total of 68,981, or, if we use the population returns *relativement aux subsistances* of Pluviôse Year III, about one person in every nine obtained relief from the authorities in Paris. The pressure

[7] *Journal de la Montagne*, 17 Germinal Year II.

exerted by these unfortunate people varied from Section to Section. It was particularly strong in the historic *faubourgs*, throwing light upon their political activity during the Revolution. The three Sections of the *faubourg* Saint-Antoine had 14,742 destitute persons requiring assistance—one out of every three inhabitants. From these figures, we can readily appreciate why the problem of daily bread assumed a greater importance than any other in these Sections. When the *faubourg* was disarmed on 4 Prairial Year III, the wheelwright L. Delormé, captain of the *canonniers* in the Section de Popincourt, was asked by General Menou if he was a republican. Standing at the head of his artillery, Delormé replied: 'Have you any bread to give me?' The Section des Quinze-Vingts headed the list of Parisian Sections giving help to the destitute with a total of 6,601, followed by the Section de Finistère with 4,951, or one person out of every 2·3 of the inhabitants: the proportion was higher in the *faubourg* Saint-Marcel than in the *faubourg* Saint-Antoine. On the left bank again, the Chalier, Panthéon-Français, Observatoire and Sans-Culottes Sections had 10,625 *indigents secourus*—approximately one in six of the total number of inhabitants. These Sections were amongst the most politically active in the Year II. Similarly, also on the left bank, the Section du Bonnet-Rouge had 2,037 destitute citizens—one in eight of the population. In the west, however, there were fewer *indigents*, but the proportion rises again on the northern outskirts of Paris. The number of destitute in the Faubourg-Montmartre, Faubourg-Poissonnière, Faubourg-du-Nord, Bondy, and Temple Sections totalled 8,448—one out of every 6·4 inhabitants. In the centre of the capital, the worst situation was to be found in the Section de la Maison-Commune which was third on the list with a total of 4,258, a proportion of 2·9 of all its inhabitants. As a contrast, only one person in 16·5 received assistance in the Section des Gravilliers—a total of 1,616 out of 24,774 inhabitants.

From these figures, we can build a social picture of the Parisian sans-culotterie which emphasizes the essential feature of popular movements during the Revolution—that of hunger.

If in times of crisis, the complex and solid mass of the Parisian sans-culotterie provided the impetus behind the more violent episodes in the Revolution, in calmer times, less worried about the provision of its food, it paid only a fluctuating attention to political affairs. Not every sans-culotte was a militant. A study of the sectionary political personnel in the Year II will give us a more complete and more balanced social description of the Parisian sans-culotterie.

For this study, the most important material has been taken from the collection of dossiers forming the alphabetical series of papers of the Committee of General Security.[8] Based primarily on the repression of Prairial Year III, in some respects they throw as much light on the Thermidorean psychology of the property-owning classes as on the terrorist mentality of the sans-culottes themselves. We need, therefore, to be very careful about accepting the many denunciations contained in these documents. As the class struggle intensified during the spring of the Year III, the least word was exaggerated and used as evidence to justify arrests, explaining why so many people were arrested as *septembriseurs* when it is perfectly clear that they had taken no part whatsoever in the massacres of September 1792. Bitterness and personal vengeance were given free rein. There was also the very real fear experienced by many of the *honnêtes gens* in the Year II of seeing themselves deprived of their social and political status: the repression was particularly severe for this reason. The numerous files dealing with disarmament and arrests present an equally valuable documentation, the only one which gives us direct information on the political personnel of the Sections as a whole.

The nature of this evidence does not, by any means, enable us to make an exact statistical study—the age of the militant sans-culottes is rarely indicated; their profession is often omitted; the vocabulary is loose and misleading. Any study of the social composition of the sans-culotterie is, therefore, beset by many uncertainties. At the end of the eighteenth century, manual workers were frequently referred to, rather disdainfully, as *le peuple* by the propertied-classes, aristocrats and the bourgeoisie. The bookseller Hardy writing in his *Journal* unites under the same phase—*menu peuple*—the non-propertied-classes and the lower middle class Parisians who were, in fact, often property-owners—small tradesmen and workshop masters as well as *compagnons*, labourers and the destitute. In fact, there are as many shades of difference between the lower middle-classes and the proletariat as

[8] *A.N.*, F[7] 4577–4775[53]: a collection of 348 boxes.

there are varieties of social conflict. Jean-Jacques Rousseau had written in his *Confessions* that he had been born 'in a family which distinguished itself from the "people" by its manners and social customs'. Robespierre's host, the cabinet-maker Duplay, provides another example of this kind of attitude. The remark of his daughter, wife of the *conventionnel* Lebas, recalling that her father had never, out of a sense of his bourgeois dignity, eaten with any of his *serviteurs* (referring to his workmen) has often been quoted. Jaurès reminds us that Duplay received not less than ten to twelve thousand *livres* from house-letting alone, not to mention the earnings from his own trade. The vocabulary reflects the faint lines of demarcation between social groups and the indelible mark imprinted upon those who belonged to the artisan class: it was the trade or guild which supplied the qualification, not the kind of work a man did, nor yet what his position was in his chosen profession. The 'cabinet-maker' Duplay certainly had his connexions with the working population, but he was never the less a furniture-contractor on a large scale. Had he ever used a jointing-plane in his youth? Or his father? Or his grandfather? It may appear to be only a small detail, but the question would have to be considered before we could write a true social history of the Revolution. The head of a business concern kept his professional qualification and still described himself as a 'cabinet-maker' or a 'carpenter' even when he was employing dozens of workers. This was the case with the 'fan-maker' Mauvage, a militant sans-culotte in the Section du Faubourg-du-Nord: we have to study his dossier carefully before we discover that he owned a factory which employed sixty people. The same word is used to describe social realities which are basically different, and we have to decide in each case exactly where these artisans and shopkeepers belonged in the social hierarchy. At what point does the work of a craftsman become a business concern? More often than not, the documents of the period fail to distinguish between the *compagnon*, the small crafts-man and the contractor: the degrees of difference between them are multiple, and the transition from one to the other is graded into many stages. Any attempt to fix a rigid system of classification upon so fluid a society must be arbitrary. In any case, it would not be possible to make a really satisfactory study if we were to rely solely on the political documents: we need to determine the financial resources of the militants. However, the absence of fiscal documents for the Parisian Sections makes this extremely difficult. Intensive research into the notarial records might perhaps compensate for this loss, at least for those sans-culottes whose social standing bordered on the edge of the middle bourgeoisie. As for the records dealing with the lowest strata of Parisian society, they have disappeared altogether unless reference to them can be found in the dossiers of the anti-terrorist repression.

The political personnel of the Parisian Sections in the Year II may be divided, according to their functions and their social background, into three categories illustrating the social diversity of the sans-culotterie. The personnel of the *comités civils* represented the oldest, most stable and most prosperous category, and were often considered as belonging to the middle bourgeoisie. A later institution, the *comités révolutionnaires* were more popular in origin. The personnel of these committees were very soon paid for their services. From March 1793 to Fructidor Year II, they suffered from the repercussions of political upheavals, becoming more and more democratic until the autumn of 1793. The third category was that of the ordinary militant sans-culottes, mostly to be found after the autumn in the *sociétées sectionnaires*, representing the most popular elements of the sans-culotterie.

Created by the municipal law of 21 May–27 June 1790, and composed of citizens with the necessary qualifications for voting, the *comités civils* were largely renewed after 10 August 1792. Most of the *commissaires* on these committees kept their posts from this date to the Year III, some of them even escaping the reprisals in Prairial. Their purely administrative function provided them with the opportunity to stand aloof from political terrorist activities. Moreover, although the committees received money from the municipality for their expenses, the *commissaires* were for a long time unpaid. It was only on 6 Floréal Year II that the Convention voted the payment of three *livres* a day in recognition of their public services. This allowance came too late for the personnel of these committees to be democratized. The *commissaires civils* belonged mostly to the higher ranks of the sans-culotterie. The money which they earned from their workshops, or from their business interests, permitted them to devote their time to their administrative tasks.

The *comités révolutionnaires*, at first paid only their expenses, but later salaried, were more democratically recruited than the *comités*

civils. They represented the more popular elements of the sans-
culotterie. Few of the *commissaires* lived off their own incomes—
only 20, or 4·6 per cent. of the total number of 454; whereas
26·2 per cent. of the members of the *comités civils* did so. Amongst
them only 4 were *rentiers* in the full sense of the word (0·8 per
cent.); 11 belonged to the liberal professions (2·4 per cent.), and 6
were former shopkeepers or artisans (1·3 per cent.). Although
there were few heads of business concerns, there were also no
really popular elements. Manufacturers, contractors, or master-
craftsmen accounted for 13 (2·8 per cent. as compared with 2·3
per cent. for the *comités civils*). On the other hand, we find 22
wage-earners, operatives, *compagnons* or apprentices, and 23
domestic servants or former domestic servants—a total of 9·9 per
cent. The liberal professions were represented by 52 *commissaires*—artists, sculptors, painters, musicians, and schoolteachers: lawyers were relatively few. To this group we can add
22 lower-grade civil servants (*employés*), 7 of whom were employed
by the Post Office (4·8 per cent.).

Here again, most of the *commissaires* were craftsmen or
shopkeepers: 290 out of the total of 454, or 63·8 per cent. of the
personnel of the *comités révolutionnaires*. Altogether, 206 *commissaires* (45·3 per cent.) could be considered as having some
connexion with the artisan class; 84 were engaged in commerce
(18·5 per cent.). The craftsmen are relatively more numerous than
in the *comités civils*: for many of them, expenses of three, and later
of five *livres* a day, compensated for the decline or total loss of
their trade: this is substantiated by the number of craftsmen
connected with the luxury or art trades. The 28 shoemakers form
the most important group (6·1 per cent.), followed by the 18
cabinet-makers (3·9 per cent.), then 16 wig-makers or hairdressers
(3·5 per cent.). But there were 42 *commissaires* connected with
some branch or other of the art trade (9·2 per cent.). A group of
37 *commissaires* were builders (8·1 per cent.), and 29 were
timber-merchants or furniture-makers (6·3 per cent.).

Amongst the 84 persons engaged in trade, 41 described as
merchants appear to have held a status above that of an ordinary
shopkeeper. Ten wine merchants, whether wholesale or retail
traders, headed the list, to which we can add six who sold soft
drinks. The sale of drinks played an important part in the political
life of the Sections. Another 15 dealt in the provision of food

supplies: there were 6 grocers, 3 pastry-cooks, a baker, a fruiterer, also 2 restaurant-owners and 2 inn-keepers.

Scattered hints in individual dossiers sometimes enable us to discover the social standing of these *commissaires*. Many craftsmen and shopkeepers who had been more or less ruined by the loss of customers found a means of livelihood in the salaried duties of a *commissaire*. This explains the large numbers of wig-makers, hairdressers and shoemakers to be found on the *comités révolutionnaires*, as well as the domestic servants who had lost their positions, particularly numerous in the committee of the Section du Bonnet-Rouge in what used to be the *faubourg* Saint-Germain. Noel, a wig-maker from the Section de Bon-Conseil had lost his job 'because of the Revolution', and he had three children and an old mother to care for. A similar case was that of Jean-Baptiste Moulin, also a wig-maker, *commissaire* of the Section de la Republique and a juror on the Revolutionary Tribunal from 22 Prairial Year II. Arrested in the Year III, he defended himself by the following statement: 'having lost my position as a wig-maker I was forced to enter the *comité de surveillance* in my Section so that I could live'. Miel, a sans-culotte from the Section des Marchés held in custody since 5 Prairial, had according to the *comité civil* in Messidor Year III 'accepted a place on the *comité révolutionnaire* so that he could procure the means of livelihood for himself, his wife and his children'.[9]

If many of the *commissaires* found that their duties rewarded them with an income which they could no longer derive from their occupations, some on the other hand, still enjoyed either a modest income or a situation of some importance. Lambert, a *commissaire* in the Section de l'Arsenal, was a former domestic servant living on his small private income. Etienne Fournier, *commissaire* for the Section de l'Indivisibilité who had been a crockery-dealer, enjoyed an income of 1,700 *livres*, the yearly salary of an ordinary *employé*. In the Section Révolutionnaire, *commissaire* Tarreau considered that his position as a jeweller did not give him 'what one might call a fortune'; 'it only provided me with the everyday necessities of life to keep my wife and children'. This meant that Tarreau's social status lay about half-way between the wealthy and the popular classes. The dyer Barrucand from the Section de l'Arsenal, 'conqueror of the

---

[9] *A.N.*, F⁷ 4774⁵⁸, 4774⁵⁴, 4774⁴⁵.

Bastille', a *commissaire* dealing with the manufacture of pikes, member of the *comité révolutionnaire*, admitted that he was worth 21,600 *livres*. He had bought a house valued at 47,300 *livres*: doubtless, to do this, he must have borrowed money and sold his silverware, but this does not mean that he was any the less comfortably situated.[1]

Other *commissaires* were important business men. In the Section des Gardes-Françaises, Maron, a plaster-manufacturer, employed twenty workmen in the quarry which he owned. As for Mauvage, *commissaire* in the Section du Faubourg-du-Nord, a really militant sans-culotte, we have seen that he was responsible for a fan-making concern employing sixty workers: nevertheless, he still called himself a 'fan-maker'. Some profited from their circumstances to put themselves on their feet financially and to rise in the social scale. Candolle, *commissaire* in the Section de l'Arsenal, previously a porter, became a wine-merchant. Larue, a member of the *comité révolutionnaire* of the Section des Lombards, did even better—an apprentice mason in 1789, he had become a building-contractor by the Year II. According to those who informed against him in the following year, 'The Commune had given him work on various projects which helped him to make his money.'[2]

Although the *comités révolutionnaires* drew more upon the popular classes than the *comités civils*, they still reveal very much the same social pattern—from wage-earner to the large employer. The sans-culotterie did, indeed, represent a coalition of socially heterogeneous elements.

If we look at the third category of the political personnel in the Sections in the Year II—that of the militants, we arrive at the same conclusion, with the slight difference, however, that the wage-earning element in this group is more important. Out of the total number of 514 militants counted (and by the word 'militant' we mean every citizen who played an active political role, whether in the popular society or in the general assembly, and who, for this reason, became a victim of the reaction of the Year III), 64 were wage-earners—*compagnons*, operatives, apprentices, journeymen or day-labourers—a percentage of 12·4. If we add to this list domestic servants, odd-job men, office-boys and

---

[1] *A.N.*, F⁷ 3688², 4759, 4775²⁶, 4774³³.
[2] *A.N.*, F⁷ 4774³⁵, 4774⁴⁰, 3688², 4766.

shop-assistants, 40 in all (7·7 per cent.), the popular element forms
20·1 per cent. of the militant group, as opposed to 9·9 per cent.
of the personnel of the *comités révolutionnaires*, and 0·8 per cent. of
the *comités civils*. As a contrast, we find only one *rentier* and one
landlord, 8 shopkeepers or retired traders (1·9 per cent.), whereas
on the *comités révolutionnaires* and *comités civils* this group represented 4·6 per cent. and 26·2 per cent. respectively. The number
of contractors or manufacturers is also quite small—only 4, or
0·7. On the *comités civils*, this percentage rises to 2·3 per cent. and
to 2·8 per cent. on the *comités révolutionnaires*. As for the liberal
professions, they are represented by 35 militants (6·8 per cent.), to
which we can add 45 *employés*, making a total percentage 15·5.
This group of *employés* is particularly important for, more often
than not, they formed the life-blood of the *sociétés sectionnaires*.

The shopkeeper and, above all, the artisan class predominate
amongst the militants, although the proportion is lower than for
either of the two committees—81 tradesmen (15·7 per cent.), and
214 craftsmen, (41·6 per cent.). Amongst the tradesmen, 34
(6·6 per cent.) are described as merchants. The 18 engaged in the
grocery trade were the most numerous, but the 10 wine-merchants
are placed on top of the list, confirming the importance of their
contribution to the political life of the Sections.

Amongst the 214 artisans, the shoemakers form a compact
group of 41 militants (7·9 per cent. of the whole), followed by 24
hairdressers and wig-makers, and 20 tailors: should we, perhaps,
establish a relationship between the militant activity of these small
craftsmen and their professional difficulties? The building trade
accounts for 30 militants (5·8 per cent.), there were 29 engaged in
the timber and furniture trades (5·6 per cent.), but only 23 from
the art and luxury trades (4·4 per cent.). Thus the trades which
demanded fewer professional qualifications provided a large
number of militants. For the *comités civils* and *comités révolutionnaires* the proportion was reversed: the artisans were really an
élite to which the sans-culottes in many of the Sections looked for
leadership.

Although the wage-earning element predominated amongst the
militants, there were also many citizens who were comfortably
situated, financially and socially. In the Section des Droits-de-
l'Homme, Varlet possessed an income of 5,800 *livres*. In addition
to his salary as a postal clerk, this *enragé* had a small income of his

own, and could obviously be regarded as a representative of the middle classes. François Mercier in the Section Marat, formerly an assistant in a hat shop, was a juror on the Revolutionary Tribunal. He had invested the 12,150 *livres* which he had inherited from his mother in 1780 in a life insurance policy. He said that he had taken an interest 'in the business affairs of different people', and had also saved from his income, and from his fees as a juror, the sum of 9,430 *livres*. In the Year III, he stated that he was worth 21,580 *livres*. Bouland, an active militant from the *société de Lazowski* and the Section du Finistère, who never stopped 'condemning the activities of merchants', had bought a house at the beginning of the Revolution in the boulevard Hôpital. Damoye, a saddle-merchant in the Section de Montreuil was arrested in Pluviôse Year III for his terrorist activities in the previous year. In his defence statement, he described himself as a well-to-do property-owner, adding that 'he has his living to think of, and, for this reason, has suffered great anxiety since he was put under arrest two months ago'. In the Year IV, the same man was asked for a forced loan of 3,000 *livres* (hard currency).[3] Damoye was a typical example of the bourgeois sans-culotte.

Thus, if we analyse the composition of the political personnel of the Sections in the Year II, as well as the part played by the *faubourg* Saint-Antoine and to a lesser extent by the *faubourg* Saint-Marcel in the revolutionary movement and the important *journées* from July 1789 to Prairial Year III, we must conclude that the revolutionary *avant-garde* of the Parisian sans-culotterie did not constitute an industrial proletariat, but a coalition of small master-craftsmen and *compagnons* who worked and lived with them. This explains certain characteristics of the popular movement, as well as certain contradictions, arising from the ambiguous situation in which the sans-culottes often found themselves.

The small master-craftsman, working and living with his *compagnons*, very often a former *compagnon* himself, exercised a decisive ideological influence on the latter. Through him, bourgeois influences penetrated into the world of the workman. Even if he was in conflict with him, the small workshop *compagnon* inevitably derived many of his ideas from his employer, and often living and eating under the same roof had basically the same

[3] *A.N.*, F[7] 4775[40], 4774[42], 4611, d. 5, 4660.

attitude to the great problems of the day. It was the lower middle-class craftsman who fashioned the mentality of the worker. However, having said this, many small problems remain to be solved. In particular, we must distinguish between the 'independent' craftsman of Paris and the 'dependent' craftsman, the classic example of the latter being the silk-weavers of Lyons—*le canut lyonnais*. Juridically free and head of his concern, possessing his own machine, even in a position to hire his own labour, the latter has all the appearance of an employer. But economically he is only a wage-earner, strictly dependent upon the merchant who supplies him with the raw material and who distributes the finished article. The interests of the 'dependent' craftsman and the *compagnon* are the same—confronted with merchant capitalism they demanded price-controls and a basic minimum wage. But they did not go so far as to work out a direct relationship between the nature of the work and the rate of pay: wages were determined by the cost of living, not by the value of the work done. The social function of labour is not clearly understood. The dependent craftsman stands in an intermediate position between the *compagnon* and the independent craftsman aspiring towards the status of a lower middle-class citizen.

As for the wage-earning worker in the large manufacturing concerns, more important in the centre of Paris between the Seine and the *barrières*, less widespread in the *faubourgs*, they sometimes showed a more independent spirit which, to some extent, foreshadowed that of the proletariat of the great modern industrial concerns: the Réveillon affair, which turned into a riot on 28 April 1789, was a case in point. But more often than not the wage-earners in these larger manufacturing ventures had begun employment in small workshops. The spirit of the craftsman which they retained was strengthened by the environment in which they lived—a small minority of factory-workers surrounded by far greater numbers of *compagnons*. Labour as a whole carried the imprint of lower middle-class artisan mentality, and like it, the Parisian labour-force shared its bourgeois ideology. Neither in thought, nor deed, could the Parisian workman become an independent element during the Revolution.

There was a serious contradiction in this situation which affected the sans-culotte's attitude to his work, his position in society and his political activity. Although they shared their mode of living with their *compagnons*, craftsmen still owned their work-shops, their equipment, and looked upon themselves as indepen-dent producers. The fact that they exercised authority over *com-pagnons* and apprentices accentuated their bourgeois mentality. Nevertheless the system of small production and direct sale was diametrically opposed to the ideas of the merchant bourgeoisie and commercial capitalism. In consequence, these craftsmen and shopkeepers who formed the more articulate section of the sans-culotterie cherished a social ideal which was incompatible with the evolution of the economic system. They campaigned against the concentration of the means of production, but they were themselves property-owners. When the more extreme sans-culottes demanded a maximum of wealth in the Year II, the contradiction between their own social position and this demand escaped them. They expressed their feelings in passionate outcries and bursts of revolt, but never in a coherent programme. The same was true of the individuals and political groups which shared their outlook—Jacques Roux, Hébert, even Robespierre and Saint-Just.

Failing to define their place in society as a working population, the sans-culottes had no clear and precise idea of the nature of labour itself. They did not appreciate that it had a social function of its own; they only considered it in relation to property. The bourgeoisie in a century of enlightenment had restored the arts and crafts to their rightful place, they had given an incomparable impetus to the forces of invention; but, concentrating their attention mainly upon the problems of technique and production, they had not conceived of the idea of labour as part of the social structure. From 1789 to 1794, the bourgeoisie had never thought about labour problems in themselves or in relation to the workers, but always with regard to the interests of their own class: the Le Chapelier law is evidence of this. If the Convention decreed the General Maximum on 29 September 1793 after constant pressure from the sans-culotterie, it was, as far as the montagnard bour-geoisie were concerned, simply a tactical move. Price-controls were related essentially to food supplies; salaries were not in any way determined by the amount of work a man performed. Divided between a predominantly artisan economy and nascent industrial-ism, lacking all sense of class-consciousness, how could the Parisian labour-force fail to be influenced by the bourgeoisie into whose hands it had largely entrusted the defence of its interests in the vital struggle against the aristocracy: its attitude to the problems of labour could only reflect prevailing political and social conditions. For the bourgeoisie, property was the key to the problem. The Declaration of 1793, like that of 1789, had established it as the first of the imprescriptible Rights of Man, after the abolition of feudalism had made it an absolute right. For the sans-culottes in the Year II, the problem of labour was not their primary social preoccupation. They were far too aware of their interests as consumers—it was not the question of strike-action or demands for higher wages which roused the sans-culotterie, but the question of food supplies. A rise or fall in the cost of the main products of popular consumption, grain and, above all, bread, which accounted for at least half of the family expenditure, was the decisive factor which tightened or eased the wage-earner's budget. The sans-culottes looked for a fixed system of price-controls on basic commodities; the demand for a sliding-scale of prices was exceptional. This perspective reflects economic and social conditions, as well as the ideology of the period.

Price-controls on basic commodities were demanded with all the more insistence by the militants because they were subjected to pressure in their respective Sections, not only from wage-earners, but also from the thousands of destitute Parisians, tormented by hunger. Hunger—an essential factor in all popular movements—was the cement which held together the artisan, the shopkeeper, and the workman, just as a common interest united them against the wealthy merchant, the contractor, the noble, and the bourgeois monopolist. From a sociological point of view, the term 'sans-culotte' may appear to be vague, but from the standpoint of the social conditions of the time, it reflects a reality. It is true that the political motives explaining popular behaviour must not be excluded—particularly hatred of the nobility, the belief in the 'aristocratic plot', the desire to destroy privilege and to establish equality before the law. How else can we account for the enthusiasm and disinterestedness of the sans-culotte volunteers? But the riots of February 1793, like the popular movement of the following summer, do not entirely fit into the general pattern of the bourgeois revolution: to quote Robespierre himself, these events were due to the popular demand for cheap and shoddy goods. The aim of the maximum, so stubbornly insisted upon and finally imposed on 29 September 1793, was to provide the wage-earners with their daily bread, not to facilitate the problems of national defence: the permanent motive behind popular action is to be found in the hardship of everyday life. In the last analysis, it can be said that economic fluctuations provided the rhythm of the revolutionary movement.

On 1 Prairial Year III, the tailor Jacob Clique from the Section des Gardes-Françaises was arrested for having said: 'One would think that the buyers and the farmers are plotting together to sell everything as dearly as possible in order to starve the workman.' Questioned about this statement, he replied: 'I am embittered by misfortune. The father of three young children, without any resources, my daily work has to provide a living for five people. I was given hardly any work throughout the difficult winter we have just faced.' Political demands were linked in a confused way with the demand for bread. 'Under Robespierre,' the cabinet-maker Richer from the Section de la République was alleged to have said on 1 Prairial, 'blood flowed and there was enough bread to go round. Today, blood no longer flows and there is a shortage of it. It seems, therefore, that we must spill a little blood before we can get bread.'[4] The sans-culottes could not forget that during the Terror, despite every difficulty, there was no shortage. The political behaviour of the terrorist is intimately linked with the demand for bread, and it was this dual factor which cemented the unity of the Parisian sans-culotterie.

[4] *A.N.*, F⁷ 4649, 4618, d. 3.

II

SOCIAL ASPIRATIONS

THE conditions in which they lived, as well as the particular circumstances of the period, together explain why the sans-culotterie should have laid such emphasis on bread in their programme of social priorities. This same preoccupation led them to assert, in a rather confused manner, what they called the *droit à l'existence*—the right of every citizen to receive the means of providing for himself and his family: the right to receive at least enough to satisfy his hunger. It would be unwise to try and construct a coherent doctrinal system out of such demands, since it was only during periods of crisis they were expressed in any positive manner; but the factor which unified them is to be found in the deep-rooted egalitarianism, both in thought and action, which characterized the attitude of the lower classes, firmly convinced that the conditions of existence should be the same for all. They rejected the unlimited right of ownership—the fundamental cause of inequality—in favour of the principle that every citizen should have an equal opportunity to enjoy the benefits which society conferred upon its members (*l'égalité des jouissances*). From this principle sprang their various social demands, including the right to receive public relief, and the right to education.

The Declaration of Rights of June 1793 announced that the aim of society was to ensure the happiness of all citizens; the sans-culottes took this principle a step further. They believed that as the Revolution was the work of the people, its first duty was to guarantee them *le droit à l'existence*. Since the most informed militant could hardly have been described as a theorist, the documents do not present us with any theoretical justification for this statement; it was only as a result of the pressure of events, particularly when food was scarce, that it clearly emerges as an expression of sans-culotte aspirations. From this premiss the sans-culottes went on to formulate the principle of *l'égalité des jouissances*.

During the first months of 1793, the increasing shortage of food supplies prompted the militant sans-culottes to clarify their attitude towards social questions. On 7 February, the Section des Gardes-Françaises stated that steps should be taken to end the oppression by the rich of the poor. 'If this were not done', the Section pointed out, 'citizens would cease to be equal in rights . . . and the lives of the poor would be threatened from one moment to the next, whilst the rich enforced the most rigorous laws against them.'[1] In a petition to the Convention dated 9 May 1793, a citizen from the Section des Arcis ranked as enemies of the Republic 'those who, using liberty and their rights as property-owners for an excuse, think that they can squeeze the last drop of blood from the miserable and starving section of the population, satisfying their vile coveteousness and hardly leaving the destitute the right to breathe or complain'.[2] Even more significant was the petition of the same date from a citizen in the Section du Marais who was convinced that 'It is time the workman was assured of his bread—a modest tribute to his long and tedious labour. It is time that a republican government put an end to speculation on the lives of men and women.'

These ideas reflect the general trend of popular thought. Jacques Roux developed them in his petition of 23 June 1793 when he wrote: 'Liberty is nothing but a figment of the imagination when one class can deprive another of food with impunity. Liberty becomes meaningless when the rich exercise the power of life and death over their fellow-creatures by means of monopolies.' During the crisis of the summer of 1793, these same ideas were more forcibly expressed. Felix Lepeletier, speaking on behalf of the *commissaires* of the primary assemblies, told the Convention on 20 August: 'It is not enough that the French Republic should be founded upon equality. We must still ensure that its laws and the moral conduct of its citizens lead, by a happy agreement, to the disappearance of *l'inégalité des jouissances*; we must make certain that every Frenchman is assured of a full and happy life.'[3] According-ing to the *Commission temporaire de Commune-Affranchie* on 26 Brumaire Year II, it was nothing less than a mockery to refer constantly to equality 'when so many degrees of happiness have always separated man from man'. The extent to which the *droit à*

---

[1] *B.N.*, MSS. new acq. fr. 2684, f. 113.
[2] *A.N.*, D XL 23, d. 77.
[3] *Journal de la Montagne*, 21 August 1793.

l'existence and its corollary, even if they were not clearly formulated corresponded to the deepest aspirations of the sans-culottes can be seen from a petition drawn up by the Section des Quinze-Vingts during the period of great shortage in the Year III. Demanding that coercive measures should be taken against grain-producers, the Section added that 'the poor, who only have their *assignats*, should be able to live in every way like the rich'.[4]

Since the inequality of wealth naturally became more apparent during periods of shortage, the sans-culottes demanded that the principle of equality should be observed first of all in the distribution of food supplies. But this stage was soon passed. 'Equality' was only a meaningless word unless it could be applied to every aspect of life. The rich must not live any better than the poor; they should surrender any surplus they possessed to the latter, and soon, even share their own goods with them: 'Take away everything which a citizen has no use for,' declared the *Commission temporaire de Commune-Affranchie*, 'because excess is an open violation of the rights of the people. Every man who has more than he needs cannot use his surplus, he can only abuse it. Consequently, after leaving him simply what he needs and no more, the remainder belongs to the Republic, and to its less fortunate citizens.' The sans-culotte has already become a *partageux*.

The fixing of food prices tended to reduce the advantage of wealth in favour of the workers. The same was true for the market-producer who now sold his goods 'without making any distinction between the rich and the poor', since every customer bought his food at a fixed price. The demand for equality went further still. The sans-culottes decided that no one, on account of his wealth, should be able to buy better quality goods than the poor, even at a fixed price. After listening to a report which had been prepared by Fouché and Collot d'Herbois during the course of their mission to Lyons, the General Council of the Commune, on the instigation of Chaumette, decided on 3 Frimaire Year II that in future only one kind of bread—the 'bread of equality'—would be sold: 'Wealth and poverty must disappear in a world based on equality,' it was announced: 'In future the rich will not have their bread made from wheaten flour whilst the poor have their's made from bran.'[5]

In their ardent desire to make the conditions of life the same for all, the sans-culottes reached the point at which the rich were to

[4] *A.P.P.*, AA/266, p. 254.   [5] *Affiches*, 4 Frimaire Year II.

be made to contribute towards the upkeep of the poor. Leclerc demanded in *l'Ami du peuple* on 10 August 1793 that grain should be supplied free of charge to the destitute, 'society must provide them with their living': it should take 'from the luxury at the disposal of the wealthy that which was necessary to ensure that penniless citizens were supplied with the basic necessities of life'.

Popular egalitarianism was not only concerned with the question of food supplies, but with all the possessions of the rich which confirmed their social superiority. An irrational reaction urged the sans-culottes, *non-possédant* or even the small owner, to conceive a strong attachment for whatever they did not happen to possess themselves, an attitude which faithfully reflects the popular mentality of the period, as well as a certain idea of social relationships. It emerges spontaneously in opinions or chance remarks which were eagerly seized upon by police-informers and used as evidence of terrorist sympathies in the Year III.

A report prepared by the police-agent Prévost on 9 Brumaire Year II stated that a woman who described herself as a Jacobin had told a friend: 'You have a very nice dressing-gown, but never mind, before long you might have another, and then you can give me one of them and in this way we shall get along well together; we can make a similar arrangement with other things.'[6] Towards the middle of Ventôse, when a shortage of food supplies began to rouse the sans-culottes to action once again, a citizen named Ancard declared in a café in the rue de Thionville 'that the rich must share their resources with the sans-culottes'. Many similar opinions were being expressed at this time: one citizen was reported by Bacon to have said on 25 Ventôse in the general assembly of the Section du Contrat-Social: 'The time has come when the rich must be made to pay; when the man who owns two plates gives one of them to the person who has none at all.' This statement was loudly applauded.[7]

During every period of shortage we find that pressure of this egalitarian nature is being exerted. An example may be quoted from the spring of the Year III. On 1 Germinal, during a disturbance on the boulevard Montmartre a carter named Gervais Béguin attempted to overturn a cabriolet belonging to a button-manufacturer supplying the armies, informing the latter as he did so, 'there is no more reason why you should have a cabriolet than

[6] *A.N.*, D XLII, 11.   [7] *A.N.*, W 78 and W 112.

I'. On 12 Germinal, citizen Caillau from the Section du Muséum climbed on to the roof of a shed and delivered a speech in praise of pillage, saying, 'that only those who owned anything had reason to be afraid, and in any case, they certainly deserved to be pillaged'. When an officer of the National Guard asked him to get down, pointing out that he was standing on national property, Caillou replied, 'in that case he would stand on the part which belonged to him'.[8]

In the course of the anti-terrorist repression such remarks were often invoked as grounds for arrest. On 5 Ventôse, a minor official in the War Office, Cordebar, was denounced in the general assembly of the Section de la Halle-au-Blé as 'a friend of the Héberts and Chaumettes', and for having said in Floréal of the preceding year that 'if he ever had the opportunity, he would visit the homes of the people who were more fortunate than himself and tell them, "You are richer than I, so you must share your wealth with me", and if they refused, then he would be obliged to use force'. The stationer Potin, former *commissaire de police* of the Section du Contrat-Social was arrested on 5 Prairial. He had stated in May 1793 'that the *loi agraire* would have to be enforced against those with an income of more than 4–5,000 *livres* a year'. Five days later Oudard, a schoolmaster from the Halle-au-Blé, was arrested for having maintained that it was necessary to guillotine 'all the really wealthy citizens who are no better than aristocrats, and to share out their goods'. Listing all the grievances of the *possédants* against the militant sans-culottes, the *commissaires* of the Section de la Butte-des-Moulins wrote in a report dated 30 Pluviôse Year III: 'Finally, seeing that all resistance had been broken, they conceived the idea of overrunning everything; of utterly destroying, not property, but property-owners, so that afterwards they could divide their property among themselves.'[9]

As the Thermidorean *commissaires* of the conservative Section de la Butte-des-Moulins pointed out in the Year III, the sans-culottes did not in fact object to the principle of owning property; they simply wanted to profit from this right themselves, and not become the victims of any abuses which ownership on a

[8] *A.N.*, F⁷ 4631, d. 2.
[9] *A.N.*, F⁷ 4653, 4774⁸⁰, 4774⁶⁰.

large scale entailed. The natural outcome of their demand for *l'égalité des jouissances* was the decision to ask for a limitation of the right of ownership, not its abolition.

As consumers, the sans-culottes first attacked the principle that the farmer was the rightful owner of the crops he cultivated. The theory that the people had a right to their basic subsistence was never formulated in the abstract as we have seen, but always as a result of a concrete situation: sometimes they used this right to justify price-fixing on basic commodities. This was thought to be the only way of guaranteeing *l'égalité des jouissances*. It followed that the cultivator's right of ownership over his crops should be limited and that controls should be placed on trade in agricultural produce—another common link in the chain of popular thought.

The principle was explained very clearly by the Section du Panthéon-Français on 22 September 1792, when they announced that, 'When abuses begin to appear, particularly in these three branches of trade (grain, meat, and wine), they cannot be justified by any reference to a decision, judgement, law or right of ownership which does not have immediate repercussions upon the life of the poor, society as a whole, and public order.' The inviolable nature of the right of ownership could not be invoked to justify freedom of trade in essential food supplies, since this was a matter which involved the very existence of the people. On 7 February 1793, the Section des Gardes-Françaises agreed that agricultural produce should be regarded by the cultivator or property-owner 'only as a reserve supply, of which an account must be made to the Republic': and since the possession of agricultural supplies was no longer an imprescriptible right, the Convention could pass legislation to deal with such matters. In particular, it should not be afraid to restrict freedom of trade by fixing a maximum for the price of wheat. Such a move could only make things more difficult for speculators 'who want to grow rich off the food which the people must eat, seeking to put a price on the lives of thousands of citizens'. Jacques Roux in a petition dated 26 June justified the fixing of prices on basic commodities by the *droit à l'existence*: 'Can the property of scoundrels be considered more sacred than the life of Man?' Leclerc, writing in *l'Ami du peuple* on 14 August 1793, thought that 'grain and, in general, all vital food supplies, belong to the Republic, after a fair indemnity has been paid to the producer for the labour and the sweat which went in to their cultivation'. Again, on 17 August, Leclerc wrote: 'Food supplies belong to everyone.' A petition from the Section des Sans-Culottes on 2 September 1793 expressed the opinion that, 'ownership has no foundation other than the demands made by Man's physical needs'. The statement issued by the *Commission temporaire de Commune-Affranchie* declared that 'the produce of French soil belongs to France, provided that a fair price has been paid to the farmer; and therefore the people have a definite right to the crops which have been produced'. As late as 10 Floréal Year III, the Section des Quinze-Vingts stated that 'The products of the soil belong to all men: we must only ensure that those who cultivate them are paid a fair indemnity.'

Once again, the problem was how to put these theories into practice. The most informed sans-culottes realized that the fixing of prices was only a temporary measure and foresaw that a radical solution would mean placing the distribution of agricultural supplies into the hands of the nation. Again, it was during a period of crisis that popular thinking was reorientated along these lines.

Departing from the principle that 'all men have an equal right to their subsistence and to all the products of the soil, representing as they do the indispensable needs which assures them of their existence', Leclerc came to the conclusion in *l'Ami du peuple* of 10 August 1793, that the Republic must assume the responsibilities of a buyer: 'in future, no one will be able to sell these basic commodities to anyone but the State'. The Jacobins of the Section des Arcis also demanded a form of nationalization on 18 Brumaire Year II, not only for essential food supplies, but for all consumer goods—'social' laws should determine how liberty should be interpreted, particularly in matters of commerce: speculation and hoarding would only disappear by setting up national warehouses, 'where growers, owners, and manufacturers would be obliged to deposit the surplus of their output in all kinds of goods at a reasonable price, and where the nation would then distribute these same goods'.[1] The general assembly of the Section des Champs-Elysées, debating the problem of distributing a stock of oil in Ventôse which had been found in the cellar of an *émigré*, also questioned the ethics of private enterprise: 'What is a merchant? He is the trustee, and not, as some have foolishly believed

[1] *A.N.*, AD I 70.

until now, the owner of those things which are essential to life. He is the trustee of such goods, just as other citizens share an interest in them. He is, therefore, a public servant and the most important of all since he holds in his hands the very lives of the people.' 'One citizen has suggested that one of the best and quickest ways of unmasking the selfish or counter-revolutionary attitude of merchants would be to bring as many goods as possible into Paris, distribute them amongst the Sections, and then sell them to citizens on a scale fixed by the law.'[2]

The crisis in the spring of the Year III again prompted the sans-culottes to conceive of similar schemes of municipalization or nationalization of the trade in essential food supplies. The wheelwright Journet, *commissaire civil* of the Section de l'Indivisibilité, proposed on 25 Floréal that the State should control the trade in all edible goods. The State would buy the food from merchants so that it could be distributed 'equally amongst all citizens'. The unemployed and workers in the lower-income group who earned less than 1,500 *livres* a year would pay half the amount which it had cost the government to purchase them, 'and the rich would pay the original price'. Journet justified this plan, not by any theoretical consideration, but by the critical circumstances of the period. To him, Paris and the Republic represented a besieged fortress, 'where every inhabitant was forced to share everything alike'.[3]

Journet's scheme was egalitarian in two ways: it was designed to ensure that every citizen received an equal amount of food, and to compensate social inequality by exploiting the resources of the rich. Circumstances forced the sans-culottes to define their aims more clearly; the outline of a social theory emerged as a consequence of day-to-day experience. From the principle of *l'égalité des jouissances* they conceived the idea of limiting the right of ownership of agricultural produce. The next logical step was to criticize the free exercise of the right of ownership as it had been defined in the Declaration of Rights of August 1789 and of June 1793.

Firmly believing in ownership on a limited scale, the sans-culottes never challenged the principle of ownership itself. But, as small producers, they based this principle upon personal

[2] *A.N.*, W 112.   [3] *A.N.*, F⁷ 4751.

labour. The worker's 'private ownership' of the means of his production corresponds to the artisanat structure of industry, still characteristic of France at the end of the eighteenth century: a mode of production which can only expand when the worker is the independent owner of his business—the peasant owning his field, the artisan his workshop and tools. On 27 Nivôse Year II, the *société Poissonnière* asked the *Administration des subsistances* to indemnify a baker for expenses which he had incurred, adding that 'small resources which have been saved as a result of work which benefits society should be highly respected and safeguarded from any attack'.[4] The *Commission temporaire de Commune-Affranchie* thought that work should 'always be rewarded by some degree of comfort'.

It was against the rich and the *gros* that the sans-culottes really directed their hatred. In their rather confused way, they thought that if they failed to challenge the supremacy of wealth by putting no limitation on the right of ownership, the principle of *l'égalité des jouissances* would become meaningless. In their addresses and petitions, particularly in times of crisis, their desire for an egalitarian society can be seen in the various, and sometimes quite irrational, schemes which they conceived for the equalization of wealth. The sans-culottes believed that the extremes of wealth and poverty should disappear in a Republic, and that suitable laws should be drafted to prevent the concentration of ownership and the means of production. They never considered that there might be a contradiction between the preservation of the property which they already enjoyed, or thought they should enjoy, and its limitation within the narrow confines determined by their position in society.

On 18 August 1792, Gonchon, an orator from the *Société des Hommes de Quatorze-Juillet et du Dix-Août*, stated at the bar of the Assembly: 'Find a government which will lift the people above their meagre resources and deny to the rich the unrestricted exercise of their wealth and the balance of society will be perfect.'[5] A year later Leclerc repeated this theme in *l'Ami du peuple* of 10 August 1793 when he wrote: 'A State is on the verge of ruin when you find extreme poverty and abundant wealth existing side by side.' In the opinion of Felix Lepeletier, speaking on behalf of the *commissaires* of the primary assemblies on 20 August, 'the rich

---

[4] *A.D.S.*, D 989.   [5] *Moniteur*, xiii, 438.

are not so much the owners of surplus wealth intended for the happiness of their fellow-citizens, as the fortunate trustees of it'.[6] Finally, on 26 Brumaire Year II, the *Commission temporaire de Commune-Affranchie* pointed out that, 'if, unfortunately, it is impossible to create perfect equality between men, it is at least possible to narrow the gaps which separate them'.

The petition of the Section des Sans-Culottes on 2 September 1793 was more explicit. It sought not only to determine 'the profits of industry and trade' by a general scheme of price-fixing, and to limit the scope of agricultural exploitation, but also to impose a maximum on wealth. The petition did not give an exact figure, but it hinted that it would correspond with the ideas of the small artisan and shopkeeper class: 'No one should own more than one workshop, or one store.' Such radical measures, according to the authors of the petition, 'would slowly lead to the disappearance of the inequality of wealth which was far too great, and increase the number of property-owners'.[7] At no other point during the Revolution do we find such a concise and striking statement of the popular social ideal: an ideal which suited the interests of the craftsmen and shopkeepers who formed the main body of the sans-culotterie and who exercised a decisive ideological influence on their *compagnons* and clerks. It was also an ideal which satisfied the wishes of the mass of consumers and small urban producers, hostile towards tradesmen who were directly or indirectly concerned with food supplies, and contractors whose initiative and enterprise threatened to reduce them to the state of dependent workers.

The ideas which the sans-culottes proposed during periods of shortage were not always highly original. In the majority of cases they had already been expressed, sometimes in a different form, by orators from different sections of the montagnard bourgeoisie, who had themselves borrowed these ideas from the common store of eighteenth-century philosophical thought, to which Rousseau had made such a significant contribution. The idea that the producer did not possess an absolute right of ownership over his crops is an obvious example.

On 2 December 1792, speaking on the question of food supplies and the disorders which had taken place in the Eure-et-Loire

---

[6] *Journal de la Montagne*, 21 August 1793.   [7] *B.N.*, Lb⁴⁰ 2140.

department, Robespierre laid greater emphasis on the *droit à l'existence* than on the rights of ownership: 'The most important right of all', he said, 'is the right to live. It follows therefore that the most important law in society is that which guarantees the basic necessities of life to every citizen: all other laws are subordinate to this.'[8] In his *Opinion sur la fixation du maximum du prix des grains*, Momoro, who knew how to express the social ideas of the sans-culotterie although not actually a sans-culotte himself, repeats the theme that ownership involves the right of making good or bad use of something, but then goes on to ask the question: 'Does the producer have some right of ownership over the crops which grow as a result of his labours? Clearly he does not. These crops are intended for the provision of society, on condition that a fair recompense has been paid to the producer which will then represent the price at which these crops must be sold. This sum should be calculated according "to the amount of money which citizens can afford to pay".'[9] Hébert provides us with a more emphatic statement of this idea, but again no social theory. 'The soil has been created for living things', he wrote in August 1793, 'and each one, from the ant to that proud insect which we call Man, must find his subsistence in the produce of the earth which is their common source.' In conclusion Hébert adds that: 'The most important thing we possess is life itself—whatever the cost, we must eat.' Such was the widespread acceptance of these views as well as the pressure of popular opinion on the subject that, although he was an open enemy of the sans-culotterie, the Dantonist Dufourny provides us with an even more explicit statement of their aims. On 1 September he wrote: 'Since farmers have no right to do what they like with the soil, whether by not cultivating at all, or by destroying what they have cultivated, then those who own the land are not proprietors of the soil or of its produce.' They are nothing but the trustees of the harvests which must be disposed of only by the nation, after the farmer has been paid a fair indemnity. Trade must return to its original purpose—that of serving the producer and the consumer. Food supplies must never be subjected to speculation: 'every speculator who uses his stock of food supplies only to make a profit is an unnecessary "middleman", who is both dangerous and a criminal. He is the true *accapareur*, the monopolist and enemy of society'.

[8] *Moniteur*, xiv, 636.   [9] *B.N.*, Le[38] 2461.

The sans-culottes had no quarrel with Dufourny's interpretation of their aims; their only original contribution was to try and turn theory into practice and force the government to accept the idea of trade-controls and fixed prices. The Mountain only accepted a system of fixed prices after great pressure had been brought to bear upon it. Robespierre's silence on this most important problem throughout the summer of 1793 is significant in this respect. He was far too good a politician to underestimate the balance of power in society and neglect the interests of the bourgeoisie, despite his sincere concern for the lower classes. Behind the façade of unanimous declarations, the conflict of interests remained an insoluble problem.

The same was true of the right of ownership. The montagnard or jacobin leaders formulated theories on the subject which were not dissimilar to those put forward by the sans-culottes, but there was little or no attempt to embody these theories in the law. Chaumette and Hébert, regarding themselves as the spokesmen of the sans-culotterie, never failed to press this point from the tribune of the General Council of the Commune or in the pages of the *Père Duchesne*. Billaud-Varenne, who was more of a theorist, wrote in his *Eléments de républicanisme* that ownership was the pivot of social relationships, and that as a result of this 'the political system must not only be designed to assure everyone of the unhindered enjoyment of his possessions, but must be planned in such a way as to ensure as far as possible proportional, if not an absolutely equal, distribution of goods between citizens'. If the right of ownership was imprescriptible, 'it must be employed for the good of every human being who forms part of the nation'. If this were done, no one in the Republic would find himself 'under the direct and non-reciprocal dependance of any other person'.[1] On 24 April, Robespierre had spoken of property, not as a natural right, but as a social institution which every citizen should be able to enjoy. Saint-Just stated in his *Institutions* that the aim of the Republic was 'to give to every Frenchman the means of obtaining the basic necessities of life, without recourse to anything but the laws and without one person being dependent upon another within the body politic'. In other words every Frenchman should be a small proprietor and an independent producer. Moreover, 'Every man should be able to live independently . . . there must be neither

[1] *B.N.*, Lb⁴¹ 2383.

rich nor poor.' A recurrent theme in the literature of the eighteenth century from Montesquieu to Rousseau was that a Republic could not exist without a certain social equality. In this respect the montagnard leaders did not show much greater originality than the militant sans-culottes.

On one point at least, the Parisian sans-culottes did show some ideological boldness. Even the most out-spoken Montagnard never planned anything but the restriction of ownership of landed property. In his *Institutions* Saint-Just specified that 'only a limitation on the possession of land will be fixed'. Billaud-Varenne was still thinking of landed wealth when he wrote in his *Eléments de républicanisme* of 'weakening the corrosive influence (of great wealth) by forced subdivision, allowing no such subdivisions to be grouped together to form bigger estates'. He goes on to explain that: 'No citizen will be able to own . . . more than a fixed number of acres of land'—an average of twenty. Momoro was more explicit on this subject, even though he was a militant Cordelier, and much closer to the sans-culotterie. His Declaration of Rights of September 1792 only spoke of safeguarding industrial estates (*propriétés industrielles*): the estates 'that we erroneously term "territorial" only being guaranteed until such time as appropriate legislation will have been passed on this subject'.[2] Those revolutionaries, both jacobin and montagnard, who found themselves midway between the sans-culotterie and the bourgeoisie were more hostile towards landed wealth than towards any form of property. We can find evidence of this in an essay on the type of popular government which, according to the views of one citizen, would best suit France presented to the Convention in the summer of 1792. The writer thought that although the nation must decree that no one should own landed property valued at more than 120,000 *livres*, this did not mean that it should 'assign a maximum or limitation to the amount of wealth which might be derived from purely personal property such as money, personal effects, merchandise, ships, &c.'

Since the sans-culottes were represented by small urban producers attached to the independence of their store or workshop, as well as consumers of agricultural produce, their ideas went further than this. Their greatest fear was that they would be reduced to the level of the proletariat and, consequently, they

[2] *B.H.V.P.*, 109586 (article XXVII).

were just as hostile towards big commercial or industrial ownership as towards large-scale property-owners, or those who had
considerable interests in the exploitation of landed wealth. This
explains the demand from the Section des Sans-Culottes that, in
order to prevent the concentration of the means of production,
no one should own more than one workshop or one store.

Before considering the relationship between the sans-culotterie
and commercial capital, there are two important problems which
need to be taken into account. In the first place, are the social
tendencies which we have been studying, and their comparative
lack of originality characteristic of the sans-culotterie? Part of
the answer to this question at least can be found in the actual
position which the sans-culotterie held in society. Composed of
heterogeneous elements its only unifying factor was opposition to
the aristocracy. The sans-culottes could not possibly be 'class-
conscious', nor present a coherent social policy when they included
craftsmen and tradesmen recruited from the ranks of the lower,
and sometimes the middle bourgeoisie; *compagnons*, who shared
the same daily existence as the craftsman and who, as a result,
frequently adopted the same social attitude; workers in the few
big industrial concerns which were to be found in Paris at this
time; not to mention intellectuals, artists, and some who escape
classification. Their aspirations are confused and often contradictory; they present no specific character, since the sans-culottes
drew from the same well of ideas as did the majority of revolutionaries, particularly the Montagnards and Jacobins. The social ideal
of the sans-culotterie is in fact very similar to that of the Robespierrists—a community of independent producers between
whom the laws of the State would ensure an approximate equality.
On the subject of fixed prices and trade-controls, the ideas of the
militant sans-culottes conflicted with those of the montagnard
bourgeoisie, some of them even demanding a limit to the amount
of property which the craftsman or tradesman might own. They
justified the maximum, not only on theoretical grounds, but by
the demands of national defence, and perhaps even more important, as a means of re-establishing the balance between interests
which were economically antagonistic. But in spite of this, the
sans-culottes remained faithful to the montagnard Declaration of
Rights of June 1793 which saw the nation as a community of equal

citizens, everything being directed towards the common good. In the social sphere, the sans-culottes appear, therefore, to have been following, with different shades of emphasis but with the same contradictions, in the wake of the montagnard, and particularly, the jacobin bourgeoisie. Their original contribution is not to be found in such theories but in their actual political behaviour.

The second problem is to decide how far these ideas are representative of the sans-culotterie as a whole? The deliberations, addresses and petitions which have been preserved for us only reflect the opinions of a minority of militant sans-culottes who were sufficiently literate to express themselves, and who, although they did not have an intimate knowledge of the philosophical thought of the century, had been impregnated with its teaching in varying degrees. Through the clubs and popular societies, the ideas of Rousseau in particular were widely circulated, and they can be traced in diluted form in many of the texts drawn up by different organizations in the Sections. But there were still many sans-culottes, occupying positions of some importance in the Sections, who could neither read nor write as many of the documents prove. The main body of the sans-culotterie was not roused to action by ideas or theorizing, but by the miserable conditions in which they eked out an existence. Scarcity was the permanent motive behind popular agitation, from the Réveillon riots in April 1789 to the *journées* of Germinal and Prairial in the Year III, although political considerations were inextricably linked, particularly during the more important revolutionary *journées*. Practically every sans-culotte in the Year II had a confused notion of the egalitarian Republic which they described as democratic or popular. If, as a result of their education, a few militants were able to copy their montagnard or jacobin leaders and express some of the essential features of this Republic, and try to justify them theoretically, the great majority of sans-culottes were satisfied with the realization of their immediate objectives.

Actually, it is in this struggle for the implementation of their demands that the social aspirations of the sans-culotterie can best be studied. In 1793, the sans-culottes campaigned for a maximum on the price of grain so that the cost of bread would compare more favourably with their wage-rate, in fact, so that the workers could earn enough to keep alive: the *droit à l'existence* was then invoked as an argument to justify this demand. A social demand gives rise to a theoretical justification, which, in turn, intensifies the struggle. It is not statements of principle, but the measures which the sans-culottes proposed in the struggle for the recognition of their rights which help us to define their social aspirations more clearly.

The same is true of the demands presented by the Sections concerning the different branches of speculation, and, above all, the concentration of war supplies in the hands of a few big contractors. Better than any well-conceived plan, they emphasize the popular ideal of limited ownership and small-scale independent production which was to be kept within strictly defined limits by State legislation.

The hostility of the sans-culottes towards any form of commercial capital was marked in the first place by their persistent opposition to the exchange and coining of hard currency.

Such opposition was usually based upon the conviction that the use of hard currency could only increase the difficulties confronting the Republic. The circulation of gold and silver money further discredited the *assignat* and, therefore, aggravated the economic situation and the shortage of food. Hard currency had become associated with the upper classes of society who were opposed to the egalitarian republic envisaged by the sans-culotterie which is why we find so many documents in the Year II denouncing the possession of gold. A prohibition on the sale of hard currency was demanded in February 1793 in a strongly-worded petition which emphasized its repercussions on the value of the *assignat* and the rise in the cost of living. This demand was reiterated by all the Sections on 3 March. But although the Convention finally capitulated to popular pressure on 11 April, trading in money did not actually come to an end. On 27 June, the *représentant* Dentzel denounced the speculators who continued to operate in the rue de la Vivienne. On 29 August, the Section de l'Unité informed the General Council of the Commune of the dealings of money-merchants beneath the balconies of the Palais-Royal gardens. The establishment of the Terror led to more determined action, but apparently this still did not resolve the problem, for on 7 Frimaire, the General Council adopted a petition from the Cordelier club which was designed to forbid the circulation of coins until the end of the war. The petition emphasized that, 'every merchant, and every tradesman, as well as individuals who are paid by any kind of financial concern, should be made to deposit all the gold and silver which they might possess at the Mint so that they could be exchanged for *assignats*'. This would certainly have led to renewed discontent in business and trading circles, and, in view of this, the petition was simply referred to the Committee of Public Safety.[3]

But this action against speculators was not in itself enough. The sans-culottes felt that the root of the trouble lay in the financial organizations upon which commercial capitalism was founded, and for this reason they pressed for the closing of the Paris Bourse and the suppression of joint-stock companies. On 1 May 1793, the Section du Faubourg-du-Nord asked for the closure of the Stock Exchange, and on the following day, the Section du Contrat-Social gave its support to the petition. Once the Girondists had been eliminated the Convention agreed to act and on 27 June 1793, passed a decree closing the Paris Stock Exchange.[4] It only did so, however, as a direct result of popular pressure and as a concession to the reiterated demands from the Sections—on 25 June, Jacques Roux had presented his menacing petition, and on the twenty-sixth, disturbances had occurred along the quays of the Seine over the price and distribution of soap.

Just as significant of the economic position adopted by the sans-culottes was their hostility towards the share-holding societies which had multiplied towards the end of the *ancien régime*, representing the most highly evolved form of commercial capital. At the end of July 1793, a citizen from the Section des Sans-Culottes said that he was surprised to see 'a sick-fund bank in one place, a trading bank in another and a savings bank somewhere else; a little farther along, a *Tontine* for old people and another for life assurance. Then, above this door, the "Patriotic Lottery of the rue de Bac" '—all of them simply financial concerns for hoarding money. 'These wealthy people, bank directors and managers, are the real threat': they are the citizens who 'ruin' trade and make things increasingly difficult for the Republic. The Convention should seize 'these banks run by scoundrels'. On 24 August, the Assembly decided to act upon this advice and suspend the activities of finance societies. On 26 Germinal, amending its

---

[3] *Moniteur*, xv, 615; xvi, 108, 759; xvii, 521; xviii, 538, 559.
[4] *Moniteur*, xvi, 759.

decree of 17 Vendémiaire Year II, the Assembly passed a law closing down every kind of commercial and financial concern.[5]

Although the policy of national defence could be adjusted to meet the suppression of the share-holding societies, it was forced to rely upon private enterprise for the provision of supplies to the armies, nationalization being reserved solely for the manufacture of weapons. The governmental Committees were anxious to facilitate progress and, therefore, inclined to concentrate orders in the hands of a few big contractors or business men instead of scattering them around the many small workshops. This was a source of continual conflict between the Revolutionary Government and the sans-culotterie in the Year II, aggravating their differences even further.

Once the war had begun, the Sections wanted to reserve all work concerned with the manufacture of clothing for the armies for their own members in order to ease the distress of the people and reduce unemployment. On 8 September 1792, the General Council of the Commune had proposed that the task should be divided proportionately between the forty-eight Sections. The crisis at the beginning of 1793, which led to a big increase in the number or army volunteers, multiplied demands for clothing. The Sections opened workshops such as the one in the Section des Tuileries, which, in order to collect the necessary money to launch the enterprise, organized 'a public subscription in money and in kind' on 4 February 1793. The reasons for this move given by the Section are significant: 'In the first place, these grasping army contractors, who are either incompetent or deliberately obstructive, will no longer be in a position to hinder the advance of our armies and check our success; the road to liberty will not be barricaded in future by the speculations of monopolists. Secondly, a handful of these contractors will not be able to appropriate all the profits to be derived from supplying the armies on such a large scale; they will have to divide them amongst our merchants and our workers so that everyone will benefit. Thirdly, since small business concerns are always run economically and with considerable skill, added to the fact that they have a smaller initial outlay, we will be in a position to produce more, and our articles will be of a higher standard.' The Section could not have written a better eulogy of small independent production. But the question

[5] *Moniteur*, xvii, 484; xviii, 79; xx, 233.

was, did it correspond to the urgent problems of national defence? In fact, the work was still conducted according to the system current at the time—contractors received the raw material from the authorities and then proceeded to make up the required article. The Sections continually complained about this system, but since they could offer no alternative solution, they found it very difficult to alter it. On 15 June 1793, the Section du Finistère decided to set up a workshop under its own control so that the workers could take advantage of the new scale of payment for making up articles of clothing. But it was still forced to rely upon the people who could provide them with the initial capital outlay to pay for the cost of the raw material allocated to the Section, and to pay for the first few weeks of salary for the workers. Two *commissaires*, who were not concerned with any speculative enterprise, were given the responsibility of superintending the work on behalf of the Section and of receiving complaints from the workers. Only one citizen offered to provide the necessary sum of 6,000 *livres* for initial expenditure, and he was himself a contractor, although his freedom was restricted by the control which the *commissaires* exercised on behalf of the Section.

Though it satisfied the aspirations of the sans-culottes, this system did not satisfy the requirements of national defence, which demanded production on a much larger scale, and, therefore, greater concentration. The governmental department which dealt with the provision of clothing for the troops—*l'Administration de l'habillement*—was naturally in favour of organizing large workshops where production could be started on these lines, but it was always faced with the opposition of the workers who were accustomed to independent production, and who were continually putting forward claims on behalf of the small workshops in the Sections. This was not only a conflict between two ideas of economic organization, but also between popular demands and the policy adopted by the Revolutionary Government.

On 25 July 1793, the Minister of War, Bouchotte, made a new attempt to conciliate these contradictory interests and, 'for the good of the service', to obviate any difficulties between the Sections and the *Administration de l'habillement*. On 30 July, the *commissaires* of the forty-eight Sections explained to the General Council of the Commune 'how many inconveniences arose when too many citizens were assembled in one workshop'. They felt that the distribution of labour between the different Sections had far greater advantages. On 9 August, the Convention nevertheless decreed the establishment of six big workshops in Paris for cutting cloth, and for a distribution and delivery office to be attached to each workshop. After the cloth had been cut the material would then be divided amongst the various Sections, according to their needs, so that it could be turned into uniforms and other articles of clothing. The workers, however, complained more bitterly than ever about the way in which the authorities distributed the work. On 25 August, a deputation of women asked the Convention to reorganize the clothing workshops 'so that the work could be transferred to the Sections'.[6] Tired of these continual complaints, the Convention finally authorized the Minister of War on 30 August 1793 to increase the number of distribution offices to thirty-six so that it would not be necessary for workers to travel as frequently as they did away from their own Sections. The general assemblies of the Sections were asked to appoint one *commissaire* for each Section to superintend the distribution and delivery of the material which was ready to be manufactured as articles of clothing.

After the passing of this decree, workshops were opened in most of the Sections. On 9 September 1793, the general assembly of the Section des Invalides organized its own workshop. Two *commissaires* were appointed to superintend the process of finishing the various articles of clothing, and, using the new scale of prices issued by the *Administration de l'habillement*, to propose what the Sections should charge for the different jobs assigned to them so that the running costs of the workshop would be covered: the Section itself drew no profit whatsoever from the work which was designed to benefit the workers alone. By appointing and dismissing the *commissaires*, deciding on their salary, fixing the prices of the finished articles, auditing accounts and regulating expenditure, listening to the complaints of the workers, the general assembly really was in control of the undertaking which satisfied the popular ideas on the organization of production and labour. This arrangement, however, had one fundamental weakness—the general assembly had no funds to provide for current expenses. On 25 Thermidor Year II, the general assembly of the Section realized that if the *commissaires à l'habillement* had to advance the

[6] *Moniteur*, xvii, 281; xviii, 492.

necessary capital themselves to pay the wages of the workers, then these posts could only be filled by well-to-do citizens, thus excluding the sans-culottes. In view of this, the assembly invited the wealthier citizens to loan the necessary capital to the Sections without interest. Since the *Administration de l'habillement* did not put any money at the disposal of the workshops, the general assemblies were forced to rely upon private capital, which placed them once again under the control of the contractors.

The sans-culottes complained continually in the Year II about this procedure, particularly as they were eager to shake off the control of the *Administration de l'habillement* (which they felt was far too rigid). But their chief criticism was reserved for the people upon whom they were so dependent: the contractors and *soumissionnaires*—those citizens who advanced them the initial capital outlay for the workshops. On 4 Pluviôse, the *société de l'Unité* proposed 'a law to do away completely with all the *soumissionnaires* in the Republic who, by their cunning plans, worm their way into the business of providing equipment for the troops'. The society went on to explain who suffered as a result of this: 'It is the Republic; it is the destitute craftsmen and workers with no means of support who are forced by their circumstances to beg work from these selfish citizens and promise to finish articles of clothing at the lowest possible cost so that they can buy bread.' In order to do away with these 'middlemen', the society asked 'that all the supplies needed for the upkeep and provision of the armies should be deposited without delay in government warehouses, so that these supplies could then be distributed amongst the workshops in the Sections'—those which had been set up following the decree of 30 August 1793. If this were done the workers would find employment 'and the bread which they eat will rekindle the flame of their republican sentiments'. The petition denounced the profits made by the monopolist *soumissionnaires*. The business deals which they made appeared to be benefiting the Republic, but in fact 'the monopolists make the less fortunate members of society carry the full weight of their greed': they only paid sixteen to eighteen *sous* for a pair of leggings to be made up, and ten to twelve *sous* for a shirt, although they received thirty *sous* for this work, added to which the worker had to pay almost half his salary for the thread which he used.[7]

[7] *A.N.*, D iii, 255–6¹, d. 2, p. 2.

This petition was such an accurate reflection of the opposition of the sans-culotterie to commercial capitalism that it secured the adherence of all the other Sections and popular societies, such as the *société Lepeletier* on 7 Pluviôse and the general assembly of the Section des Invalides just over a week later. The workers in the latter Section renewed their attack on 30 Pluviôse when they presented a petition to the general assembly which sought 'to ensure that the material which had to be made into finished articles of clothing for the soldiers of the Republic be distributed amongst the workshops in the Sections and not given to grasping *soumissionnaires* who make a substantial profit on such articles'. The assembly thought 'that it was only right that profits which had been made on public undertakings should be devoted to the benefit of the greatest number and the poorest class', and appointed *commissaires* to accompany the petitioners to the Jacobin club. The *société de l'Unité* which had presented its petition to the Convention on 20 Pluviôse, and to the General Council of the Commune four days later without success, had won the support of the other Sections and popular societies. Their *commissaires* presented themselves at the bar of the Convention on 5 Ventôse: the petition was referred to the Committee of Public Safety.[8] The growth of social unrest provided the Government with an additional warning. Once the crisis was over, however, and the Cordelier leaders eliminated, there was no longer any need for the Committees to satisfy popular demands: such a policy would have alienated the sympathies of that section of the bourgeoisie which made a substantial profit from contracts to supply the armies, particularly as it coincided with the more liberal commercial policy which the Revolutionary Government was pursuing.

Whilst this problem remained unsolved, and despite the stiffening of governmental policy after Germinal, the sans-culottes still persisted with their demands. On 15 Floréal, the general assembly of the Section du Bonnet-Rouge denounced the arrival of a new 'aristocracy'—that of the war-contractors: 'a single one of them, always extremely wealthy, is certain to take over every paying concern within range, whereas, if such concerns were shared out fairly, they would give hundreds of deserving citizens the opportunity of keeping themselves and their families and still leave them with a small profit'. The general assembly believed that

---

[8] *Journal de la Montagne*, 6 Ventôse Year II: *Moniteur*, xix, 553.

if twelve executive commissions were constituted it would have 'the co-operation of hundreds of workers in every trade'. The assembly refused to allow a handful of contractors to monopolize all the work for themselves. In order to prevent 'this monopolization', the Convention should decree that no one should be permitted to tender contracts for any work without showing his *certificat de civisme*. This would put an end to 'all these grasping speculators who would prefer to retire discreetly into the background than run the risk of a test which could prove embarrassing for many of them'. As for the sans-culotte who, it was naturally assumed, would find no difficulty in getting the certificate he deserved, he would only accept 'that share of the work which was his, without prejudicing the position of his fellow sans-culotte'.[9] The militant sans-culottes in the Section du Bonnet-Rouge clearly wanted to direct the Terror against commercial capital— the refusal of a certificate would classify the merchant-contractor as a suspect. But this petition suffered the same fate as the preceding ones: it was submitted at the precise moment when the governmental committees were relaxing the economic aspect of the Terror in favour of the *possédant* class.

The workshops in the Sections were not immediately swept away by the Thermidorean reaction, however, for they had undoubtedly made some contribution to the war effort. It was the crushing of the Parisian sans-culotterie during the *journeés* of Prairial Year III which finally led to their suppression. On 25 Prairial, the Committee of Public Safety authorized the *Commission des approvisionnements* to liquidate the cutting workshops and distribution offices of the Paris Commune and to hand over the work of finishing articles of clothing for the troops to individual contractors.

The history of the Revolution was forced back to its original course. There was little hope for the small independent producer once the government had decided to return to an economic policy of *laissez-faire*, and when supplies for the armies seemed to be regarded by bourgeois business men as a field reserved exclusively for their capitalist initiatives.

The attitude of the Sections towards the problem of taxation reveals the social aspirations of the sans-culotterie in much the

⁹ *A.N.*, D III, 253³, d. 1, p. 13.

same way as their hostility against any move to concentrate the production of war supplies. In both cases, what motivated their actions was the desire to reduce the gap which separated the rich from the poor, and to make the conditions of life in revolutionary Paris the same, or almost the same, for all citizens.

When the sans-culottes turned their attention to matters of taxation they combined their inner social convictions with revolutionary enthusiasm: whereas the *possédants* were mostly to be found in the moderate party, the fiscal ideas of the sans-culotterie were shaped by the same mentality which produced the decrees of Ventôse. The idea was to help poorer citizens by taxing the rich; if this meant that a blow would be struck against the enemies of the Revolution at the same time then this would provide more than sufficient justification for such a policy. One of the best examples of this attitude can be found in a decree issued by Collot d'Herbois and Fouché on 24 Brumaire Year II from Lyons, stating that the revolutionary tax to be levied upon the rich would be based upon their personal resources and the degree to which they had failed as patriots.[1] The political and social consequences of this popular fiscal system were identical, to a lesser extent, with the reaction to the decrees of Ventôse—they forced the *possédants* to unite against a system which attacked the possession of wealth, and encouraged them to shake off the yoke of sans-culotte democracy.

The kind of mentality which determined the revolutionary attitude towards taxation is well expressed in *l'Instruction de la Commission temporaire de la Commune-Affranchie*, a body composed chiefly of Parisian sans-culottes—how could one pay for the cost of the war and offer everyone the benefits of the Revolution if one did not tax the rich? If such people were aristocrats, then it was only right that they should be made to contribute towards the expenses of a war which was being waged partly on their account: if they were patriots, then they would be only too happy to see their wealth being used for the good of the Republic. Every citizen who had more than enough to meet his own needs must be subjected to taxation: 'This is not the time for mathematical exactitude or a timid approach to the work of assessing the amount of public contributions.' The collectors would be authorized to take everything

[1] *Moniteur*, xviii, 505.

for which a citizen had no immediate use: 'because any surplus wealth is clearly an open violation of the rights of the people'. Motivated by this 'levelling' spirit the militant authors of the *Instruction* went on to attack personal effects: 'Every kind of material, which can be found in such plentiful supply in the homes of the rich, and which might prove of value to the defenders of the nation, must be transferred to the nation at once. For example, there are some people who have ridiculous quantities of sheets, shirts, towels, and shoes': all these articles would be requisitioned. Some of the sans-culottes carried out these instructions to the letter.

The idea that only the rich should be made to shoulder the responsibility of paying the expenses of the State, and by so doing, ease the burden of poorer citizens is characteristic: the fact that it survived the reaction of the Year III is proof of sans-culotte conviction on this point. Although such addresses as that delivered to the Convention on 20 Germinal by the Section des Piques denounced the terrorists of the Year II, this did not prevent the Section from requesting a constitution 'which, above all, does not condemn citizens with no financial resources for not fulfilling obligations which really are the duty of the rich, who too frequently neglect them. The man who owns property and other possessions which require greater safeguards from the State must consequently expect to make greater sacrifices for the State. It is time', the address continued, 'that we confronted these rich egoists, who share neither our difficulties nor our dangers, with their responsibilities. Harness them to the chariot of the Constitution. It is only the rich who are dragging their feet: farmworkers, craftsmen, and even destitute citizens, shoulder the burden with ease.'

The sectionary militants were given the opportunity on numerous occasions from 10 August to 9 Thermidor to put these ideas into practice. Loans, taxes, or 'voluntary contributions', organized by order of the general assemblies, were usually levied with the idea of sustaining the war effort, whether by arming and equipping volunteers, organizing the collection of saltpetre, or by assisting the wives and children of the troops. On rare occasions, they were used to ease the distress of the poorest citizens and the unemployed. It seems that the social aspirations of the sans-culotterie were orientated on questions of taxation to meet the demands of the revolutionary struggle. The idea that they were acting simply in accordance with fixed principles appears less frequently.

The law of 13 Frimaire Year III required that the constituted authorities who had levied revolutionary taxes, or made 'voluntary or forced' collections, should hand in an account of their activities. The Section du Théâtre-Français—formerly the Section Marat—drew up its financial report immediately. In September 1792, the assembly had decreed a 'voluntary' collection to arm and clothe the troops. There were other voluntary collections in March 1793 after the conscription of 300,000 men, and again in May during the recruitment of volunteers for the Vendée. A subscription had been opened in Frimaire Year II 'for the relief of those persons who had suffered from a fire in the rue Serpente'. Another collection was made in Nivôse to arm and equip a detachment of jacobin cavalry raised by the Section; and in Germinal there was the cost of providing this detachment with flags, as well as the expenses of a fête to commemorate the 'martyrs of liberty'. Finally, in Floréal, the assembly ordered a collection 'so that it could meet its obligations towards the defenders of the nation and their families'.[2]

If we look at the Sections as a whole, popular fiscal ideas were determined mainly by the threat from outside France. The militants began to tax the rich so that the volunteers could be armed and equipped. This taxation was based increasingly on class divisions as the popular movement grew stronger. The first demand for 'class taxation' coincided with the *journées* of September 1792. On the second of this month, the Section de Montreuil asked for 'a law to make every *rentier* who is not personally engaged in the struggle for liberty, contribute to support those women and children whose husbands and fathers are actually fighting against the enemy'. On the same day, the Section Poissonnière acknowledged a decree from the Section des Gravilliers proposing 'that rich, elderly people should be asked to look after the wives and children of those citizens who had been recruited for service on the frontiers'. Clearly such proposals were not acceptable to the *possédant* class, who were still too firmly entrenched in power to give way on such matters. Some general assemblies, such as the assembly of the Section du Théâtre-Français, organized the 'voluntary' collections levied in their Sections quite efficiently, although we do not know on what scale they were based.

[2] *B.N.*, MSS. new acq. fr. 2707, f. 230–361.

The conscription of 300,000 men was decreed on 24 February 1793, and as a result, a new campaign of revolutionary taxation was launched during the following month to clothe and arm these soldiers and assist their wives and children in their absence. However, at this time, the conflict for power between the sans-culottes and the *possédants* had not yet been resolved, so that the system upon which this new taxation was based did not reflect a marked class character, but something in the nature of a compromise. The general assembly of the Section de Bondy decided to arm and clothe all the volunteers in its Section on 9 March. However, since 'one of the causes which has checked the advance of our fearless defenders of liberty, has been the anxiety which the latter have felt on account of their parents, wives, and children,' it declared, 'that the families of poor volunteers who leave for the front will be fed, and their rents paid, at the cost of the citizens of the Section'. The Section left to the property-owners who were present at the meeting the responsibility of 'putting aside a small percentage of their wealth as a compensation for the dangers, the hazards, and sometimes even the lives of those who march against the enemy, so that the advantages of our great Revolution, and what property they may possess, will be safe-guarded for them': the assembly only reserved the right to fix the amount of an individual contribution when the property-owner himself had suggested a figure which was quite obviously too small.[3] This suggests that a compromise had been worked out between the *possédants* and the sans-culottes—the latter gave their blood, and the former their wealth, and it was, in fact, this sort of compromise which the sans-culottes objected to when they assumed absolute control of the Sections: that of 'substitution', whereby one citizen who had been chosen for recruitment to the armies could substitute another to serve in his place. Following the same principle, the general assembly of the Section du Temple decreed on 11 March 1793 that 'every citizen will voluntarily contribute, according to his means which he must evaluate himself, to support those of our brothers who leave for the frontiers'.

After 2 June, it was quite clear that the *possédants* were still unwilling to co-operate in these projects, although the Sections continued to rely upon what they were prepared to offer: this fact

[3] *A.D.S.*, D 784.

alone emphasizes the persistent weakness of the sans-culotte movement. The *comité civil* and the *comité révolutionnaire* of the Section de l'Indivisibilité warned the general assembly on 4 June that: 'many rich citizens refuse to give their time and money to maintain the principles of liberty and equality'; others were not giving the support they could have done. Despite these drawbacks, the assembly decided to pay a hundred *livres* a month to every volunteer for the duration of the war in the Vendée, as well as promising to assist their relatives. This arrangement meant that the Section had to find 30,000 *livres* a month for the fifteen companies within their sphere of jurisdiction. The committees outlined two ways of meeting this obligation: 'The first is that every rich citizen in the Section promises in writing, voluntarily and with a willing heart, to give every month as much as he thinks he can afford as long as the war in the Vendée lasts. The second, a forced tax to be levied on rich citizens.' Eventually, the committees decided for the first alternative. An account of the sums of money promised would be printed and made public. 'If it seems that some promises do not correspond with the wealth we estimate a citizen to possess . . . the general assembly will then levy the sum which it thinks fair, so that citizens will be obliged to pay according to their means.'[4]

After the *journées* of September 1793, the sans-culottes became undisputed masters in their Sections; decisions which had formerly been left to the goodwill of the *possédants* now became unequivocal commands. The system of taxation becomes revolutionary in character and assumes a definite class bias. The advent of this new order was heralded by Chaumette on 19 Brumaire when he informed the General Council of the Commune that 'Since the rich do not wish to contribute in order to support their brothers, then clearly we must force them to pay for the time and energy which the sans-culottes devote to the Revolution.' If the *possédants* refused to co-operate then force was the only alternative. Antoine Lebrun, an upholsterer and *juge de paix* from the Section du Bonnet-Rouge, was arrested in Prairial Year II for having expressed the opinion in September 1793 'that it was about time we used bayonets to get the money required to meet the desperate needs of many women and those who defend the nation'. The carpenter Antoine Maréchal, *commissaire révolutionnaire* from the

[4] *A.P.P.*, AA/266, p. 143.

Section du Mont-Blanc, was betrayed by an informer in Frimaire Year III because he had continually advocated in the Year II that 'forced revolutionary taxes' should have been levied on the rich. During the fête given by the Section in honour of Marat, one citizen had suggested that they would need a great deal of money to pay for the celebrations, to which Maréchal replied: 'We have rich people in this Section, citizens under suspicion. We shall arrest them and, if necessary, force them to pay 100,000 *écus* as a revolutionary tax.'

Since the law of 14 Frimaire announcing the organization of the Revolutionary Government prohibited the levying of such taxes, the sans-culottes contented themselves by planning 'voluntary' collections. The rich were still obliged to comply with this fiction unless they wanted to be suspected of a lack of patriotism; but they did so very reluctantly. The *commissaires* of the Section des Halles-au-Blé, authorized to collect money for the equipment of a jacobin cavalryman, called at the home of a doctor named Petit who greeted them with the remark: 'What you again? When is this business going to come to an end?' He grudgingly donated an *assignat* worth ten *sols*, although it was widely known that he received an income of about 5,000 *livres* a year. The general assembly took due note of this and unanimously denounced him as an unworthy citizen, posting the decision up in public.[5]

During the winter, 'voluntary' collections became more numerous, increasing the tension which already existed between the *possédants* and the sans-culottes. There were collections to arm jacobin cavalrymen, to collect saltpetre, ceremonies to celebrate the *decadi*, civic fêtes—all of them opportunities for indirect taxation of the rich. If they attempted to evade the taxation, the sans-culottes threatened to brand them as suspects. At the beginning of Pluviôse, the *société Lepeletier* decided to find the necessary equipment for one cavalryman, and issued a circular amongst the wealthier citizens of the Section which informed them that they were 'fortunate to be able to give more financially than the sans-culottes. We know that you will appreciate the happy situation you enjoy—which your brothers sometimes envy—particularly when you remember that instead of giving money they are prepared to give their blood for the nation.' The assembly of the Section des Lombards adopted a resolution

[5] *Journal de la Montagne,* 15 Pluviôse Year II.

on 30 Pluviôse which dealt with the collection of saltpetre. In order to cover the cost of installing a workshop, and to pay the sans-culottes a wage of six *livres* a day, a collection was organized, and by an amendment to article 3 it was resolved that if the rich did not give 'according to their means', they would be reported to the general assembly.

Since the Section had lost the power of levying taxes by the law of 14 Frimaire, and were only making 'voluntary' collections, only a few documents dated before 14 Frimaire give us any indication of the principles upon which popular fiscality was based. The taxes levied from June 1793 to Frimaire Year II were mainly designed to repay the money which the Convention had authorized the Treasury to advance the Sections so that they could fulfil their obligations towards the volunteers who had fought in the Vendée.

On 11 June 1793, the general assembly of the Section du Panthéon-Français, finding itself in debt, levied a contribution on all personal and landed property in the Section, although this did not include 'the indigent class of the workers'. The rate of assessment was moderate enough, and even more important, it did not depart from the accepted ideas on taxation. A tenth of income derived from landed property was levied, although there were deductions for expenses which could be legally proved, and 150 *livres* a month allowance for every child under fifteen. The same percentage was levied on personal property, but this was based upon rents. Solicitors and lawyers were asked to give a tenth of their salary, schoolteachers a twentieth, and the rate for public officials was fixed at six *deniers* for every *livre* of their pay (2·5 per cent.). Finally, citizens 'living only off their income as manual labourers' were taxed at the rate of six *deniers* for every *livre* they earned above 100 *livres*; below this figure they could contribute what they wished. Although workers and civil servants were privileged, the rate levied on landed and personal property, in the absence of any progressive tax, was still reasonable. After all, many of the sans-culottes were themselves owners of shops or possessed capital of some kind.

The Section des Gravilliers adopted a progressive tax system. On 6, 7, and 8 June the *comité révolutionnaire* discussed 'a method of taxing the rich' in order to repay the 180,000 *livres* which the Section had borrowed. Finally, the assembly agreed that 1,200 *livres* should be the minimum taxable figure for landed property,

300 for salaries, and that the basic assessment should be fixed at a twentieth (5 per cent.) 'to rise progressively from this percentage'. Unfortunately the details of this progressive taxation were not given.[6] The minutes of a resolution passed in the Section des Lombards on 6 September, referring to the repayment of a loan borrowed from the national Treasury on behalf of volunteers serving in the Vendée, records an identical minimum figure upon which the taxation would be based, but gives us more detailed information. Every citizen in the Section would be taxed if they knew, or anticipated, that their salaries, or their private income from landed or industrial property, would exceed 1,200 *livres* a year. Wealthy citizens 'living solely off their private incomes', which meant that they did not work, would pay half as much again as other citizens. Bachelors were classified two categories above that to which they would have belonged had they been taxed on their income alone. In contrast, the head of every family, with at least four children below the age of 12, was taxed at half the rate, every aged relative or invalid being counted as a child. Finally, 'apprentice tradesmen, clerks working for bankers, notaries or solicitors, living with their employers' and who were eligible for recruitment at the time of the departure of the volunteers for the Vendée, would be penalized: they would pay, according to their circumstances, ten to fifteen *livres*.[7] Here again two essential factors are missing which prevent us from appreciating the full significance of popular fiscal ideas: the rate of assessment and the progressive scale.

Some light is thrown upon this in the 'contribution' scheme devised by the Section de Bonne-Nouvelle. Property-owners, and people living off income derived from rents, would be taxed at one-fifth of their net profit. There was no assessable minimum figure or progressive scale of taxation envisaged for this category. Every tenant would be eligible for taxation according to the amount of rent he paid, and in this case the tax was to be a progressive or 'sliding-scale' tax—from the minimum taxable figure to a rental of 300 *livres* they would pay 1 sol on every *livre*; from 300 to 600 *livres*, 1 sol 6 *deniers;* from 600 to 1000 *livres*, 2 sols; and above 1000 *livres*, 2 sols 6 *deniers*. Public officials and lower-grade civil servants, as well as citizens living on pensions, would be taxed according to their salary—1 sol for every *livre* up to a salary of

[6] *A.N.*, F⁷ 2486.   [7] *A.P.P.*, AA/266, p. 174.

2,000 *livres*; 1 *sol* 6 *deniers* from 2,000 to 4,000 *livres*; and 2 *sols* on every *livre* if their salary exceeded 4,000 *livres* a year.

One of the most striking features of this popular system of taxation is its moderation. The Parisian Sections were constantly asking the Commune and the Convention to levy a progressive tax on the rich, disguised as a forced loan, but an exceptional forced loan was finally decreed only with the greatest reluctance. When it arose for discussion on 21 June, Robespierre thought that it did not deal sufficiently with people of 'average wealth', but at the same time he advised the assembly that they should take care not to alarm the rich. Popular fiscal schemes betray this same contradiction: the sans-culottes were anxious that the burden of taxation should not weigh too heavily upon the *non-possédants*, but they also had no desire to oppress those who derived their income from landed or personal property, since there were many shopkeepers and craftsmen amongst the sans-culottes who could be classified as belonging to the lower section of this income group.

If it proved impossible to redistribute property by fixing a maximum on wealth, then the sans-culottes believed that the fiscal system should be designed to remedy social inequality. The demand for the recognition of the right to work and the right to public relief were intended to serve the same purpose—to assure every citizen of his subsistance and an independent livelihood. The right to work and the right to receive assistance seemed to be the necessary corollaries to the *droit à l'existence*. They both contributed towards the realization of *l'égalité des jouissances*.

On 22 May, during the ceremony of presenting its quota of volunteers for the Vendée, the Section des Gravilliers asked the Convention to make it possible for the sans-culottes to be provided with the basic necessities of life by organizing 'public works'.[8] The Declaration of Rights of 24 June had been less explicit on this point: the right to work was not clearly asserted in its provisions, only the right to receive public relief; but, as far as the sans-culottes were concerned, the two could not be separated. A petition from the Section de la Maison-Commune on 27 July 1793 stated that this was the natural conclusion to be drawn from the *droit à l'existence*. Unemployment and the cost of living had deprived 'the class with the least resources' of the opportunities

[8] *A.N.*, C 22, d. 482, p. 4.

of providing its members with a living, and it was the duty of the legislature to restore these opportunities. According to the authors of the petition this could be done quite simply by providing 'Work, and reasonable prices for basic commodities'. In view of this the Section asked that public works should be organized. Another petition from the *société des Hommes-Libre* thought that 'In a State founded upon Liberty and Equality, work on public projects should be given to the poorest and most industrious class of society.' In other words, the sans-culottes were pressing towards the recognition of the right to work.

The pressure exerted upon the authorities concerning the right to receive assistance was more persistent and more explicit. Since before 31 May, the progressive Sections had looked upon the organization of public relief as the first of their priorities during the struggle with the moderates, convinced that the Revolution should do everything possible to attract the support of the poorest sans-culotte. By a decree passed on 26 November 1792, the Convention had already voted assistance for the relatives and children of volunteers, and this measure had been extended on 4 May 1793 to cover the families of all military personnel. On 8 May, however, the Section des Invalides went a stage further and requested a pension for widows, orphans, disabled servicemen and those who had lost their source of livelihood; the necessary funds to cover this scheme would be raised by a levy of one-twelfth of the annual income of all citizens liable for service in the armies. This scheme did not only provide aid for the relatives and children of volunteers, but also for the needy who would then be supported by the contributions of the rich. Such projects were not without a certain element of hostility towards the *possédants*. The forced loan on the rich demanded by the Sections of the *faubourg* Saint-Antoine on 1 May 1793 was also planned to assist the poor as well as to equip volunteers.[9]

After 2 June, the tone of these petitions changes and becomes more menacing. The *canonniers* of the Section de Quatre-Vingt-Douze demanded a Constitution eight days later 'which embodies the principle that State assistance is the right of the poor'. In the Declaration of Rights this demand was met with the provision that public relief should be considered as 'a sacred obligation'. But there was still the problem of organizing such relief. In March

[9] *Moniteur*, xvi, 288.

of the same year, the Convention had made a good start by laying the foundations of a general scheme of public assistance. On 28 June, it adopted a resolution on the relief to be given annually to children, the aged and the destitute; and on 15 October, it discussed the possibilities of suppressing begging. But despite the continual promptings of the Sections, there was no sign that the Convention was actually planning to put these general resolutions into operation.

At the time of the acceptance of the Constitution, many of the primary assemblies in Paris, particularly those in the *faubourg* Saint-Antoine, congratulated the Convention for having recognized that the people had a right to receive assistance from the State, but they pressed it 'to complete its work'. The Quinze-Vingts, Popincourt, and Montreuil Sections, where the number of destitute citizens was particularly high, stated on 4 July 1793 that it was time that the poor, who had so far been supporting the Revolution alone, 'began to enjoy its benefits'. They asked for 'the establishment of workshops, which had been talked about for too long, where an industrious citizen will always be able to find work, whenever and wherever he needs it; and alms-houses where the aged, the sick, and the infirm will receive the sympathetic and charitable attention which humanity owes to them'. On 17 July, the *société des Républicaines-Révolutionnaires* demanded the organization of public relief. On 14 August, all the Paris Sections delivered to the General Council of the Commune a petition to the Convention dealing with the organization of alms-houses and hospitals. Young men recruited at the beginning of September included the same demands in their patriotic addresses: those from the Section de Montreuil took the liberty of reminding the Convention on 11 September of its 'sacred promise', adding that: 'The wealth at the disposal of the nation should be used to provide (our parents) with assistance to relieve the state of destitution in which we leave them.'[1]

In Brumaire, the measures adopted by Fouché in the Nièvre, enthusiastically supported by Chaumette in the General Council of the Commune, awakened new claims. 'They tell me', the *procureur* of the Commune wrote on 11 Brumaire, 'that there are no longer any nobles, priests, or rich citizens to be found in this part of France. I add the rich because they have found a way of

[1] *A.N.*, C 261, d. 573, p. 30; C 271, pl. 667, p. 36.

combating poverty by giving assistance to every wretched cripple or beggar.' Chaumette added his plea for a scheme of assistance 'to ease the distress of the aged and the infirm, and to find some way of employing the destitute so that there would be no more begging in Paris and that the suffering of humanity might be alleviated'. The money to finance this plan would, of course, come from the rich: 'The rich must be forced to play their part and made to contribute, whether they like it or not, towards the happiness of all citizens.'[2] Once again they based their claims on rather general statements of principle. The Section de Mutius-Scaevola suggested to the Convention on 22 Brumaire that the money necessary for these ideas should be found by levying a forced loan on the rich, but the suggestion was rejected. Again, it was 'at the expense of these rich egoists' that the *société populaire de Popincourt* asked for houses to be opened where the destitute and the aged could be cared for, adding that 'having little wealth at their disposal, the Section was unfortunately forced to see their brothers suffer without being able to help them'.

The deterioration in the general situation at the end of the winter of the Year II led to a renewed campaign for the organization of public relief. The police-agent Hanriot reported on 3 Ventôse that the Section du Contrat-Social had organized an alms-house 'where pregnant women would be received and where they would be given the broth and the meat which women in their condition required'. The Section de l'Homme-Armé adopted a resolution 'on the assistance which should be given to the unfortunate', which was enthusiastically supported by the *société Lepeletier* on 14 Ventôse and the Section des Invalides on the following day. The Section de l'Homme-Armé, referring to article 21 of the Declaration of Rights, reminded the Convention 'that it is time to ensure that even penniless citizens are assured of their rights'. It demanded the establishment of an alms-house in each Section, 'so that not even the rich egoist would expect more consideration and comfort in his own home than our poor brothers will find in the refuge which will have been prepared for them by republican hands'. Only the genuinely poor would be received in these alms-houses; they would only be given their immediate needs; but, above all, work would be found for them, or the

[2] *Affiches*, 12 Brumaire Year II; *Journal de la Montagne*, 13 Brumaire Year II.

essential tools to carry on their own trades. On 15 Ventôse, the *société populaire de Bonne-Nouvelle* was the next to present its ideas to the Convention: these were concerned with 'the ways of making different classes contribute proportionately towards the relief of the destitute'. On 29 Ventôse, the *société populaire des Lombards* discussed the merits of a scheme for a benevolent fund whereby, 'every member, according to the proposed scale, will be assured of receiving assistance from the society in case of sickness'.[3] Already, we can detect the principle of social security. The decree of 22 Floréal which dealt with the opening of a register of public charity in every department outlined this scheme of social security which the sans-culottes had only just begun to distinguish from traditional ideas of charity. Of all this, nothing was to survive Thermidor, except the realization that a great hope had not been fulfilled.

The sans-culottes also believed that the organization of public instruction would play a significant part in the realization of *l'égalité des jouissances*, but here again it was disillusionment, not fulfilment, which confronted them after Thermidor. Influenced by the prevailing ideas of the century, the sans-culottes attached great importance to the question of education, regarding it, in the same way as their other demands, as a social right. They believed that it would help them to overcome the difficulties and harshness of their existence; it would help them to improve their social standing and destroy the pervading influence and power of wealth. If the community did not ensure that everyone received the same opportunity of being instructed, then education would continue to be the jealously guarded privilege of the wealthy. As more citizens were instructed, so the Republic would grow stronger, since its future depended upon the degree to which the young were nurtured upon the same ideals as their parents. The demand for free education was an integral part of the social campaign conducted by the sans-culotterie and became in fact its most characteristic feature.

Even before 31 May, the more progressive Sections had insisted on the need for the organization of public instruction, whilst some had even tried to undertake the task themselves. On 17 March 1793, the *société patriotique du Luxembourg* decided to organize

[3] *A.N.*, W 112.

'public instruction for children, as a temporary measure'. Realizing the urgency of the problem it accepted the responsibility of teaching them to read and write. Children of both sexes from the ages of 6 to 12 would attend twice a week for instruction which would lay particular emphasis on moral and civic qualities. 'The main aim of the teaching will be to point out the duties and obligations which children owe to their country and their parents, and to explain what morals and opinions they should endeavour to cultivate in order to grow up as useful citizens. We will encourage their inherent goodness, show them the virtue of sympathy and respect for the aged. . . . We will demonstrate, with the use of simple comparisons which children of their age will understand, the aim of every society and the different forms of government which societies can choose; but we will pay particular attention to those governments which are based on Liberty and Equality. We will give them an explanation of natural, political, and civil laws, and define what is meant by the terms sovereignty, the sanction of the people, liberty, equality, and the Republic; and in addition we will show them the evils which are attached to all tyrannical régimes, and the happiness which is the natural consequence of a republican government.'

This preoccupation with civic and political questions was also observed by the Observatoire, Finistère, Sans-Culottes and Panthéon-Français Sections when they asked in May for a 'national code of education' based on the principles of the Republic. The Section des Gravilliers urged the Convention on 22 May to strengthen the unity and indivisibility of the Republic by organizing national education.[4]

After 2 June, the sans-culottes believed that the organization of public instruction was more necessary then ever to consolidate the popular victory. 'On one side we find ignorance and fanaticism, undermining the work of four years of struggle and sacrifice,' one citizen in the general assembly of the Section des Amis-de-la-Patrie stated on 16 June, 'on the other, we find instruction and enlightenment, scattering prejudice, and making us appreciate a revolution based entirely upon the indestructible foundation of virtue.' The speaker insisted upon the necessity of 'investigating every possible method of instructing the destitute section of the populace', and asked for the immediate organization of primary

[4] *A.N.*, C 255, d. 482, p. 4.

schools. The Declaration of Rights on 24 June, by recognizing that the people had a right to be instructed, provided the theoretical justification for popular demands; but, as the Section du Panthéon-Français observed three days later, 'it is not enough to make laws: they must be put into operation'. Now that the Constitution had been completed, the Republic had to build, 'the edifice which will serve as a barrier against the prejudices of the priesthood and the nobility. Let us decree the organization of a republican institution, open to every citizen, the importance of which has been overlooked for far too long in the notable measures of general security. The evil caused by the Vendée and rebel arms is far less than that caused by ignorance and fanaticism.' Again, the objective which the Section had in mind was fundamentally political—they wanted to organize 'a national institution which will make it easier for the sans-culottes to receive the necessary training which will qualify them for every kind of office'.

The congratulatory addresses on the acceptance of the *Acte constitutionnel* laid particular emphasis on the necessity of organizing public instruction as quickly as possible. The Section des Amis-de-la-Patrie referred to the problem on 4 July, and on the same day the Section des Fédérés asked for 'a wise scheme of education designed to assure the future prosperity of our children'. The young girls who presented bouquets on behalf of the Section invited the Convention to organize 'national instruction along popular lines'. On 7 July, the Section de Bon-Conseil asked for a national education which would cultivate 'the seeds of patriotic virtue': and a week later the Section des Droits-de-l'Homme expressed their wish for 'a scheme of education which would instruct citizens in their duty and the exercise of a virtuous life'.

The sans-culottes did not limit their horizons to the organization of just one form of civic education designed to shape good citizens for the future; they also wanted a practical and utilitarian education which would give the young professional training for particular occupations. The influence of eighteenth-century ideas was making itself felt—Rousseau's *Émile*, which stressed that the acquisition of intellectual learning was not as important for children as the inculcation of sound moral principles and technical training. On 4 July, the Section du Faubourg-Montmartre asked 'not for one of these metaphysical educations which tend to weaken moral and republican virtues, but an instruction designed to perfect the arts and crafts, to give greater drive to national industry, to help in the construction of our buildings and the improvement of our trade, and to destroy tyranny for ever'. On the same day the three Sections of the *faubourg* Saint-Antoine informed the Convention that they were waiting confidently for a law on education: 'We know that we shall find in such a law the means of acquainting the farmer . . . with every discovery which might simplify his work and increase the yield of his crops; that the craftsman, upon whom all trade depends, will discover how to perfect his skill, the worker his ability, and that everything which might rekindle or perpetuate the spirit of superstition will be excluded.'[5]

On 13 July, Robespierre informed the Convention of Lepeletier de Saint-Fargeau's plan of education, and on 29 July, on behalf of the *Comité d'instruction publique*, moved that it should be adopted. But the matter was not taken any further, and opponents of the Government, both inside and outside the Convention, used this inaction as a means of agitation. Lepeletier's scheme was referred to on 17 July by the *société des Républicaines-Révolutionnaires*, and a month later Leclerc paid tribute 'to the man who had conceived the idea of giving every child the same education'. Leclerc went on to ask: 'Why has the National Convention refused to adopt this sensible measure as it stands? Why is it afraid to force parents to recognize the principle of equality by sending their children to schools which make no distinction between their pupils?' Hébert expressed himself more forcibly when he wrote: 'We will never have good generals and good magistrates until an appropriate system of education has reformed people.' The Convention should hasten 'to instruct the sans-culottes so that they can shake off the tyranny of lawyers and clever-dicks'.

Given this encouragement by Hébert and others the Sections renewed their campaign. On 25 August, the Section des Lombards presented a petition to the Convention asking that national education should be 'compulsory and free'. On 12 September, the Section du Panthéon-Français laid down the principle that: 'The law punishes, learning persuades', and suggested that a school should be opened in every Section or canton offering free education to all children. It was not simply a question of educating

[5] *A.N.*, C 262, d. 578, p. 37; C 261, d. 573, p. 18 and p. 30.

infants and adolescents, even those sans-culottes who had reached the age of maturity were still subject to the 'influence of old prejudices'. On 21 October, the Convention passed a decree establishing State primary schools designed to combine the improvement of mental and physical qualities, precept, and experience; but on 4 November, this scheme was already being subjected to further discussion.[6] The wave of dechristianization created a new sense of urgency, since the sans-culottes were anxious that the Revolution should present a constructive as well as a destructive policy. On 22 Brumaire, during the presentation of their dechristianization address, the Mutius-Scaevola and Bonnet-Rouge Sections, pressed the Convention to organize 'national education which would provide the same instruction for all citizens'. On 6 Frimaire, 'the young children' of the former Section, appropriately rehearsed, returned to ask the Convention 'to organize primary schools as quickly as possible'.

The slow response of the government to this prompting sometimes forced the Section or popular societies to lead the way in organizing public instruction. The Section de Bonne-Nouvelle provided 'a course on morals and reason', and the *société populaire de Lazowski* opened 'a school of morality for young citizens'. The *société populaire de la Réunion* proposed on 27 Brumaire that 'a course of morality based on the principles of nature and truth' should be organized which was accepted by the general assembly and a commission of public instruction was created.

On 29 Frimaire, the Convention passed a decree dealing with public instruction, particularly the first stages of education—the *premières écoles*. It outlined a scheme of teaching, controlled by the State, but offering a certain measure of decentralization which was a fairly accurate reflection of the ideas of the sans-culottes themselves. But, since the Revolutionary Government continued to devote practically all its energy to the prosecution of the war, this scheme was never put into operation.

This meant that popular agitation and the flood of petitions continued. In No. 349 of the *Père Duchesne*, which appeared in Pluviôse, Hébert expresses his feeling of anger and frustration 'that education was being pushed to one side, and that there were some citizens who were anxious to monopolize the minds of the people (*accapareurs d'esprit*); who did not want to see them being

[6] *Moniteur*, xviii, 346.

taught in case the poor and the unemployed might escape the threat of being reduced to begging'. On 6 Pluviôse, schoolchildren from the Section de la Fontaine-de-Grenelle drew the attention of the Convention to their teachers 'who have fallen into the most shocking laziness. It is over three years since they last taught us anything new.' On the seventeenth of the same month, the school-children from the Section de Mutius-Scaevola returned once again to the Convention to ask for 'the immediate establishment of primary schools'.[7]

In Ventôse, the irritation caused by the inactivity of the government played a significant part in the general crisis experienced by the sans-culotterie during the course of the month. According to the police-agent Charmont on 5 Ventôse, 'they are tired of seeing their children lose the benefit of this new instruction which will ensure the happiness of future generations'; the sans-culottes, Charmont added, were anxious to see primary schools finally organized. On 10 Ventôse, the Section des Sans-Culottes adopted a strongly-worded resolution which pointed out the 'extreme urgency' of organizing these schools 'so that each individual acquires the necessary talents and virtues to enjoy the fullest expression of his natural rights'. On the fourteenth, according to the police-agent Hanriot, 'the need for public instruction is so pronounced amongst the patriots that they even complain of the fact that no schools have been opened anywhere for shaping republican principles. It would appear from this, a citizen in one society said, that some people wanted to throw spokes in the chariot wheels of the Revolution.' This petition was sent to all the general assemblies of the other Sections on 15 Ventôse, and was enthusiastically received by the Section de la Montagne in particular. In answer to this unanimous feeling amongst the sans-culottes, the Department published a decree on 21 Ventôse which promised to accelerate the organization of primary schools: according to one eyewitness, 'the keen interest with which people are reading it proves that good citizens really want to see republican schools opened as soon as possible'.[8]

This move on the part of the Department appears to be the first genuine attempt to transform the many schemes of education into practice, but the difficulties which faced the authorities, despite their good intentions, were many. The necessary books, furniture

---

[7] *A.N.*, C 292, pl. 935, p. 37; pl. 936, p. 14.   [8] *A.N.*, W 112.

and equipment were not to be found: neither the Sections nor the
Commune had sufficient resources to organize schools. On 19
Germinal, the *commissaires* of the Section de la Halle-au-Blé
informed the Department that there was not one single school-
building in their Section, and that they needed the authority to
requisition two houses, forming part of the national lands, to
open a boy's school and a girl's school; as for the benches and
tables which were needed, they asked for permission to take the
required number from the Duplessis college which had been
turned into a jail. The only thing the Department could do was to
nominate one of its officials to accompany the *commissaires* to
the *Comité d'instruction publique*. But even this body had no power
to requisition national lands.

This provides some idea of the insurmountable difficulties
which faced the popular authorities once they had decided to
organize schools in the Sections. Many gave up the struggle. The
disillusionment amongst the sans-culottes was all the keener for
their having placed so much faith in education as a means of
strengthening the Republic and of improving their own position
in society.

The fundamental belief of the sans-culottes in the *droit à
l'existence*, which was constantly being invoked, although it was
never clearly expressed, gave rise to the idea of a limitation to right
of ownership, hostility towards the concentration of industry, the
beginnings of an organized fiscal system, public relief and a plan
of education designed to realize the *égalité des jouissances*: all this
was characteristic of a social ideal which suited the economic
conditions of the period.

If they were peasants or artisans, attached to the soil or prisoners
of a guild or corporation, the first task of the sans-culotterie was
to achieve their own independence. This accounts for their hatred
of the feudal aristocracy, their hostility towards the *ancien régime*
with its corporative organization; without their assistance the
bourgeoisie would never have succeeded in overcoming these
obstacles. Since the sans-culottes produced their goods for an
immediate market, they believed that ownership should be based
upon personal labour, and their ideal society was a society of
small owners, each man possessing his own field, his own workshop, or his own store. The State should intervene by protecting

small business concerns, passing appropriate laws on inheritance, levying a progressive tax on income and organizing public assistance so that at least a relative equality could be maintained between all citizens. These measures would strengthen small ownership and compensate for the economic trends which militated against the interests of the sans-culottes. Above all, it was a question of preventing the accumulation of wealth into the hands of a privileged minority, and of protecting the sans-culottes against the threat of being depressed into the state of a dependent proletariat.

At the end of the winter of Year II, when the Revolution was entering upon its most critical phase, the general feeling amongst the sans-culotterie was that, despite its many notable achievements, the work of the Revolutionary Government left much to be desired. Had the confiscation of the lands of the clergy and the nobility led to the distribution of one acre more to landless peasants? Had the abolition of corporations and guilds allowed *compagnons* to become masters in their own workshops?

The economic structure based upon small independent producers favoured the parcelling out of land and the scattering of property: it excluded social co-operation and the concentration of the means of production. The sans-culottes did not forsee that having reached a certain stage of development, this society would create the very factors which would lead to its own destruction—individual forms of production, scattered into small units would, almost inevitably, transform themselves into socially concentrated forms of production, the small ownership of thousands of independent craftsmen, producing for an immediate market, would be supplanted by the large ownership of a capitalist minority. A form of ownership dependent upon the wage-earner replaces the idea of ownership based upon personal labour.

The sans-culottes struggled vainly to resolve insoluble contradictions. Although they were hostile towards the rich and the big business man, they associated themselves with the bourgeoisie either because they were, or wanted to become, property-owners themselves. They demanded the fixing of prices and the limitation of ownership, but at the same time they were working to achieve the independence of the shop, an artisan economy, and the rural property of the peasant, borrowing these ideas from the policy of economic liberalism which was so vital to the interests of the capitalist bourgeoisie. These same contradictions are reflected in the social composition of the sans-culotterie which did not constitute a class in society, and therefore failed to agree upon a coherent economic and social programme. The majority of craftsmen, not wishing to depart from a method of production which was founded upon personal labour, were condemned to lose their importance as the capitalist organization of the economy grew stronger: only a minority, receptive to the impetus of industrial capitalism, was destined to succeed.

The most advanced Montagnards—particularly the Robespierrists—whose social ideas were not far from being identical with those of the sans-culottes, were also the victims of the same contradictions. Thus we are confronted with the irreducible antagonism which arises between the aspirations of a social group and objective historical necessity. From the winter of the Year II, this antagonism lay beneath the tragic conflict which led to the collapse of the egalitarian Republic—the cherished dream of the sans-culotterie—and the triumph of the revolutionary bourgeoisie.

III

POLITICAL LEANINGS

ALTHOUGH the sans-culotte militants were unable to devise an original and effective social programme, the coherent pattern of political ideas which they adopted distinguishes them as the most progressive group to emerge during the Revolution. Their demands for the autonomy and permanence of the Sections, the right to approve legislation, the exercise of control over their elected representatives and the power of revoking their mandate, based upon a wide interpretation of the expression 'popular sovereignty', moved the sans-culotterie nearer the exercise of direct government and popular democracy.[1] But could the bourgeois conception of democracy and the exigencies of the Revolutionary Government be reconciled with the political leanings of the sans-culotterie?

The political behaviour of the militant sans-culotte can only be explained by his unqualified acceptance of the principle that sovereignty resides in the people. For the sans-culotte, this was not an abstract idea, but a concrete reality of the people gathered together in the assemblies of the Sections exercising the totality of their rights.

Popular sovereignty was 'imprescriptible and inalienable; a right which could be delegated to no one', and on 3 November 1792, the Section de la Cité announced that 'anyone who claims that he is invested with this right will be regarded as a tyrant, a usurper of the people's freedom who deserves to be punished by death'. On 13 March 1793, after a citizen in the general assembly of the Section du Panthéon-Français had stated that 'people are threatening us with a dictator', the assembly rose to its feet and swore to kill 'any director, protector, tribune, triumvire, or any other kind of ruler, whatever title he chooses for himself, who attacks the principle of the people's sovereignty'. This anxiety to

---

[1] The expression 'popular republic' can be found in Etienne Barry's *Essai sur la dénonciation politique.*

defend the sovereignty of the people clearly explains why so many proposals by Marat to nominate a tribune of the people, or a dictator, were so unsuccessful, as well as the importance of the accusation that Hébert and others were planning to create an office of *grand juge*, a charge designed to weaken their popularity in the eyes of the people.

The imprescriptible and inalienable nature of popular sovereignty became a reality after June 1792 when the sans-culottes took their place in the general assemblies of the Sections, ignoring the distinction which had previously been made between 'active' and 'passive' citizens. An address from the Section du Théâtre-Français on 30 July 1792 stated that 'A particular class of citizens cannot assume the exclusive right of defending the interests of the nation,' and, in view of this, it called upon citizens, 'aristocratically known as passive citizens', to do their service in the National Guard and to deliberate in the general assemblies: in fact, to share 'the exercise of that part of the people's sovereignty which belongs to the Section'. Supporting these views, Hanriot simplified the question when, on 31 May, he announced from the parade ground of the Section du Finistère; 'The rich have been making laws for too long: it is about time the poor were given their turn so that inequality between the rich and the poor might disappear.'[2]

The principle of popular sovereignty was unrestricted: it applied, in its entirety, to every sphere of government. In legislative affairs, a law was only valid if it had been drafted, or sanctioned, by the people. When the Constituent Assembly forbade collective petitions on 10 May 1791—favouring the right of the individual against the sovereignty of the group—and tried to limit the deliberations of the communal assemblies to 'purely municipal aspects of administration', the *société fraternelle de deux sexes* meeting at the Jacobin club protested against this limitation, explaining that, in their opinion, 'this deprives the *communes*—in other words, the sovereign people—of the exercise of their most important public right; it deprives them of the very reason for their existence'. Sovereignty resides in the assembled citizens, and one cannot forbid them the practice, or deny them the right, of rejecting laws which did not meet with their approval. To the sans-culottes, every law was an arbitrary law if they had not

[2] *A.N.*, F⁷ 4774⁷⁸.

co-operated in its making. The formulation of this principle led to the practice of direct government, particularly in times of crisis when the sans-culottes were determined to press for the full exercise of their rights. The address of the Section du Théâtre-Français on 30 July 1792 proclaimed the belief that when the nation was threatened, 'the people automatically enter into the exercise of their sovereign vigilance', and, even more significant, it advanced the principle that 'every department should be allowed to pass laws within its own sphere of jurisdiction so long as the safety of the nation was threatened'. This anarchical tendency was in direct contradiction with the demand for action on a collective and national basis. A pamphlet, which appeared in the summer of 1792, stated that the people should never be satisfied with the practice of electing representatives and delegating their powers to them in times of crisis: the assemblies of the sovereign people should meet as long as the National Convention remained in session: 'When the country is in danger, the sovereign must stay at his post, at the head of his armies, in control of its affairs: he must be everywhere.'[3]

In exceptional circumstances, the sans-culottes effectively reasserted their control of the legislative power. This was particularly true of periods of insurrection as well as for the acceptance of the Constitution. On 14 July 1793, several Sections appeared at the bar of the Convention to signify their approval of the *Acte constitutionnel*: the Assembly, yielding to pressure, decreed that those who spoke on behalf of their Sections would be allowed to remain in the assembly hall 'because they do not appear before us as petitioners, but as members of the sovereign power'.[4] Again, when the assembly-room of the General Council of the Commune was invaded on 4 September 1793, the people mingled with the members in order to participate in their deliberations. The *Moniteur*, on this occasion, noted simply that 'a fraternal discussion took place between the people and their magistrates'; the *Journal de la Montagne*, on the other hand, reported more accurately: 'the assembly-room being crowded, and the people finding themselves seated alongside the magistrates, they begun to share in their deliberations'. On 21 August 1793, in *l'Ami du peuple*, Leclerc wrote unequivocally: 'Sovereign, claim your rightful place. Delegates of the sovereign, leave the seats on

[3] *A.N.*, AD 1, 69.   [4] *Moniteur*, xvii, 48.

the terraces—they belong to the people. Your place is on the floor
of the amphitheatre.'

The principle of popular sovereignty, which had already given
rise to a rather vague theory of direct government, was also invoked
to justify the right of the people to approve laws drafted by the
legislature. The militants considered this to be one of their most
important demands and made repeated attempts to secure its
recognition.

Rousseau had already proclaimed that since sovereignty was
inalienable, and laws were an expression of the General Will,
'every law which is not ratified by the people themselves is
invalid'. Nicolas de Bonneville had developed these same principles in the *Bouche de fer*. On 30 May 1791, the Cordeliers had
asserted that the nation could only be governed by laws which had
received its 'assent', or laws which had been 'requested by the
nation'; they added that even the Constitution could not become
law until it had been ratified by the people. If the primary assemblies were to be deprived of their right of criticizing laws and of
making their opinions known, then an 'aristocracy of deputies'
would take the place of the aristocracy of the nobility.

During the crisis of the summer of 1792, when the sans-culottes
were making a positive impact upon political life and the insurrection of 10 August had given the nation some idea of the actual
meaning of popular sovereignty, these principles were advanced
once again, but this time in a particularly striking form. On 9
August, the general assembly of the Section du Marché-des-
Innocents proposed that even the basic principles upon which a
National Convention should legislate demanded that 'the provisions made for the drafting of a Constitution and the passing of
such permanent laws as those governing marriage, inheritance and
the judiciary' should not be considered as binding until they had
been accepted by the primary assemblies. On 27 August, the
Section de Bondy claimed the right of accepting or rejecting the
Constitution decreed by the National Convention. In the electoral
assembly of the department of Paris on 9 September, a representative from the Section des Halles proposed that the decrees passed
by the Convention should not receive the force of law until they
had been approved by the primary assemblies. On 18 September,
the Section de la Halle-au-Blé delegated to deputies elected to the

Convention, 'the necessary powers for proposing what kind of laws and form of government should be accepted by the nation', reminding them that sovereignty resided in the people alone. The same day, the Section Poissonnière adopted a petition which demanded that the Constitution should be approved by the people. On 29 September, the Section de la Cité announced that since 'there could be no such thing as a constitution which had not been freely accepted by the people', it had decided to express its approval of the abolition of royalty by the Convention, and its proclamation concerning the unity and indivisibility of the Republic. The Section went on to ask that before it even began to deal with constitutional laws, the Convention 'should acquaint the primary assemblies as soon as possible with the manner in which its decrees would be approved'. The people's right to sanction laws, therefore, was not only to be invoked during periods of crisis, or when discussing the acceptance of the Constitution, but extended over the whole range of legislation. On 2 November 1792, the general assembly of the Section des Piques again adopted a draft resolution 'on the method of approving laws'. Since sovereignty was inalienable, 'only the people can dictate our laws: their (the deputies) sole function is to propose what laws should be passed'. Laws were to be submitted to the people in their primary assemblies, and not to an *assemblée sanctionnante* composed of the people's representatives.

The sans-culottes were not satisfied simply with a theoretical assertion of their rights; they were frequently used to justify opposition to decrees issued by the National Convention and to legitimize those violations of the law which furthered their own political aims. When, on 5 June 1793, the president of the general assembly of the Section du Mont-Blanc tried to close a debate by referring to a law stipulating ten o'clock as a time-limit for their meetings, Auvray, a battalion commanding officer, objected 'that there was, in fact, no such law, since the one referred to had not been approved by the people'. According to a denunciation made on 29 Ventôse Year II against the *comité révolutionnaire* of the Section du Bonnet-Rouge, the *commissaires* were frequently supposed to have said that 'even if the National Convention passed a decree favouring the release of any detained citizen, and it had been invoked by the president, they would only act upon it if it had been approved by the committee'. A citizen named Cailleux from the Section des Amis-de-la-Patrie was denounced on 2 Brumaire Year III for his conviction 'that he could question a law'.[5]

The popular conception of sovereignty was completely at variance with the doctrine of the separation of powers: the sovereignty of the people extended over both the legislature and the judiciary. 'Justice always dwells amongst the people' announced Leclerc to the General Council of the Commune on 16 May 1793. The general assembly of the Section du Finistère was told by the sans-culotte Bouland on several occasions after 10 August: 'in times of crisis such as these, we have no need of tribunals. The people are sovereign; it is within their authority to judge and pass sentence on the guilty.' The sans-culottes pointed out that justice had always been one of the essential attributes of sovereignty throughout the centuries. In the system of democracy practised by the Sections, it naturally became the prerogative of the people. The tribunals which had been created during the September *journées* had exercised power on behalf of the people who had simply delegated their authority, not abdicated it: the tribunals were prepared to bow to the will of the people whenever they wished to reassert their sovereignty. This is why the Fontaine-de-Grenelle, Sans-Culottes and Quatre-Nations Sections had declared themselves in favour of the tribunals set up within their respective spheres of jurisdiction—they had been created by the people; they represented the will of the people. One of the *commissaires* of the General Council of the Commune told the Legislative Assembly during the night of 3 September: 'The people were executing justice by exercising their vengeance.'[6]

The popular exercise of justice—an attribute of sovereignty—had been one of the distinguishing features of the crisis of September 1792 when few people, indeed, had been prepared to challenge it. The sans-culottes had to legitimize the insurrection of 10 August and surmount the danger which threatened the nation. However, similar claims were made during other critical phases of the Revolution. In March 1793, when 300,000 conscripts were levied, Pouxlandry, soon to be appointed *commissaire révolutionnaire*, called for a new *septembrisation* in the general assembly of the Section de Bonne-Nouvelle, saying that the people had to exercise justice on those deputies who had not voted for the death

[5] *A.N.*, F[7] 699.   [6] *Moniteur*, xiii, 603.

penalty outright during the king's trial. In Prairial Year III, the shoemaker Duval asked for a people's tribunal in order to save the Republic.

The force of arms was the one other important attribute of popular sovereignty for which the sans-culottes repeatedly demanded recognition, and which, from July 1789 to Prairial Year III, almost inevitably led to disastrous consequences. According to the sans-culottes, the people could only really exercise their sovereignty if they were allowed to carry arms.

Defining the 'pillars' of liberty in an address to the electoral body, a pamphlet which appeared in August 1792 enumerated the permanence of the Sections, the freedom of the press, and 'the arming of all citizens, without cost and without distinction'. The sans-culottes forced their way into the ranks of the National Guard at the same time as they invaded the general assemblies of the Sections. The pike became the object of lavish praise—the 'holy pike'—and was finally identified with the sans-culottes themselves. Their political success appears to have depended upon the degree to which they were armed: certainly, when they were disarmed, their influence was no longer apparent. The sans-culottes made repeated requests for rifles or similar weapons owing to their increased effectiveness over the pike. There was a considerable outcry in the autumn of 1792 when the government proposed to relieve the Sections of their canons and transfer them to the armies. On 4 November, the general assembly of the Section des Champs-Elysées adhered to a decree issued by the Section de Bonne-Nouvelle announcing that it would never consent 'to its canons—its conquest of 14 July—leaving the Section except as part of its armed force'. The attitude of the Section de la Cité on 6 November was precisely the same—the canons belonged to the Section, and only the general assembly could authorize its artillery company to leave the service of the Section. An address by the Section des Quinze-Vingts reminded the Convention in December 1792 that only citizens had the right to carry arms in the capital, and that regular troops should never be employed in Paris.[7] The 31 May 1793 is a date which marks not only the arming of the majority of the sans-culottes, but also their political victory. The Section de la Réunion on the same day disarmed all aristocrats and moderates 'so that those citizens who

[7] *A.D.S.*, D 926 and 691.

are truly worthy of fighting for liberty can be armed'. This move
was copied by all the Sections under the control of the sans-
culottes. Similarly, when it was the turn of the sans-culottes
themselves to be disarmed in the Year III, this was not only
regarded as a precautionary measure, but the symbol of a political
reaction: disarmament was usually followed by their exclusion
from the general assemblies. One of the first demands made by the
insurgents of Prairial was the restitution of arms to citizens who
had been deprived of them. The proposition was actually made by
Duroy, and it became one of the more serious charges levelled
against him after the failure of the insurrection. The right of the
people to carry arms, and to exercise their other rights by means
of insurrection, was the extreme application of the principle of
popular sovereignty which the Thermidoreans rejected.

The very ideas which the sans-culottes held on the question of
popular sovereignty, as well as the situations arising from their
practical application, were revolutionary in content. Backed by the
force of the *sections en armes*, this revolutionary aspect can be
traced throughout the course of the Revolution, but particularly
during the summer of 1792. One year later, however, the contradiction between the aspirations and political behaviour of the
sans-culotterie and the urgent problems facing the Revolutionary
Government burst into the open, revealing an incompatibility
which, equally as important as the social question, lay at the very
root of the crisis which finally led to the collapse of both the
Revolutionary Government and the popular movement.

The popular conception of sovereignty was a decisive weapon
in the struggle against the monarchy. On 31 July 1792, the famous
decree issued by the Section de Mauconseil declared that the
Section had reassumed the exercise of its rights and no longer
recognized Louis XVI as 'king of the French', and although it
remained faithful to the nation, it intended to renounce 'those
oaths of allegiance which, in good faith, it could no longer observe'.
Principles based on popular sovereignty and the autonomy of the
Sections were also carried to their logical conclusion—the dissolution of the body politic. On 4 August, after hearing Vergniaud's report, the Legislative Assembly annulled the decree issued
by the Section de Mauconseil. In the opinion of the Assembly,
sovereignty belonged to the people as a whole, not to a section of

the people. Two conceptions of sovereignty clashed, and the only way of resolving the problem was by means of insurrection. The Sections accepted the challenge.

After 10 August, popular sovereignty was invested in the Convention, and later into the hands of its governmental Committees. The difficulty which presented itself in August 1792 was basically that which arose in the Year II—how to reconcile the uncompromising claims of popular sovereignty as interpreted by the militants in the Sections, with the immediate problems which faced the Revolutionary Government, completely absorbed in the task of organizing national defence.

In the Year II, the very expression 'popular sovereignty', which had been used so frequently in 1792 and 1793, disappeared from the political vocabulary of the government. There is no mention of it in the speech made by Saint-Just on 10 October 1793 concerning the need for a 'revolutionary' government until the end of the war, nor in the decree of 14 Frimaire actually creating such a government, nor in Robespierre's speech of 5 Nivôse outlining its policy. After the decree of Frimaire, the Sections played no part whatsoever in the work of the Revolutionary Government. A decree of 5 Brumaire had previously suspended the election of the municipalities, and the whole elective system gradually fell into disuse. In order to replace magistrates and public officials, *représentants en mission* and *agents nationaux* simply consulted the popular societies. Thus the sovereignty of the people was no longer to be found 'in the clubs, or the party which happens to be in power' as Albert Mathiez puts it, but in the hands of the administrative machinery of the government. The sans-culottes held on as long as they could to their electoral power—the symbol of their sovereignty—but it finally fell from their grasp in the Year III. The *comités révolutionnaires*, elected by the general assemblies in the spring of 1793, and re-elected in September, purged in the autumn by the General Council of the Commune, eventually came under the control of the Committee of General Security during the course of the winter: in the spring of the Year II, the members of the committees were appointed by the Committee of Public Safety. The General Council of the Commune suffered a similar fate. After Germinal and the execution of Hébert and Chaumette, the Committee dismissed the members of the Council and chose their successors without consulting the Sections. On 16 Floréal, the *agent national* of the Paris Commune, Payan, reminded the Sections that 'under the Revolutionary Government, there are no primary assemblies: we only recognize the general assembly'. As far as the sans-culottes were concerned, this meant that their sovereign rights had been transferred to the Revolutionary Government. The shoemaker Potel, *commissaire* in the Section du Contrat-Social, was promptly arrested in Germinal for telling the *société des Amis-de-la-République* that since the society represented a part of the people's sovereignty, it had the right to legislate. The refusal to satisfy popular aspirations on the question of sovereignty largely explains the indifferent attitude of the sans-culottes towards the Revolutionary Government during the spring of the Year II.

The Thermidoreans, realizing the threat to the ultimate success of the bourgeoisie inherent in the notion of popular sovereignty, denounced the manner in which it had allegedly been misused. The people had a concrete conception of sovereignty vested in the general assemblies of the Section: the bourgeoisie advanced a more abstract interpretation which was more in keeping with their particular interests. On 12 Vendémiaire Year III, Lambert, a *représentant en mission*, complained to the Committee of Public Safety about the indiscriminate usage of such words as 'people' and 'sovereign': 'Real sovereignty belongs to the people, collectively, and, therefore, the "sovereign" is a single and indivisible unit. It should be regarded as a purely metaphysical term, that is to say, the General Will.' For the sans-culottes, sovereignty was expressed in flesh and blood; the people themselves exercising their rights in the assemblies of the Sections. There can be no doubt that this interpretation persisted. On 1 Prairial, Jean Thévenin, a haberdashery merchant from the Section de l'Arsenal, declared that the Convention no longer had the right to legislate, and 'that no laws would be passed today, other than those proposed by the people themselves'. Having invaded the Convention, the sans-culottes sat down on the benches reserved for the deputies, one of them shouting: 'Clear the assembly hall! We are going to constitute ourselves as the Convention.'[8] Their elected representatives had failed to carry out their duties and the people had recovered the exercise of their sovereignty.

When the National Convention was about to complete its work,

[8] *Moniteur*, xxiv, 505.

those citizens who had been given the privilege of voting by the Constitution of the Year II borrowed similar arguments from the sans-culottes when they protested against the decree by which two-thirds of the Conventionnels were made eligible for re-election. 'When the sovereign people is assembled', the Section de la Fidelité announced on 20 Fructidor Year III, 'it cannot, and must not, recognize any higher authority. At such a time, the people alone can make laws, and are not called upon to recognize laws made by anyone else.'[9] This was a rather strange assertion for citizens whose very qualifications as voters were a denial of the principle of popular sovereignty.

Since popular sovereignty was inalienable and could not be delegated to any other authority, the sans-culottes held that the people had the right to criticize, control, and in the last resort, to change their elected representatives. This belief constituted one of the motivating factors of the popular movement.

Here again, the origin of these ideas can be traced back to Rousseau and the *Contrat-Social*. Rousseau had strongly criticized the contemporary system of electoral representation in England: 'The English deceive themselves if they think that they are free,' he wrote, 'the only freedom they exercise is during the actual election of deputies to parliament. As soon as they have elected their representatives they lose this freedom entirely and become nothing more than slaves. . . . As a result the deputies of the people are not, indeed, cannot be their representatives: they are simply their "mandatories".' According to a citizen from the Section des Tuileries on 22 September 1792, deputies to the Convention 'should not be called representatives, but mandatories of the people'. Leclerc defined the rather confused ideas which the sans-culottes held on this question, when, paraphrasing Rousseau, he wrote in *l'Ami du peuple* on 21 August 1793: 'Above all, remember that when people are "represented" they are not free, so do not use this term loosely . . . there is no way of "representing" the General Will . . . your magistrates, whatever their function, are only your mandatories.' Many of the sans-culottes in the Year II signed letters which they had written to their deputies, 'your equal in rights'.

In order to reconcile the system of elective representation with

[9] *A.D.S.*, 4 AZ 698.

the need for a true democracy the sans-culottes had asked for the right to approve legislation: the control which they sought to exercise over their elected representatives was intended to serve the same purpose. These demands were forcibly expressed at the time of the elections to the Convention. From the standpoint of popular sovereignty, the system of indirect election which was adopted only emphasized the drawbacks of the representative system and a number of Sections set out to remedy this defect by criticizing the choice of deputies made by the electoral assembly of the department of Paris, and by exercising their right of control and dismissal.

Since the Legislative Assembly had abolished the distinction between 'active' and 'passive' citizens, but retained the system of indirect election, the more radical Sections demanded direct universal suffrage. In a pamphlet entitled *Ways of Establishing Liberty on Permanent Foundations . . . presented to the Section de Marseille*, Lacroix denounced indirect election as 'immoral, tending towards the destruction of the people's sovereignty, and favouring the growth of intrigue and factions'. On 21 August 1792, the Section des Quinze-Vingts adhered to a draft petition drawn up by the Section de Montreuil, 'to ask that there should be no electoral bodies, but that all kinds of elections should be conducted in the primary assemblies'. On 27 August, the Section de la Place-Vendôme—which was under the influence of Robespierre—declared itself in favour of indirect election, although it went on to state, that 'in principle, every mandatory of the people must be named directly by the people—in other words, by the primary assemblies'. To overcome the drawbacks which arose as a result of indirect election, the electors would name their deputies aloud in the presence of the people. The same day the primary assembly of the Section de Bondy affirmed 'that the sovereign people must not entrust anyone with the exercise of rights which cannot be delegated without ensuing harm, and that true representation is only reached when it is derived directly from the represented'. The General Council of the Commune indicated its approval of these views by the decree of 27 August announcing that, in future, electors would be asked to vote aloud in the presence of the people, and that the names of those deputies chosen by the electoral assembly would be submitted for the approval of the various Sections.

On 12 September, the electoral assembly, conscious of the strength of popular feeling on this subject, decided to present the Sections with the list of deputies elected to the Convention, 'with a view to securing the approval of the people by the "purifying vote" (*scrutin épuratoire*), and also in the hope that it will revive the spirit of sovereignty in every member of the body politic'.[1] On the following day, the Section de la Fontaine-de-Grenelle again insisted that the most careful precautions should be taken, 'to ensure that the sovereignty of the people is safeguarded against those who are driven by ambition to attack it'. Finally, on 15 September, the Section de Marseille decided to proceed with the 'revision' of deputies nominated by the electoral assembly: they asked the assembly not to invest deputies with any of their powers before their names had been approved by the Sections.

Despite the conviction of the people concerning the importance of their sovereignty, it is difficult to ignore the fact that even the most solemnly worded principles tended to be revised in the light of prevailing political circumstances. When, before actual nominations had been made, the Sections demanded the recognition of their right to censure the election of deputies, they were simply providing themselves with a safeguard in advance in case the electoral assembly should make—what was in their opinion—an unsatisfactory choice: the people would then be in a position to rectify the decision of the electors. The general assembly of the Section des Quatre-Nations was clearly thinking along these lines when, on 9 September 1792, after reminding its members that no deputies should be chosen from the ranks of 'the feuillants, signatories of anti-civic petitions, chaplains, or any other intriguing faction', it decreed that, 'if by some error one of the above mentioned individuals was voted as a representative of the people', it would reserve the right to reject his nomination and procede with a new election. The idea of holding a vote of censure over the choice of deputies was not determined, therefore, by the principle of popular sovereignty alone, but also as a matter of political expediency. When it appeared that the deputies named by the electoral assembly were being chosen mainly from the supporters of the Mountain, the more politically conscious Sections adjusted their principle accordingly, since, in this case, there was a risk that they would be defeating their own ends if they allowed members

[1] *A.N.*, F⁷ 4718.

to censure the subsequent choice of deputies. The General
Council of the Commune had demanded on 27 August that the
Sections should be allowed to approve the nominations made by
the electoral body, but towards the middle of September it did not
hesitate to publish an address 'on the drawbacks involved in
submitting deputies chosen for the Convention to the test of a
scrutin épuratoire'.

In fact, certain leading political figures, whose patriotism was
undisputed, were already being subjected to criticism from
popular agitators or from some of the Sections. On 19 September,
the Section des Marchés only accepted Marat's nomination to the
Convention after a long discussion, denouncing in the course of
the meeting, the 'anarchical principles' contained in *l'Ami du
peuple*. Méhée *fils* complained that some people were trying to
deprive ordinary citizens of the right to accept or reject deputies
chosen by the electors, which was clearly intended as an attack on
Robespierre. Realizing that there might, indeed, be some danger
of the people losing this right altogether, some of the Sections,
although they renounced it on certain favourable occasions, were
very careful to point out that this was only a temporary measure,
and that they still upheld the general principle that the people
should approve the names of deputies chosen by the electors. The
general assembly of the Section de la Réunion stated on 18
September 1792 that it was renouncing, 'on this occasion only',
the exercise of its vote of censure on nominations made by the
electoral assembly; and, on the same day, in order to reconcile
'the rights of the people with the problems of safeguarding the
nation', the Section Poissonnière decided to postpone discussion
on the choice of deputies 'until the return of our brothers who
have left to fight on the frontiers'.

The purging of the electoral list of deputies, which counter-
balanced the evils of indirect elections, was not in itself enough to
satisfy the principle of popular sovereignty as far as the sans-
culottes were concerned: elected representatives still had to be
faithful to the mandate which they had received from the people.
Without actually returning to the theory of the *mandat impératif*
which had been much in evidence at the time of the elections
to the States General and in the drawing up of the *cahiers
de doléances*, the Parisian Sections clearly stated the principle
that the sovereign people had the right to withdraw their

mandate should any representative fail in his duty towards the people. By adopting this principle, the sans-culottes hoped to decrease the number of defects which they detected in the representative system. On 25 August 1792, the general assembly of the Section du Marché-des-Innocents suggested that the National Convention should adopt as its guiding principle the idea that 'deputies may be recalled at the will of their departments', and that 'public officials may be recalled from office by those citizens who had voted for them; and that these officials must carry out their resolutions'.[2] On the same day, the general assembly of the Section de Bonne-Nouvelle decided that in case the right of the Sections to withdraw their support from their elected representatives whenever it pleased them might possibly have been overlooked, the Sections of Paris should 'remind their delegates of the true nature of their mission, and of the imprescriptible right which they possess to deprive them of their authority'. On 9 September, an elector for the Section des Halles proposed in the electoral assembly of the department of Paris that it 'should accept the principle that the imprescriptible sovereignty of the people includes the inalienable right and authority to recall their representatives whenever the people are convinced that such an action is in their own interests'. The electoral assembly adopted this resolution, although, three days earlier, it had only referred a similar resolution dealing with the removal of deputies 'in the event of their negligence or prevarication' to the primary assemblies. On 18 September, the general assembly of the Section des Droits-de-l'Homme announced that it would reserve the right to recall deputies 'if, during their term of office, their patriotism was called in question'.[3]

The right to recall and control the activity of deputies was not in any way regarded as an abstract consideration by the Parisian Sections. During the tense months of the summer of 1792, it met the requirement, in much the same way as the purging of the electoral lists, for a definite tactical programme of action; the aim being to ensure the success of the more radical revolutionary party. The principle of the people's control over their elected representatives was raised each time revolutionary policy was threatened. A pamphlet, which appeared in the summer of 1792, stated that deputies were only mandatories, responsible for carrying

    [2] *B.N.*, Lb⁴⁰ 3166.   [3] *B.V.C.*, MS. 120.

out orders given to them by ordinary citizens; in view of this it was their duty to observe these orders to the letter, never to pursue an independent policy, and to report to their constituents on everything they had said, written or performed during the exercise of their powers. During the struggle between the Girondins and the Montagnards in the autumn of 1792, the more progressive Sections claimed the right to censure representatives who displeased them, and make all deputies responsible for their actions; whilst the moderate Sections protested that such claims were without foundation.

In March 1793, as the crisis became more acute, extreme patriots demanded that the right of the people to recall their representatives should be implemented in order to crush 'the wicked faction'. On 10 March—a date which marks the first attempt to overthrow the Girondins—the Cordelier club invited the department of Paris—'an integral part of the sovereign power'—to assume the powers of sovereignty. The Cordeliers wanted the electoral assembly of Paris to be convoked so that it could replace 'those deputies who have betrayed the cause of the people'.[4] On the same day, the Section des Quatre-Nations asked for a meeting of all the Sections—'the supreme, and only possible measure to be taken in the present circumstances'—to authorize the electoral assembly of the department of Paris 'to remove unfaithful and unworthy mandatories as legislators of the people's interests', since they had betrayed their mandate by voting 'in favour of a referendum for the tyrant (Louis XVI), and not for the death penalty outright'.

The Girondins had refused to accept the theory that the people had the right to recall their representatives from the Convention, and defended themselves by invoking the principle of the 'inviolability of deputies'. On 10 April, the Section des Tuileries announced that since such an idea 'had originally been conceived under a monarchy', it could not be adopted by a republican government—'mandatories must be accountable for their actions to a free people'. The Section demanded that the principle be abolished 'since it is nothing but an odious privilege, a cloak of treachery worn by a corrupt mandatory so that he can betray the interests of the people with impunity'. On 12 May, the Section du

[4] *Moniteur*, xv, 704; quoted by Vergniaud in his speech to the Convention, 13 March 1793.

Finistère, sympathizing with these views, witnessed 'its dissatisfaction . . . concerning the misfortunes which afflict us as a
result of the negligence, ineptitude, or bad faith of the Convention', and summoned its representatives to 'give a unequivocal
answer—yes or no—whether they believe that they can save the
nation or not'.[5]

The theoretical justification for the *journées* of 31 May and 2
June 1793 is to be found in this conviction on the part of the people
concerning the responsibility and revocability of elected representatives. Since the Convention had refused to obey the orders of
the sovereign people over deputies who had betrayed their
mandate, the people had recovered the direct exercise of their
sovereign rights in order to force the removal of the Girondins.
On 31 May, Luillier, *procureur-général* of the department, called
upon the Convention, in the name of the authorities constituted
by the Revolution, to yield to the wishes of the nation: the deputation responsible for delivering this message had come to the
Convention accompanied by a crowd of fellow-citizens in order
to mingle 'fraternally with the members on the Left'. On 2 June,
the spokesman for the deputation of revolutionary authorities
stated that the citizens of Paris 'demand from their mandatories,
the rights which they have shamefully betrayed'.[6] Insurrection was
the final conclusion to be drawn from the principle of popular
sovereignty.

After the fall of the Girondins, the sans-culottes waited to see
if the Montagnards, who had helped to formulate and support
popular ideas on sovereignty since August 1792, were going to give
these ideas legal sanction. On 25 May, the Section de l'Unité,
'seeing that the responsibility of deputies is one of the essential
features of a republic', had asked 'that a "Tribunal of Ephors",
composed of members of the eighty-six departments, should,
sometime during the re-election of deputies, give an account of
those deputies who had sat during the preceding session, and that
those who had not deserved their place should be . . . excluded
permanently from any office in the Republic'. A deputation from
the Sections of Arras emphasized the urgency of the problem when
they told the Convention on 18 June that five deputies from the
department of the Pas-de-Calais had lost their confidence—the

[5] *A.N.*, C 255, d. 480, p. 14; *A.P.P.*, AA/266, p. 44.
[6] *Moniteur*, xvi, 537 and 548.

Assembly took no action. Six days later Hérault de Séchelle returned to this question when, during a debate on the framing of the Constitution, he presented a work entitled: *On the Criticism of Deputies by the People, and its Guarantee against Oppression by the Legislative Body*. It roused considerable opposition, and Couthon rejected it on behalf of the Committee of Public Safety.[7] Once again, political expediency had triumphed over the sanctity of principles.

The strengthening of the Committee of Public Safety, followed by the gradual establishment of the Revolutionary Government, did not, however, completely silence the Sections, supported by the popular press. In *l'Ami du peuple*, Leclerc reminded the deputies on 21 August 1793, that they were under the 'watchful eye' of the people and that 'its arm will be a rewarding, or an avenging arm, according to the people's verdict on your conduct, determined only by your actions'. On 4 August, the Section des Amis-de-la-Patrie had asked the General Council of the Commune for deputies to be judged after each session, suggesting 'that we reward them according to their actions'. On 29 September, the Section de la Halle-au-Blé solemnly announced that 'the duty of investigating the conduct of members of legally constituted authorities elected by the sovereign people, belonged to the sovereign people alone'. In the beginning of the Year II, *l'Observatoire* again pointed out 'that the sovereignty of the people obviously includes the right of recalling representatives who had proved unfaithful, as well as every other public official unworthy of their confidence'.

However, in one way, the control exercised by the people strengthened the authority of representatives who had gained their confidence. Some of the Montagnards, who thought it expedient to justify their actions to the Sections during the crisis of the summer of 1793, were obviously aware of this. On 4 September, Collot d'Herbois, a member of the Section Lepeletier, *en mission* to the departments of the Oise and Aisne, sent a statement of his conduct, as well as an account of the decrees he had issued from Senlis, which was thrown open for debate and approved by the general assembly. This kind of correspondence allowed the people to exercise a measure of control over their representatives, but it also gave the latter the opportunity of influencing and directing opinion in the Sections.

[7] *Moniteur*, xvi, 739.

Once the Revolutionary Government had been definitely established by the decree of 14 Frimaire, and the authority of the Committee of Public Safety no longer challenged, debate on the principles of popular sovereignty died away. The Committee was determined to construct a centralized and efficient system of government, and, for this reason, was not prepared to tolerate any reference to the people's right to control and recall their elected representatives. Principles were subordinated to the urgent problems facing the government during a period of national emergency.

The sans-culottes sought to extend their revolutionary vigilance to include control of the executive and its agents. As long as the conflict between the Girondins and the Montagnards lasted and danger from the moderates still threatened, the sans-culottes made determined efforts to secure the recognition of this right. Once again, it was the consolidation of the Revolutionary Government which upset their plans.

On 14 December 1792, the Section de Bon-Conseil, complaining that there was far too much inefficiency in the system of equipping volunteers, stated that it was necessary 'to maintain a ceaseless vigilance over the activity of the executive power concerning every aspect of its administration'. It invited the other Sections, 'in order to further the interests of public safety and liberty', to form a committee charged with the supervision of government ministers.[8] The Section des Quatre-Nations adhered to this decree on 17 December, but the Section des Gardes-Françaises, where the moderates were in a majority, denounced on 11 January 'every kind of organization which tended to weaken the individual responsibility of ministers'.

The sans-culottes sought to extend their supervision over government ministers as far as the military sphere, even to the actual conduct of military operations. The Section de Bon-Conseil, where the sans-culottes appear to have been particularly sensitive to any attack on the rights of the people, summoned Santerre, Commander of the Parisian National Guard, to appear before the general assembly in order to settle a difference of opinion which had arisen over the question of service in the Guard. He obeyed on 10 February, explaining 'that it was the fear that the people

[8] *A.D.S.*, D 916.

might think he was trying to curry personal favour which prevented him from coming to the Section as often as he would
have liked'.

In March 1793, announcing that 'treason can only be prevented
by means of a strict, enlightened, and constant vigilance', the
Section des Lombards proposed that a permanent commission
should be created which would send representatives to the Vendée
to report on 'the conduct of generals, the position of the armies,
and the morale of the soldiers': guided by these reports, the
commission would then decide upon the 'denunciations, advice
and solution to problems' which the commission felt competent
to deal with. This proposition does not appear to have attracted
widespread support; but on 17 June 1793, the Section des Gardes-
Françaises sent two of its own *commissaires* to Tours, where
they reported on the situation of the army, its successes and its
failures. They held consultations with the captains of companies
belonging to the Section, and kept an eye on the conduct of both
officers and soldiers. They had been charged by the Section 'to use
every possible means of fraternal persuasion to encourage those
officers and soldiers who have swerved from the path of duty'.
This mission was actually sanctioned by the authorities. On 25
June, the powers of the two *commissaires* were endorsed at
Tours by the government's *représentants en mission* to the armies
of the Côtes-de-la-Rochelle. On 4 September, at the army headquarters in Saumur, the commanding officer issued a 'permit to
go anywhere he wishes' to François Lemaître, *commissaire* of
the Section des Gardes-Françaises in Paris, deputy to the army
of the Vendée. On 21 September, General Bournet again endorsed
Lemaître's powers at Saumur.[9]

After 2 June, the exercise of power by the Sections strengthened
the conviction of the sans-culotterie that public officials were
dependent for their authority upon the people, and upon the
people alone. A denunciation made in the Year III reported that
'many citizens thought, and, perhaps, still think, that it is quite
natural for them to appoint and dismiss public officials'. The
Section des Amis-de-la-Patrie had elected a citizen named Bailly
as *commissaire aux accaparements*, but wished to remove him from
office owing to his indecision. The General Council of the Commune on 23 August 1793 discussed the problem of whether or

⁹ *A.N.*, F⁷ 4774¹⁶.

not a *commissaire* could be dismissed by the Section which had appointed him. It was eventually decided that the Section could not: 'If it allowed the Sections to act in this way, the stability of the Republic would clearly be endangered.' The Section des Amis-de-la-Patrie were not deterred by this decision, and on 1 September the affair was brought before the Convention. The Convention did not endorse the decision of the Commune and decreed that the choice of *commissaires*, including the right to dismiss them, lay in the hands of the Sections alone.

It was in the autumn of 1793, when the threat from the moderates had been eliminated and an attempt was being made to consolidate the Revolutionary Government, that the right to censure the conduct of public officials was advanced with even greater determination. As early as 28 August, the Section des Arcis had asked for the creation of a commission—to be supervised directly by the Sections—authorized to examine the conduct of all State employees. In the course of the great purge which gained momentum after the popular *journées* of 4 and 5 September, some administrative authorities had incurred the anger of the more politically active Sections by announcing their intention to conduct their own purges. On 29 September, the Section de la Halle-au-Blé declared that the purge carried out by the department of Paris was 'void and illusory': 'only the sovereign power can judge the conduct of members of the constituted authorities elected by its authority'. At approximately the same time, the Section de l'Observatoire stated that the sovereignty of the people clearly included the right to recall, not only unfaithful representatives, but 'every public official who has proved himself unworthy of the people's confidence', and that 'this principle was being tacitly violated because it was legally impossible to observe it'. The Section asked the Convention for 'the power to recall every public official who failed to carry out his duty'.[1]

Once the danger from the moderates had been swept aside, the right of censuring the activities of public officials and the administrative authorities passed out of the hands of the general assemblies and popular societies: the decree of 14 Frimaire entrusted this responsibility to the Committee of Public Safety and to the *représentants en mission* in the departments. The Sections lost all right of control and dismissal: stability and centralization were

[1] *A.D.S.*, D 933.

now of greater importance than the popular exercise of democratic principles. This loss contributed towards the dissatisfaction shown by the sans-culottes for the Revolutionary Government, increasingly evident after Germinal. They had clearly attached great importance to this question. As one citizen from the Section du Contrat-Social exclaimed on 25 Pluviôse: 'Where would we be if we were not allowed to examine most carefully the conduct of those who govern us.'

It is perhaps true to say that the sans-culottes were more interested in local affairs than in influencing policy on a national level, which explains the importance they attached to the fundamental organizations of political life—the communal assemblies, and, particularly, the general assemblies and popular societies in the Sections. They rejected the indirect exercise of their sovereignty by a National Assembly in favour of the concrete reality of the people gathered together in the general assemblies of the Sections. Here, the sans-culottes were fully conscious of their sovereignty and its application. Of all the attributes of their sovereignty, that which concerned the permanence and autonomy of the Sections was thought to be of the greatest importance.

Sans-culotte demands in the Year II were very similar to those made by 'active' citizens in 1790; only their interpretation differed. On 18 March 1790, the district of la Chaussée-d'Antin had recalled 'that patriotism and the permanence of the districts have proved to be the very foundations of liberty in France', and in view of this, the Sections should retain 'their imprescriptible right of meeting freely, whether to settle their own particular problems, or to resist measures taken by the municipality, or for any other just and reasonable cause'. Out of sixty districts, fifty-three adopted a resolution demanding that their sittings should be considered permanent 'through assemblies authorized to meet regularly every month', and on 23 March, the Mayor of Paris presented these views to the Constituent Assembly. The districts made a new move on 10 April 1790, but in the meantime the campaign was being continued through the publication of pamphlets. One anonymous pamphleteer interpreted the word 'permanence' to mean the right of the Sections to meet every month as well as 'on those occasions when important problems require emergency meetings of the general assemblies'. These assemblies would also form permanent committees 'to carry out the orders of the municipality and the police'. Another pamphlet answered the criticism that the permanence of the Sections would transform Paris into so many 'sovereign republics', and that to assign all the acts of the administrative power to the Sections would make the Commune itself unnecessary, by pointing out the advantages of allowing the Sections to conduct vital investigations into every department of public life, and how this would help to shape the civic virtues of citizens.

The demands presented by the sans-culottes for the permanence and autonomy of the Sections were too close to the exercise of direct government for them to find any sympathy amongst the members of an assembly hostile to the democratic movement and jealous of their own prerogatives. After the passing of the municipal law of 21 May–27 June 1790, the Sections—which now replaced the districts—were authorized to meet for almost exclusively electoral purpose; citizens only assembled in order to vote, and once they had performed this civic duty, the intention was that they should immediately disperse. This clearly dealt a firm blow at the notion of the permanence of the Sections. The districts protested vainly against these provisions in the law and demanded that they should be allowed to retain the privileges which they had, in fact, conferred upon themselves. The supporters of the law, particularly Demeunier, who had introduced it to the Assembly, defended it on 3 May by emphasizing that no authority which existed in opposition to the Assembly could be tolerated. Robespierre, recalling the services rendered by the districts at the beginning of the Revolutions, asked that the Sections be given the right of discussing and deliberating matters freely. Mirabeau on the other hand was afraid that if the Assembly allowed these sovereign Sections to exist the result would be 'a chain of action and reaction which might eventually destroy the Constitution'. However, the law did not deprive the Sections of all possibility of meeting other than for electoral purposes. The president of the Section could convoke the general assembly at the request of fifty active citizens. The Sections also enjoyed a certain administrative autonomy—*commissaires* were empowered to see that laws were carried out; they corresponded with the municipal authorities and held certain minor police powers alongside the *commissaire de police* elected by the general assembly. The law did not, however, closely define the competence of the general assembly to deal with such questions as the duration and frequency of its meetings.

But the political apprenticeship which the districts had served since the beginning of the Revolution had not been wasted. Reports which appeared in the *Moniteur* on 11 January and 18 February bear witness to the continued political preoccupations of the Sections, preoccupations which they inherited from the districts: 'The anarchy produced by the districts', wrote the municipal administrator Peuchet, 'will soon be repeated by the activity of the Sections, if, going beyond the prescribed limits of their authority, they continue to pass resolutions when the law which created them stated that they should concern themselves solely with electoral procedure.'[2] In order to keep the Sections within the limits prescribed by the municipal law of 21 May 1790, the Constituent Assembly decided to redefine their position by an additional law on 18 May 1791. Dealing with the right of the Sections to petition the Assembly, and offering a more precise interpretation of the provision whereby citizens were permitted to call for a meeting of the general assembly, this decree was aimed primarily at the Sections of Paris—their assemblies could only be convoked to deal with matters of municipal administration. However, this new restriction was to prove as futile as preceding ones. On 21 January 1791, the General Council of the Commune was forced to annul a decree issued by the Section des Théâtre-Français 'ordering the Saint-André-des-Arts battalion to obey no authority other than of the permanent committee of the Section, and to arrest any aide-de-camp who appeared within the Section'. In order to justify this somewhat extreme interpretation of the autonomy of the Sections it was announced that such an order was necessary in the interests of public safety—Louis XVI had just fled from Paris.

The aggravation of the political crisis in the spring of 1792 gave a renewed impetus to patriot demands for the permanence of the Sections. According to a petition presented by the *société fraternelle*, this measure alone would provide adequate surveillance over 'the agents of the Austrian cabinet and the Coblentz committee'. On 28 May, the Théâtre-Français, Croix-Rouge and Fontaine-de-Grenelle Sections asked the Legislative Assembly to

[2] *Moniteur*, vii, 85 and 401.

recognize them as being 'in a state of surveillance necessitated by prevailing circumstances'. On 28 June, the Section de Montreuil offered its support with an address 'for the permanence of the forty-eight Sections of Paris, having the authority to pass resolutions on all matters concerning the safety of the people'. On 2 July, a deputation of Parisian citizens again requested the permanence of the Sections.[3]

The decision to declare *la patrie en danger* on 11 July meant that the legally constituted authorities would now sit permanently, but the Sections were not included in this category since they had no clearly defined authority and no special functions. However, in the course of July, the permanence of the Sections became an established fact—they met every day, the assembly halls being open to anyone who wished to attend. On 3 July, the Section des Postes had decreed that its meetings would be made public, and on 24 July, it stated in a petition to the Legislative Assembly that one way to avert the danger which threatened the nation was to authorize the permanence of the Sections. On the same day, it decided to meet three times a week 'until the National Assembly orders otherwise'. On 25 July, the Legislative Assembly finally capitulated and decreed that the Sections should meet *en permanence*.

From this time on, the permanence of the Sections became one of the foundations of the popular political system and one of the main features of the direct government which the militants attempted to install without any precise programme. In times of crisis, it became an effective weapon of action, and was jealously guarded against attack. At the beginning of September 1792, an elector from the Section des Thermes-de-Julien in an appeal to the electoral body, described it as one of the 'four pillars of liberty'. On 16 November 1792, the general assembly of the Section de la Butte-des-Moulins decided to meet only three times a week, but was careful to add that the Section still considered itself to be *en permanence*.

The permanence of the Sections became a decisive weapon in the armoury of the sans-culottes during the struggle between the Girondins and the Montagnards. From the beginning of 1793, the Girondins did everything possible to secure its suppression: Salles was of the opinion that the permanence of the Sections was a

[3] *Moniteur*, xiii, 31.

'potentially revolutionary weapon' and as such could not continue indefinitely without endangering public safety—Richaud supported this view on 6 January. Marat, on the other hand, believed quite the opposite, and asked that the Sections should continue to be *en permanence* until the danger which threatened the nation had disappeared—Robespierre was of the same opinion. In May, when the conflict had reached an acute stage, the debate was renewed. On 20 May, a citizen proposed in the general assembly of the Section Poissonnière that 'considering the small number of people who attend', the meetings should no longer be permanent. The assembly hastily rejected the proposal which was thought to be far too dangerous, convinced that 'it would take endless days of debate to end the permanence of the assembly'. On 24 May, the *Commission des Douze* decided that, in future, general assemblies in the Sections would terminate their meetings at ten o'clock, an indirect way of destroying the advantages of permanence as exercized by the sans-culottes. The more politically active Sections completely ignored this decree: On 2 May, the Section des Marchés announced that it had no intention of submitting to this ruling, whilst the Section de Bonne-Nouvelle decided, after a proposal by Hébert, to meet after ten o'clock as a club 'in order to discuss the problems which affected it'.[4]

The permanence of the Section involved one serious drawback: although the sans-culottes flocked to the general assemblies in times of crisis, they were inclined to desert them once the immediate danger had passed. Their adversaries had only to be more assiduous in their attendance to secure a moderate majority. One can actually see this happening in many of the Parisian Sections after 2 June. The moderates who had been defeated in the wider political struggle attempted to take their revenge by invading the general assemblies. The inevitable result was a concealed, but very real, civil war on a sectionary level. In some of the Sections, the sans-culottes did not definitely seize power until the summer or the beginning of the autumn of 1793. In the big cities such as Lyons or Marseilles, the permanence of the Sections became a counter-revolutionary weapon. The danger was referred to by Marat, always conscious of the realities of the political struggle. In a letter written to the Convention on 21 June, he asked that t he permanence of the Sections should be suppressed, since he

[4] *B.V.C.*, MS. 120.

was convinced that it was largely responsible for the disasters which had overtaken the great cities: 'the rich, intriguers and trouble-makers are flocking to the Sections, forming a majority, and passing the most dangerous laws; whilst day-labourers, operatives, craftsmen, small shopkeepers, farm-labourers, in fact, all those unfortunate citizens who are forced to work in order to live, cannot find the time to attend the assemblies in order to check this threat to freedom'.[5]

This argument was used by Danton to influence the debate and subsequent vote in the Assembly on 9 September 1793 which reduced the meetings of the general assemblies to two a week. Despite the factors favouring this decision, the end of permanence in the Sections dealt a very hard blow to the popular political system. It marked another step in the evolution of the Revolutionary Government which aimed at controlling the popular movement and harnessing it to the newly-formed jacobin dictatorship.

If the concession of the forty *sous* indemnity sowed discord amongst the sans-culottes and divided the Sections, the suppression of the permanence of the Sections aroused unanimous opposition. The sans-culottes managed to circumvent the provisions of the decree of 9 September by organizing *sociétés sectionnaires*, but, throughout the Year II, they pressed continually for more frequent meetings of the general assemblies. The communal authorities were not prepared to make the least concession, the Robespierrist Commune surpassing the work of its predecessor in enforcing the strictest application of the law.

The reason why the sans-culottes were so passionately concerned with the question of permanence was that they regarded the Sections not only as regulating units in the political machine, representing and interpreting the will of the people, but also as autonomous self-administrative units. The Section was sovereign; its internal affairs were the concern of the general assemblies alone.

In 1790, whilst the new law on municipal organization was being prepared, a certain Boileau de Beaulieu asked that each Section or district should be organized as a municipality, having control of police affairs, administration and the assessment and collection of taxes. He believed that this was a particularly

[5] *Moniteur*, xvi, 706.

practical demand in view of the fact that the Commune could not make 'any ruling, whether it deals with administrative or police affairs, until it had been raised, discussed, and agreed upon in each Section or district; and that no law dealing with regulations or administration could be promulgated or put into effect until the various Sections or districts had given a majority vote in favour of such a law'.

Again, we can trace the thread of continuity which links the qualified voter of 1790 to the popular militants of the Year II. The anxiety for complete autonomy prompted the Section des Sans-Culottes on 3 May 1793 to demand that the register of births, marriages, and deaths, should be transferred to the Sections. It was the same reason which led the Section de la Cité to protest on 4 May against the right of Santerre, Commander-in-Chief of the Parisan National Guard, to nominate aides-de-camp, adjutants, generals, and other subordinate officers for the new battalion which was being raised in the Section: this protest was justified by the excuse that 'volunteers are not to be exposed to the danger of being sacrificed to the defects of their commanding officers'. Santerre's action was interpreted as an attack upon the liberty of the Sections. The Section de la Cité did not want to see any officers in command of its company other than those nominated by the general assembly. On 26 June 1793, the Section de l'Unité announced that it was not in favour of Raffet's election to command the Parisian National Guard, and added that if he was elected, it would not obey his orders.

The most striking demands for the complete autonomy of the Sections dealt with the administration of police affairs. As early as 4 February 1791, the Section du Théâtre-Français stated that the method of administration adopted by the police department was unconstitutional and undermined liberty. In the opinion of the Sections, police duties should have been divided amongst the forty-eight Sections. The Section de Mirabeau asserted on 12 September 1792 'that it is the natural right . . . of every detained person to be placed provisionally under the protection of the Section in which he lives'. The Section was 'the chief tribunal based on natural rights': it was the only authority, within the geographic limits of the Section, which should have the power to issue search warrants and warrants of arrest. The Sections were so sensitive of their authority in this field that on 8 September 1792, the Section des Quinze-Vingts issued a decree stating 'that it was not within the power of the Commune to send its *commissaires* into any Section whatsoever without first having warned the Section in writing, and unless they are instructed to produce their identification papers upon demand'.[6] On 24 December, the Section du Louvre officially announced that only the Section had the right to exercise police powers within its territory. The Section du Contrat-Social stated on 11 May 1793 that a Section was not accountable to the police in its *arrondissement*, and, in order to apply this principle, *commissaires de police* chosen by the general assemblies, but placed under the control of the Commune, should take their orders from the committees in the Section. If this were not done the Section was afraid that 'it would mean a return to the terrible police régime which all citizens justifiably abhor'. At the height of the crisis on March 1793, Marat informed the Jacobins that 'within its limits, a Section is sovereign'. The incompatibility of these principles with those adopted by the Revolutionary Government, can readily be appreciated.

The importance which the sans-culottes attached to the permanence and autonomy of the Sections can be seen by their obstinate demands for more frequent meetings of the general assemblies, even after 9 Thermidor, and by their return to the practice of meeting *en permanence* during the insurrection of Prairial Year III.

Unfortunately for the sans-culottes, the Thermidoreans kept an even tighter grip on the general assemblies, finally suppressing them altogether. On 9 Thermidor, the Convention was forbidden from convoking the Sections without the authorization of the governmental Committees. On 4 Fructidor, it abolished the forty *sous* indemnity and reduced the meetings of the general assemblies to one in every *décade*. Thuriot, who had actually proposed the permanence of the Sections on 25 July 1792, now emphasized the 'inconvenience of holding too many meetings in the Sections'.[7]

The sans-culottes protested in vain. On 28 Fructidor, François Paris, a wool-scourer from the Section des Piques, was arrested for his remark 'that they have already reduced the number of meetings of the general assembly to one in every *décade*, and that within a couple of days they will do away with them altogether . . .

---

[6] *A.P.P.*, AA/266, p. 252.   [7] *Moniteur*, xxi, 556.

that the assemblies were the foundation of the Republic'. On 30 Fructidor, the Section des Gravilliers invited the Convention 'to take into consideration the need for the people to be instructed, to discuss matters which concern them, and to put their resolutions into effect; that three assemblies a month did not satisfy their patriotic zeal and their civic devotion; and to decree that the Sections of Paris can assemble as previously'. The Section de Montreuil adopted a similar resolution on the same day which was welcomed by the Montagne, Tuileries, and Popincourt Sections on 10 Vendémiaire. Three days earlier the *société populaire de la salle électorale* invited the Convention to give the people the full expression of their rights: 'Give Paris two assemblies a *décade* for each Section, which is hardly enough to settle current business.' On 10 Vendémiaire, the same request was made by the Lepeletier and Invalides Sections, followed on the twentieth by the Section de Montmartre.[8]

In the spring of the Year III, the general assemblies, which still met every ten days, became potentially dangerous since they provided the sans-culottes with the machinery for concerted action. On 10 Ventôse, the Section de la République, which was composed mainly 'of labourers, carters, and others', proposed to eliminate the sans-culottes by holding its meetings, not from six to ten o'clock in the evenings, but from eleven o'clock in the morning to three in the afternoon. Since the sans-culottes would generally be at work during these hours, the supporters of the motion felt that 'we would not in future have so much to fear from combined terrorist activity'. On 8 Germinal, one of the first measures adopted by the Convention to put an end to the disorders in the capital was to decree that the general assemblies in the Sections should meet from one o'clock to four o'clock in the afternoon: this again would practically have eliminated the sans-culottes. The Sections rebelled against this decision and declared themselves *en permanence*. On 13 Germinal, the citizens of the Section Popincourt assembled in the evening, fully armed, to declare their adherence to a resolution issued by the Section de la Cité 'establishing itself in permanent session'. The former Section invited 'their brothers from other Sections to do the same in order to discuss what action should be taken to save the nation, and to communicate amongst themselves the steps which they

[8] *A.N.*, F[7] 4648.

consider to be most effective in producing this result'. On 10 Floréal, the Section de Montreuil decided to meet *en permanence* in order to discuss the problem of food supplies. On 1 Prairial, one of the grievances presented to the Parisians who invaded the Convention dealt with the question of the permanence of the Sections. After a few decrees had been voted by the minority which had kept their seats in the Assembly, Romme pointed out 'that it was not enough to pass beneficial decrees; there must be some way of executing them'. Romme's solution was that the Sections should be convoked and that they should deliberate *en permanence.*[9]

It was the last time that the Sections had the opportunity of forcing its will upon the Assembly. On 4 Prairial, the Convention decreed that women should no longer be admitted to the general assemblies of the Sections. They had first been admitted in the summer of 1792, and had often participated in the discussion held in the assemblies during the summer of 1793. However, the assemblies were still allowed to meet once every ten days. On 24 Thermidor, after a petition had been presented to the Assembly by the Section de Bonne-Nouvelle, an anonymous deputy said that he was surprised to learn that the Parisian Sections were still meeting. The next day, Boissy d'Anglas remarked that it would be foolish to make innovations in the little time which remained before the Constitution received its final draft suggesting legislation to deal with this question. It was after the royalists had used the Sections to further their counter-revolutionary activity in Vendémiaire Year IV that Merlin de Douai proposed the immediate application of article 363 of this same Constitution which finally suppressed all meetings of the general assemblies in the Sections. This move anticipated the setting up of the constitutional government arranged for 5 Brumaire.

Thus, the general assemblies of the Sections disappeared. They had provided the framework for the political activity of the sans-culotterie, and, meeting *en permanence*, had symbolized the very essence of popular sovereignty.

Insurrection is the final resort of the sovereign people. The Constituent Assembly had not inscribed this right in the Declaration of August 1789, but the Convention—in order to justify

[9] *A.N.*, W 547 *acte d'accusation*; *Moniteur*, xxiv, 506.

10 August and 31 May as much as to arm the people against oppression—had asserted it in article 35 of the Declaration of June 1793.

Again, the sans-culottes did not interpret this as a theoretical and formal affirmation of their sovereignty. Convinced of their rights, and practising without a coherent policy the methods of direct government, they were naturally inclined to assume the exercise of sovereignty whenever they felt that the rights of the people had been betrayed by their mandatories. It is noticeable that popular statements on the right of insurrection tended to multiply during every period of crisis up to the Year III. In 1 Prairial Year III, the shoemaker Duval from the Section de l'Arsenal, after reading the petition presented to the Convention by the insurgents, summoned the president of the Assembly, Boissy d'Anglas, to recognize the fact that insurrection was the most sacred duty of all, and asked him to ensure that these words were included in the Declaration of Rights.[1]

The word insurrection, however, assumed a different shade of meaning according to prevailing circumstances. Insurrection, as the sans-culottes understood it, did not always mean armed action. On 6 October 1792, the general assembly of the Section des Gravilliers declared that the sovereignty of the people was being challenged by the claims of the Convention, and 'by the exercise of a ridiculous and unlimited power over the Sections of Paris'. 'Let us rise', the declaration concluded, 'for the last time and remain in arms until we have proved to our mandatories that, by that proud and fearless bearing which is the attribute of sovereignty alone, the men of '89, and those of 10 August and 3 September, can recall them to a sense of their duty and remind them of the rights of the people which they have had the insolence to ignore.' On 27 December 1792, the Section du Théâtre-Français declared itself to be in a state of insurrection until 'such time as France is purged of her tyrants'. By the term 'state of insurrection', the Section meant 'a continual state of positive defiance, of activity, surveillance and patriotic alertness which every good republican should adopt until liberty has been consolidated upon unshakeable foundations'. This interpretation was accepted by the Section de l'Unité when, in May 1793, it refused to submit its registers to the *Commission des Douze* and went on to

[1] *A.N.*, W 546.

discuss the day's business 'justified by our right to resist oppression'; it was also sanctioned by the *juge de paix* Hu, president of the Section du Panthéon-Français. On 25 Frimaire Year II, one citizen, referring to the law which had been passed on the fourteenth, and particularly to the article prohibiting all commissions and central reunions, refused to believe that such a law would be enforced; 'if it was, then the people should rise *en masse*, and he would have the courage to lead them to the Convention himself so that they could force it to rescind this law, since the Convention had clearly lost sight of its duty'. When the Cordeliers announced that they were in a state of insurrection on 14 Ventôse, they were thinking more along the lines of a mass demonstration than of armed action. Finally, when the *Commission militaire* in the Year III, referring to his plan for a 'pacific insurrection', described its surprise at the unusual juxtaposition of these two words, Brutus Magnier replied that a pacific insurrection meant 'the majestic action of a people who tell their mandatories—do that because we wish it!'[2] Insurrection to the sans-culottes, therefore, signified the resistance of the people who rise, refuse to obey unacceptable laws, recover possession of their sovereign rights, demand a reckoning from their mandatories, and, finally, dictate to the latter their wishes. At this stage, insurrection is a mass demonstration which reflects both the unanimity and the majesty of the popular movement.

But pacificism does not always produce the desired effect, with the result that, in the last resort, the implicit threat of force and of violence becomes necessary. On 1 May 1793, a deputation from the Sections of the *faubourg* Saint-Antoine, after suggesting a few measures of public safety to the Convention, issued what really amounts to an ultimatum: 'If you do not accept them, we—citizens who wish to save the nation—inform you that we are in a state of insurrection; ten thousand men are at the door of this hall.' Also in May, the Sections of the *faubourg* Saint-Marcel informed their representatives that the people were determined to defend their rights, 'that they can rise *en masse* in a moment; that they are watching your every move, and demand that you give an account of the honourable mission which has been entrusted to you'. Sometimes the threat is more precise. During the night of 9 Thermidor, a sans-culotte in the Section des Quinze-Vingts

[2] *A.N.*, W 546.

stated that when 'the agents (he does not use the word "representative" or even "*mandataire*"), acting on the authority of the people, do not perform their duty, the people have the right to drive them from office'.[3]

Armed insurrection proved to be the extreme manifestation of popular sovereignty. The first warning of armed insurrection came with the sounding of the alarm on the drum—the *générale*—and the ringing of the tocsin, which meant that the people had recovered the exercise of their rights and were determined to impose their will by the force of arms. Pitton, a steel polisher from the Section Poissonnière, stated that during the insurrection of 12 Germinal Year III 'that the sovereign people had the right to beat the *générale* and throw open their assemblies'. After 10 August, Cordas, an embroiderer from the Section des Lombards, who became a police official in the Year II, was alleged to have said 'that since the people had risen in rebellion, he could recognize no law other than that of the sovereign will'. During the night of 9 Thermidor, Lévrivain, a former member of the Committee of Public Safety of the department of Paris, chief clerk of the Revolutionary Tribunal, stated 'that it was no longer necessary to obey the orders issued by the Committees of the Convention, for when the tocsin rang, the Convention counted for nothing'. Through their emotional appeal, through the memory of the great *journées* of 14 July, 10 August and 31 May, when the people appeared in all the majesty of their sovereign power, insurrection for many of the sans-culottes assumed an air of exaltation: for them the atmosphere of these *journées* remained unforgettable. The raising of the barricades, the beating of the drum, the ringing of the tocsin and the warning shot from the cannon contributed to the tremendous feeling of excitement, ever-stimulating their imagination and straining their nerves. There was also the dim awareness amongst the more simple and humble citizens of an act which raised them above their station in life, which gave them the opportunity of making their own impression upon the destiny of a nation. During the night of 9 Thermidor, a man named Pellecat from the Section des Quinze-Vingts told a young National Guard: 'You have not had much experience of revolution, and cannot realize what it means in a commune when they beat the *générale* and ring the tocsin!'[4]

[3] *A.N.*, F[7] 4775[34].   [4] *A.N.*, F[7] 4775[34].

Having recovered the exercise of their sovereign right by means of insurrection, the people then assumed complete legislative, judicial, and executive powers. From the moment they announced that they were in a state of insurrection, the people recognized no other authority. The *commissaire* Marchand, a poor sans-culotte from the Section de l'Indivisibilité who was unable to read, said on 1 Prairial Year III that, 'Authority no longer exists—the people have risen in insurrection. There is no longer any need for orders to be given; the people alone will command.' The following day, Lallemand a gauze-maker from the Section Mont-Blanc, refused to obey the instructions of the authorities, 'because, from today, he no longer recognized the Convention—he was in insurrection'. Again on 2 Prairial, Louis Vian, a doorkeeper of the *tribunal du paix*, notified the *comité civil* in the Section du Finistère: 'That it had been deprived of all authority, for the sovereign people had reconquered their rights.' During the *journées* of September 1792, the people had exercised the right of justice as one of the essential attributes of their sovereignty. But once the people had clearly manifested their complete sovereign power, they were quite happy to lay down their arms, and delegate the exercise of their sovereignty to their mandatories, who were again invested with the confidence of the people. In its address of 31 May 1793, the Section des Sans-Culottes said, 'Although our Section has chosen the very moment when the people are rising in insurrection to address you once again, it is in the hope that, by placing our arms at your disposal, by conferring upon you the exercise of our sovereignty, you will use it to ensure the happiness of the people.'[5]

A document of the Year III gives us an idea of how the sans-culottes actually set the machinery of insurrection in motion. Towards five o'clock in the evening of 11 Floréal, a large crowd of men and women in the Section du Bonnet-Rouge after unsuccessfully besieging empty bakeries in their search for bread, decided to present themselves before the *comité civil*: they announced, 'in the name of the sovereign people and the law', that the *comité* was in a state of insurrection. A sans-culotte then told a citizen of the Section: 'Go and find your tambour so that we can beat the *générale* and declare the Section to be in insurrection.' Another stated that, 'When the people is in a state of insurrection, and when it finds that it has unfaithful mandatories, we must arrest

[5] *A.N.*, C 258, d. 528, p. 2.

them, judge and punish them on the spot.' The people, *en insurrection*, then nominated four *commissaires* to investigate the conduct of the officially constituted authorities in the Section. For many, this act by which the people placed their confidence in their new mandatories and delegated to them the exercise of their sovereign power was sufficient, and several of the sans-culottes immediately returned to their homes: for them the insurrection was over. Towards midnight an armed force accompanied by four officials had little difficulty in dispersing the remainder of the crowd and in liberating the imprisoned *comité civil*.[6]

We can see in the above instance both the strength and the weakness of popular ideas of sovereignty and insurrection conceived in the name of the rights of the sovereign people—no organized plan of action had yet been evolved. It was not enough to invest new mandatories with the confidence of the people; they still had to control the situation by armed force. The 10 August and 31 May prove what the sans-culottes could achieve with the sanction of force: the *journeés* of Prairial are a tragic commentary on their ineffectiveness without it.

Thus we are able to assess the political maturity of the sans-culotterie and throw some light on the way in which the bourgeoisie directed the course of the Revolution. The sans-culottes provided the striking force necessary for the attack: the bourgeoisie or, at least, that fraction of the bourgeoisie who realized that the success of the Revolution depended upon an alliance with the people, planned and organized the great revolutionary *journées*, particularly 10 August and 31 May, and then exploited the resulting situation for its own ends. The great popular *journées*, therefore, are, from this point of view, nothing more than bourgeois revolutionary *journées*.

Was there any other possible alternative? The insurrection organized by the sans-culotterie alone in Ventôse Year II, as well as the attempts in Germinal and Prairial Year III, were little more than tragic failures. It seemed as if the sans-culottes, when left to their own devices, and dependent upon their own strength, would always be powerless. But there was also the contradiction which existed between popular action and the objective necessity of the bourgeois revolution. On the political level, this contradiction

[6] *B.N.*, Lb[40] 1747.

emerged between the attitude of the sans-culottes, intent upon the full recognition of their rights, and the nature of bourgeois democracy, for which the rights of the sovereign people were only to be exercised during the nomination of representatives. Vergniaud, speaking on behalf of the Gironde on 13 March 1793, protested against the abuse of the word 'sovereignty' by *anarchistes*, 'they do not realize how close they come to overthrowing the Republic when they convince the Sections that sovereignty resides in their midst'.[7]

Popular ideas on sovereignty provided the montagnard bourgeoisie with the justification for the insurrections of 10 August and 31 May. But they were none the less incompatible with the consolidation of the Revolutionary Government and an effective policy of national defence; a contradiction which, in the objective conditions of the time, could only be resolved by disciplining the Parisian Sections. But this was the very act which broke the enthusiasm of the popular movement responsible for bringing the Revolutionary Government to power. The seriousness of the crisis can be measured by the fact that it was upon the popular movement alone that the Revolutionary Government had relied for its continued support.

[7] *Moniteur*, xv, 705.

IV

PRACTICAL APPLICATION OF
SANS-CULOTTE POLITICS

IT was not only the orientation of sans-culotte political thought which alarmed the bourgeoisie and aroused the opposition of the Revolutionary Government concerned, primarily, with efficacy and equilibrium, but the behaviour and political methods adopted by the sans-culotterie.

Two basic principles guided the political activity of the people, for whom violence was the last resort—'publicity', which protected them against the possibility of intrigue, becoming the corollary of revolutionary vigilance in the Year II; and 'unity', which, based upon unanimity of mind and purpose, led to the realization of 'concerted action', assuring the sans-culottes of their ultimate success. These two principles help to explain many of the actions which characterize the political behaviour of the people and distinguish it from that of the bourgeoisie. Forged and tested in the heat of the struggle, they contributed towards the progress of the Revolution and the consolidation of the Committees. But were they compatible with the problems confronting the latter and the underlying forces dictating the course of the former.

'There is nothing "personal" in the attitude of the patriot,' the Section de la Fontaine-de-Grenelle wrote to the *société populaire d'Auxerre* on 25 Ventôse Year II, 'his joy and his sadness mingle with the common sentiments of the people. He pours out his soul in the company of his brothers. This is the origin of the idea of conducting our affairs in public which is a distinguishing feature of the fraternal, or republican, form of government.'[1]

'Publicity' has its roots in the fraternal conception of social relationships accepted by the sans-culotterie. The consequences of this were of considerable political significance: the patriot has no reason to hide his opinions or his actions, particularly as his sole

[1] *B.N.*, Lb⁴⁰ 1831.

objective is the good of society. Political life must unfold in the open, under the watchful eye of the sovereign people. Administrative bodies like the general assemblies must throw their meetings open to the public, and electors must vote aloud in the presence of the people. According to the sans-culottes, citizens only acted in secret when their motives were suspect: denunciation, therefore, became a civic duty. 'Publicity' was clearly 'the people's safeguard', and this conviction, advanced during every period of crisis from 1792 to 1794, was to prove an effective revolutionary weapon in the hands of the sans-culottes.

On 22 February 1792, more than 200 Parisian citizens explained to the Legislative Assembly 'how important it is for administrative meetings to be made public so that the people can distinguish between those who seek only their happiness, and those who have wormed their way into the confidence of the people simply to further their own ambition or caprice'. Once war had been declared, 'publicity' becomes even more important as a means of defending the Revolution. On 1 July, in order to compel the administrative bodies 'to be more mature in their judgement, and swifter in settling their affairs', and so that the people could exercise their right 'of supervising the conduct of their administrators', the Legislative Assembly ordered that meetings of administrative bodies should be made public.[2] Under the pressure of popular opinion, this practice spread rapidly to every aspect of political life. In the Year II, it became an integral feature of revolutionary vigilance. On 13 March 1792, the general assembly of the Section des Postes passed quickly to discuss the business of the day after a citizen had asked that its meetings should be made public; the reason being that such a move would have led to the admittance of passive citizens. But on 3 July, the general assembly, recognizing 'how important it is for every citizen to be a witness of what is being debated in our midst', announced that in future its meetings would be thrown open to the public. On 20 July, the Section du Roule followed this example, and very soon it became the practice in every one of the Sections. The sans-culottes invaded the general assemblies, not content simply with the rôle of spectators. Galleries were built in the meeting halls where women, children, and strangers to the Section crowded together

[2] *Moniteur*, xiii, 19.

every evening to listen to the discussions. In future, the Section deliberated in the presence of the people.

But the publicity which was now given to the meetings in the Sections was not enough. The sans-culottes felt that the supervision of the people should be extended to cover the most important political operations—elections and voting procedure. In order to eliminate their enemies, the patriots first of all ensured that voting would be conducted aloud by applauding or cheering when the names of proposed candidates were announced—the vote *par acclamation.*

Voting aloud became the accustomed practice after 10 August. A week later, after two municipal officials had read the law dealing with the creation of the Extraordinary Criminal Tribunal to the general assembly of the Section du Théâtre-Français, it was decided, 'after taking into consideration the necessity and urgency of organizing this tribunal promptly', that the Section would nominate its own representative *par acclamation.* During the elections to the Convention, the system of voting aloud was adopted for all electoral purposes. This meant that electors had to think twice before casting their votes, and it did remedy, to a certain extent, the unfavourable aspects of indirect election which —according to the sans-culottes—undermined the principle of popular sovereignty and provided an opportunity for intrigue. Robespierre's influence is noticeable in the resolution adopted by the Section de la Place-Vendôme on 27 August 1792, which stated that, in order to overcome the disadvantages of indirect election, electors would be called upon to vote aloud, and in the presence of the people. To make this latter precaution effective, it was planned that all electoral procedure would take place in the assembly hall of the Jacobin club. The same day, the Section de Bondy decided that all elections would be made by citizens voting aloud, and that the electoral assembly should ask as many citizens as possible 'to witness the choice of each elector'. In the opinion of the Sections, this was the only possible way 'of unmasking intrigue, and of forcing the electors not to abuse their powers'.[3] The General Council of the Commune approved these measures on the same day—elections would be made by voting aloud and *par acclamation*; meetings would be held in the presence of the people, and, since the salle de l'Evêché had not been built to accommodate

³ *A.N.*, B 115.

a large audience, the electoral assembly would move to the Jacobin club. The assembly acted in accordance with this decree.

The renewed crisis in March 1793 led the sans-culottes to press once again for elections to be made by voting aloud as an effective weapon in the struggle against the moderates. But it soon became apparent that this method did not satisfy the desire for unanimity which was so important to the sans-culotterie, and during the summer of 1793, voting *par acclamation* became the accepted practice. This, along with the system of voting by standing or remaining seated, was a more satisfactory way of bringing pressure to bear upon citizens who were inclined to hesitate over their choice, and of eliminating all opposition. Soon the sans-culottes became convinced that this was, in fact, the only way of registering a revolutionary vote.

In March 1793, when the Parisian Sections nominated the members of their *comités révolutionnaires*, at first without official sanction, but later in accordance with the law of 21 March, the practice was usually that of voting aloud, but sometimes by standing or remaining seated. On 29 March, the Section du Contrat-Social adopted the latter procedure. Such nominations were subsequently judged to be illegal and, during the repression of the Year III, they became one of the major grievances levelled against former *commissaires*. In May and June, during the bitter struggle between the sans-culottes and the moderates for control of the general assemblies, voting procedure was a weapon hotly disputed by the contending factions. On 21 May, a sans-culotte from the Section du Mail declared that: 'A closed vote will mean the triumph of the cabal.' When the question of electing a Commander-in-Chief of the Parisian National Guard arose, the sans-culottes, anxious to secure the election of Hanriot, forced the system of voting aloud upon citizens in all the Sections under their control. The moderates, who preferred Raffet's nomination, declared themselves in favour of a secret ballot. The Section Lepeletier, which was threatened at this time by the moderates, kept within the letter of the law, but the sans-culottes in the Section voted aloud. La Merlière, a gunner, stated: 'I have no wish to be called a coward: I am voting out loud for Hanriot.' Where the sans-culottes were in a position to influence elections, a compromise was agreed upon. In the Section de l'Unité a citizen drew up a report on 27 June on the decree by which the general assembly had adopted the secret ballot: the significant provision was that unless citizens wanted their nominations to be declared void, they were required to sign their voting-slips. In this way the principle that decisions should be submitted to the scrutiny of the public was upheld.

During the summer of 1793, the system of voting aloud became more common as the political influence of the sans-culotterie increased. The *société populaire des Hommes-Libres* in the Section du Pont-Neuf adopted it on 7 August—the society was convinced that this was, without question, 'the vote of free men'—followed by the general assembly of the Section on 4 September when popular pressure was at its height. In Brumaire, the remaining Sections or popular societies under moderate influence fell to the sans-culottes. On 27 Brumaire, the *société Lepeletier* announced that in future all its nominations would be made by voting aloud. Those moderates who continued to press for the secret ballot were arrested as suspects. At the beginning of Brumaire, Bourdon, a citizen from the Section de Bonne-Nouvelle, was arrested for 'voting in the plain (of the assembly) in a low voice during elections'. Louis Maillet, a copper-plate engraver in the Section du Panthéon-Français, was arrested on 12 Frimaire, 'for expressing bitter opposition to the patriot proposal of voting aloud in the general assemblies'.[4] The practice of voting in secret, denounced as unpatriotic, disappeared from the political life of the Sections at the beginning of the Year II.

Once the sans-culottes had assumed complete control of the general assemblies, they introduced the practice of voting *par acclamation*, a procedure more in keeping with their revolutionary mentality and their ardent desire for unity of thought and action. The sans-culottes had, in fact, already employed this system of voting in times of crisis so that this change was not unprecedented. On 2 August 1792, the general assembly of the Section des Postes had chosen its president by acclamation, rejecting the idea of a ballot. From September 1793, voting by acclamation became the accepted practice. About this time, the general assembly of the Section du Beaurepaire, 'not to waste its time on elections by ballot', adopted the custom of nominating its president *par acclamation*, a procedure 'which it also hastened to adopt when the

<hr>

[4] *A.N.*, F⁷ 4774³⁰.

president of the committee received orders which had to be brought before the assembly for immediate attention'. But urgency was not the only motive; it was also welcome as a means of crushing opposition—a manifestation of revolutionary unity which was particularly pleasing to the sans-culotterie. The vote *par acclamation* was adopted until the spring of the Year II, concurrently with the practice of voting by standing or remaining seated, equally effective, but adopted less frequently. Although the general assembly of the Section de la Butte-des-Moulins on 20 Brumaire decided to nominate its officers by 'the revolutionary practice of standing or remaining seated', on 25 Frimaire it reverted to the system of renewing the members of its committee by 'the revolutionary practice of voting *par acclamation*'.[5] This was the method which was usually adopted by the Section des Invalides and the *société populaire de la section Poissonnière*. Voting by acclamation was finally imposed upon the General Council of the Commune after strong popular pressure had been exerted. On 2 Ventôse, Lubin, its president, asked to be replaced. Practically all the members of the Council immediately began to shout 'Lubin! Lubin!', and this cry was soon taken up by the people in the galleries. Lubin pointed out that such a nomination would not be legal, but those who favoured his nomination replied that, 'On consulting the laws issued by the provisional government, we find that the General Council has the right to appoint and renew its president when it pleases and "in any way it pleases".' As to the possibility of nominating tellers and making arrangements for a ballot: 'This would be a dreadful waste of valuable time.' Lubin was duly elected.[6]

At this time, however, the popular exercise of the ballot was already being threatened: it was not destined to survive the crisis of Ventôse and the criticism of the Cordelier group. Once the jacobin dictatorship had been strengthened a system of voting which was more satisfactory from the standpoint of the bourgeoisie was put into operation. Voting by acclamation, even voting aloud, was officially proscribed by Payan—*agent national* of the purged Commune—for nominations made in the general assemblies. The Sections were forced to obey. But the sans-culottes preferred to desert the general assemblies rather than accept a method of voting

[5] *B.V.C.*, MS. 120.
[6] *Journal de la Montagne*, 4 Ventôse Year II.

believed to be considerably weighted in favour of their enemies. On 30 Messidor, a discussion arose in the general assembly of the Section des Invalides over the election of two *commissaires de l'habillement*. The argument was based upon whether these officials should have been nominated by acclamation or by a secret ballot: 'When it was announced that the two *commissaires* would be nominated by means of a ballot, many citizens walked out of the assembly without bothering to participate in the discussion.' One of the measures which marked the reaction in the spring of the Year II is the return of the secret ballot. This played its part in further alienating sans-culotte sympathies for the Revolutionary Government.

The Thermidorians continued the policy of the Robespierrist Commune on the question of voting. In fact, in Prairial Year III, they even arrested individuals who had praised the advantages of voting aloud, by standing or remaining seated, or *par acclamation*, as well as officials who had been elected according to these methods. The last mention of this popular exercise of the vote comes from the Section de l'Indivisibilité. When, on the first day of the Year III, a citizen named Berger proposed in the primary assembly of the above Section that they should adopt the method of voting aloud, it was almost unanimously agreed that he should be expelled 'as one of the most fanatical terrorist agents'.[7]

By allowing citizens to attend meetings of the administrative authorities, as well as by the proscription of the secret ballot, political life was conducted in the open. Citizens were called upon to verify the acts, opinions, and even the intentions of their friends and enemies alike; this meant that nothing could be ignored which might, in their opinion, involve some threat to the safety of the State. For this reason, 'denunciation' evolved as the extreme application of the decision to conduct all the affairs of the Sections in public: as far as the sans-culottes were concerned, it was a civic obligation.

One of the most common revolutionary symbols was the 'eye of vigilance'—an eye set in a triangle which was carried in demonstrations and posted up in public exhorting citizens to maintain their constant surveillance. Citizens often had to promise to make 'denunciations' when they took the republican oath, and they

[7] *A.N.*, F⁷ 4595, pl. 1, p. 10.

claimed an important part of the meetings of the general assemblies and popular societies. The law itself encouraged people in this civic duty. The decree of 16 September 1791 made it obligatory for citizens to make 'civic denunciations' if they had been the witnesses of any crime. On 26 Ventôse Year II, the General Council of the Commune, after receiving a proposal from the Jacobin club, invited all faithful citizens to sharpen their vigilance, emphasizing the 'urgent' need to denounce the enemies of the State.[8]

The sans-culottes repeatedly tried to justify the act of denunciation itself. In his *Essay on Political Denunciation*, read to the *société de la Section Guillaume-Tell* on 25 July 1793, Etienne Barry defined it as an act by which 'without being called upon to sign anything if we do not wish to, and without responsibility, we reveal to the constituted authorities those crimes against the people of which we have any knowledge'. Under the *ancien régime*, the informer had been cursed 'because under a despotic government, what we call public order is nothing but the preservation and extension of despotism'. Since the Revolution, 'denunciation for political reasons, far from being a moral crime, has become a virtue and a duty': its objective is to safeguard the Rights of Man from any attack. What more effective measure could be adopted against 'noble or bourgeois' aristocrats? Marat's death was an incontrovertible proof of this. Barry concludes: 'denunciation is the shield of liberty in a popular republic'. According to a sans-culotte from the Section Chalier on 27 Floréal Year II, denunciation, like 'publicity', was the 'safeguard of the sovereign people'; it should be placed 'on a level of integrity and honour'. Those who keep silent are not good citizens; those who denounce intrigues deserve to be rewarded. All that was necessary was to declare that one had been a witness of the facts: 'it will be for the juries and judges—born defenders of the accused—to assess the value of your statements'.

In the Year II, therefore, denunciation became one of the manifestations of revolutionary vigilance. There was nothing odious in being an informer as far as the sans-culottes were concerned; they were performing a civic duty justified by its objective. The wig-maker Marrans warned the *comité révolutionnaire* in the Section Chalier on 26 September 1793 'that he was on the track of

---

[8] *Moniteur*, xix, 733; *Jacobins*, V 693.

one, perhaps several, counter-revolutionary societies; that he will try to get enough information to denounce them; and that he would agree to take part in anything they might do in case he might be suspected of being a traitor . . .'. In this same Section, the militant sans-culotte Montain-Lambain, a member of the *comité de bienfaisance*, was according help to one woman at the same time as he was denouncing her to the authorities 'for holding opinions which were contrary to the principles of the Revolution'. In the Section du Muséum, Chassant, an ex-priest from Saint Germain-l'Auxerrois, was convinced that it was the duty of children to denounce their parents if they showed signs of wishing to practise the Catholic cult.[9]

When sans-culottes were arrested as informers in the Year III they made no attempt to defend themselves, but expressed astonishment at the accusation of having committed any crime. In the Section des Thermes, Landru, a laundryman, was arrested on 9 Prairial for having denounced a citizen named Duhamel for his royalist opinions. Admitting the fact, Landru stated in reply that: 'he was under the impression that it was his duty to do it'. The painter Michel was arrested for the same reason in the Section de Bonne-Nouvelle on 5 Prairial, and in a petition which he wrote to the Committee of General Security he asked: 'Is it then a crime to have revealed and denounced true facts which help to safeguard the safety of the State? Would disorder, anarchy and confusion be so widespread if civic "denunciations" were received by the authorities on the same scale as information motivated by personal interest, vengeance or cupidity?' He had given information, but not from motives of hatred, personal interest or vengeance: 'The love of my country alone was responsible for my denunciation. If the majority of citizens had sufficient moral courage to denounce all the enemies of the nation, it would no longer be in danger.' Similarly, the carpenter Gentil, a former *commissaire* in the Section du Contrat-Social, condemned to death on 5 Prairial Year II, when asked 'Why had he denounced several people in this Section?', replied that it was 'Because he believed that they were acting contrary to the best interests of the nation.'[1]

The principle that every political act should be witnessed by the public, even when taken to extreme lengths, emphasizes the

[9] *A.N.*, F⁷ 4641.   [1] *A.N.*, W 146.

strong desire for unanimity of action amongst the sans-culotterie: it brought the people into contact with the realities of the political struggle; no detachment on their part was possible. Conformity of feeling, of opinion and of voting was not only desirable, but necessary. One of the factors which motivated the political activity of the sans-culotterie, therefore, was the desire for unity; it assumed a quasi-mystical quality. But sans-culotte unity must not be identified with that manifested by the National Assembly on the night of 4 August, proclaimed by the Constitution of 1791, then by the Convention, and, finally, solemnly celebrated on 10 August 1793. In the hands of the sans-culottes, unity became a political weapon; it offered the certainty and the means of victory. The sans-culotterie sought the closest possible association, not only between popular organizations, but also between the different social groups interested in the downfall of the aristocracy. Correspondence and fraternization were the means by which unity could be achieved; the fraternal kiss was its symbol; the oath conferred upon it a religious significance.

The need for uniting all the forces of the Revolution was felt, at first, on the sectionary level—'The greater the danger to the nation, the greater the need for all citizens to unite' the Section de Beaubourg announced on 6 September 1792 in a 'fraternal proclamation', which also stated that the Section was abandoning the 'meaningless' name of Beaubourg for that of the Section de la Réunion. The proclamation expressed the hope that soon all lines of demarcation between citizens would disappear, and that the entire Section would become 'one great family in which all the members are perfectly united'. The 'kiss of peace' followed this solemn declaration.

The sans-culottes made a particular point of inviting every citizen to participate in the political life of the Section, refusing to believe that one could be indifferent or neutral. There were frequent appeals for united action, but they did not always manage to convince those citizens who had suffered personal loss as a result of the Revolution. But if the sans-culottes could not persuade, they were quite prepared to punish. Having gained complete control of the Sections, they turned their attention to those citizens who, indifferent to the dangers threatening the nation, were simply waiting for the storm to blow over. In the autumn of 1793, indifference, carelessness and selfishness became grounds for suspicion: there could be no division of opinion in the Republic. The tireless campaign for unity played its part in intensifying the Terror.

Appeals for regular attendance at the meetings of the general assemblies, coupled with threats against indifference, increase noticeably at the beginning of 1793 when the crisis mobilized the militant sans-culottes for more determined action. On 13 December 1792, the Section de l'Arsenal had urged citizens to attend its meetings more assiduously. On 2 January 1793, the Section returned to this theme to point out, with some bitterness, that those who attended most regularly were usually the less affluent citizens: 'they are the workers . . . those who, in trying circumstances, are the first to expose themselves to danger'. This self-sacrificing attitude was compared with 'well-do-to citizens from all classes', some indifferent, others 'completely absorbed in trade, or other rewarding speculations, spending practically all their time attending to their personal wealth'. It appears, then, that only a popular minority frequented the general assemblies. The Section des Gardes-Françaises, following the example of the Section de l'Arsenal, decreed that voters would be required to sign a register: this would enable it to distinguish 'citizens who fulfil the sacred obligations imposed upon them by the nation, from those who, offering a variety of excuses, do everything they can to evade them'.[2]

On 14 February 1793, the Section des Marchés called upon citizens to contribute towards the cost of national defence, pointing out that 'Amongst a free people, there are no uncommitted citizens—there are only brothers and enemies.' A republic could not include 'a single individual who does not concern himself with the advance of freedom, or a single soul who does not do his utmost to propagate it amongst his own people and respect it in others; and that, finally, there is no one who can say that he is not personally involved in its success'. The Section de Bondy soon passed from exhortations to threats. On 8 March, it was decided to call all citizens together 'under pain of being forcibly conducted to the meeting if they refused'. The Section announced that 'all those who refused to share the dangers which seem to threaten us, either by their courage, their wealth or their activity'

---

[2] *B.N.*, Lb[40] 1844.

would be regarded as enemies of the public good and unworthy of their country. On 22 March, the Section de la Théâtre-Français told the *possédant* class: 'property-owners are finally persuaded that only the continuation of the Revolution can safeguard their interests', and that they should, therefore, attend the meetings of the general assemblies regularly—'the safety of the nation depends upon the union of all citizens'.

Exhortations and threats had little effect. On 1 April, the Section de Bondy vainly launched a new appeal to the *insouciants* —citizens who simply could not be bothered to participate in the political activity of the Section. On 10 April, the *Last word of the Section de Bondy* gave an early hint of sanctions: if anyone failed to attend three consecutive meetings of the general assembly he would be regarded as a bad citizen. The name of the *insouciant* would be sent to the committee of the Section which would, upon this information, refuse to supply references to their character for *certificats de civisme* or passports. The *insouciant* was already a citizen with diminished rights; he was soon to be classified as a suspect. The Section de Bondy went even further when it added to the list of persons noted for their lack of civic responsibility, 'every property-owner, *rentier*, or anyone known to enjoy a fairly substantial income who does not already hold a public office, and who, if offered any such position, refuses to accept it'. Those public officials who could be nominated by the Sections were, as yet, not paid for their services, with the result that the sans-culottes were not over-anxious to accept the responsibility of these positions; but for *possédants* to refuse them was, in the opinion of the sans-culottes, proof of their unpatriotic behaviour.

The fact that these appeals and threats had to be repeated time and time again only emphasizes their failure to evoke a positive response. The political outlook and behaviour of the sans-culotterie and the bourgeoisie were, in fact, incompatible. In-difference does not really explain why affluent citizens should have deserted the general assemblies; it was usually that the thought of having to mix with the lower-classes, of being forced to accept their political methods, was distasteful to them. Towards the end of May, the Section de Molière-et-Lafontaine again invited them 'fraternally, to share in its labours, and to bring (to the Section) that gift of wisdom which each individual owes to his country'. On 5 June, in order to symbolize their restored unity, the general assembly of the Section du Théâtre-Français decided to erase 'all lines of demarcation between citizens', and to dispense with such 'expressions as the "right" and the "left"'.[3] But appeals and invitations alike were destined to fall on stony ground.

Once the sans-culottes had won control of the Sections, they took immediate action against the *insouciants* whose public support they had failed to attract, and who, as a result, prevented the realization of national unity. From September 1793 to the fall of Robespierre in Thermidor, a citizen could be classified as a suspect simply on the grounds of his indifference, although the law of 17 September had made no reference to indifference being one of the defects of character distinguishing the suspect. In a decree of 19 January, the General Council of the Commune went a step further when it decided that citizens would have to prove that they had made a positive contribution to the cause of freedom if they wished to escape censure on the grounds of indifference or selfishness.[4]

The *comités révolutionnaires*, however, had clearly anticipated the reaction of the Commune, for no sooner had the voting on the law of suspects ended than the arrest of indifferent or *insouciant* citizens began. Blondel, a former valet in the Section du Muséum, suspected 'for his thoughtlessness and indifference', was arrested on 18 September 1793. Three days later, it was the turn of Lagrange from the Section des Invalides: 'he used to live amongst us without making any contribution towards the common good, and, as a result, we considered him to be an *insouciant*'. On 2 October, the former notary Arnoult from the Section de Bondy was arrested because 'his character is, to say the least, that of an egoist and an *insouciant*'. He had never been seen in the Section, and, in view of this, could only have been an enemy of the Revolution since he had never played any part in it. In the Section de l'Indivisibilité on 5 October, citizen Boutray, formerly a *rente* clerk, was branded as a suspect because he had 'never given the slightest indication that he wished to give the nation his support'; he had apparently made his position worse by stating at the time of his arrest 'that he was not a democrat, a royalist, nor a republican, but that he was going to sit on the fence for a time until the position became clearer'. Bluteau, a writer in the Section des

[3] *A.N.*, W 186.   [4] *Moniteur*, xviii, 90.

Arcis was arrested on 2 Brumaire because 'he had never once taken up arms during the Revolution'.[5]

The consolidation of the Revolutionary Government after Frimaire did not lead to a drop in the number of persons arrested for indifference or for trying to 'contract-out' of their obligations towards the Revolution, confirming the permanence of sans-culotte political preoccupations. André Angard, a bailiff from the Section de Bon-Conseil, was arrested on 18 Nivôse as an *insouciant*, as was Lachapelle, an unmarried rentier from the Section du Contrat-Social who 'did not lose much sleep over the Revolution, but spent all his time in good living'. Lachapelle, arrested on 6 Germinal, was told that 'today, he owes an explanation of his political conduct since 1789'. Again, on 23 Floréal, the *comité révolutionnaire* of the same Section ordered the arrest of a watch-maker named Brasseur 'on account of his negative attitude. He neglects his guard duty, dislikes the idea of serving at all, and has done nothing whatsoever for the Revolution.'

The sans-culottes were of the opinion that the more educated and talented a citizen was, the more culpable was his crime of indifference—another revealing trait of their political behaviour, their faith in education, and their conviction that knowledge could only strengthen a citizen's civic sentiments. The realization that they had been deceived largely explains the severity of the repression. On 15 Brumaire, the *comité révolutionnaire* of the Section de la Montagne decided upon the arrest of Jean-Charles Choderlos, formerly a clerk employed by the Compagnie des Indes, a 'very enlightened man'. 'What grieves us', wrote the *commissaires* at the time, 'is the need to remind you of the fact that a great many of these learned men like Choderlos have not made use of all their faculties in the struggle to overthrow the enemies of the Republic who happen to be so strong in this Section. Finally, to see that they refused to take any decisive action when sans-culottes—who could hardly read the alphabet—were energetically striving to act upon sound principles, casting aside all personal interests for the sake of the nation.' On 25 Ventôse, the committee of the same section ordered the arrest of the author Laharpe. It was true that he had done something for the cause of liberty, 'but, we have one criticism to make of him—he did not attend the general assemblies in his Section to support the sans-culottes, and to use his ability

[5] *A.N.*, F 4580, pl. 4, p. 93; 4614, d. 3; 4603, pl. 9, p. 69.

to further the great principles of natural right so that the aristocracy who, at this time, presented such a threat, could be finally crushed'.[6]

The class bias of their reaction against indifference is evident. Notaries, merchants, *rentiers* . . . who generally fell into the category of *insouciants*, were all well-to-do, if not really rich, citizens. But the frustration and resentment revealed by the sans-culottes at their failure to convert these citizens for the revolutionary cause only emphasizes their sincere desire for unity, and their inability to grasp the true nature of class differences: *insouciants* were arrested not so much on account of their social standing, but as a result of their political behaviour. The sans-culottes appear to have been totally unaware that the one could influence the other. Their search for unity, transcending class barriers, underlines the utopian aspect of their political and social aspirations.

The effectiveness of sans-culotte activity depended upon unity, not only between the Sections, but between all the popular organizations. One of the major problems which faced the militant sans-culottes, and, indeed, all subsequent revolutionary leaders, was the co-ordination of the popular movement: it was vital for the Sections and the clubs to think and act as one. Collective petitions and correspondence between the different popular organizations had long been a feature of political life in the Sections.

Practically everyone was agreed that citizens had the right to petition the authorities, and although it had not been explicitly stated in the Declaration of Rights of 1789, the 1793 version had included it in article 32. The question was how should this right be interpreted? Basically, there were two conflicting ideas: that proposed by the bourgeoisie for whom individualism was the key-word; and that proposed by the sans-culotterie, preoccupied with unity. For the bourgeoisie, petitions should be signed individually; for the sans-culotterie, they were to be signed collectively. The best account of this conflict of interpretation is to be found in the *Moniteur* of 6 April 1791: 'Every petition is an individual act on the part of the citizens who agree to sign it. It is contrary to all ideas of liberty, contrary to every known principle to draw up a petition which claims to speak on behalf of a number of citizens; to call an act of this nature—"petition from a Section,

[6] *A.N.*, F⁷ 4647; 4759.

petition from a commune", unless every citizen in that Section or commune was present and agreed to it; and this agreement must be indicated by their signatures.' On 10 May 1791, the Constituent Assembly prohibited collective petitions, and although it included the right of petition amongst the *Fundamental resolutions guaranteed by the Constitution*, it was careful to add that petitions must be signed by each individual.[7] But the practice of presenting collective petitions persisted: it corresponded to popular mentality; it served the best interests of the Revolution. On 4 February 1792, the *rapporteur* of the *Comité de législation* caused an uproar in the public galleries and amongst the deputies on the left of the Assembly by proposing that all collective petitions should be rejected. During the summer of 1792, when the sans-culottes flooded the general assemblies, making an increasingly active contribution to the political life of the Sections, collective petitions became the accepted practice. In a way, there was very little choice, since many of the sans-culottes did not know how to sign a petition.

The argument over the right of petition broke out again during the conflict between the Gironde and the Mountain. On 15 April 1793, the *commissaires* of the Parisian Sections presented themselves at the Convention to ask for the exclusion of twenty-two of their members: the Assembly ruled that they should be made to sign their petition individually. They were forced to obey, and an official, on the order of the president, collected their signatures. It was this episode which prompted the protest from the Section des Gravilliers on 18 April which pointed out that collective petitions were justified by the dangers which faced the nation and the need for unity: 'In these difficult times, far from seeking to divide citizens, everyone should be striving towards unity in order to transform the nation into an impregnable fortress.' The Sections had enjoyed the right of presenting collective petitions ever since the country had been threatened by war, the protest continued; to abolish it now would be to retard the progress of the Revolution. In any case, individual signatures were an 'immoral adherence purposely designed to destroy the fraternal unity which exists between patriotic citizens . . . they are in no way appropriate to our system of government which requires everyone, without distinction, to fulfil their civic obligations. If

[7] *Moniteur*, viii, 51; ix, 353.

petitions had to be signed individually, the greater and more reliable part of the population would be excluded, prevented from presenting their opinions on any occasion simply because they do not know how to write.'[8]

The Sections continued to present collective petitions, ignoring the criticism of the Girondins. They became the rule after 2 June, throughout the Year II and even after Thermidor. Collective petitions only disappear with the collapse of the popular movement after the Prairial *journées*. The Constitution of the Year III recognized the right of petition, but explicitly stated that 'they must be individual; no society whatsoever may present collective petitions'. The sans-culottes having been eliminated from the political scene, the right of petition was once again given an individualist and bourgeois interpretation.

The practice of presenting collective petitions, according to the Section des Lombards on 27 March 1791, would not effectively achieve 'unanimity of feeling and concerted action' if the Sections could not correspond with each other. 'Correspondence'—communicating resolutions and decrees—did in fact enable them to act in unison. Usually, however, the means of communication was by *commissaires*, which proved to be extremely slow. Often, by the time every Section had received the necessary information the time for action had passed. Correspondence, if it was to be effective, had to be swift. On 27 March 1791, the Section des Lombards proposed that a central correspondence office should be created where *commissaires* could communicate and discuss the decrees which had been passed by their respective Sections. In February 1792, the Section de Sainte-Geneviève also tried to organize, unsuccessfully, a 'correspondence office', or a 'central committee'.[9]

Finally, influenced by the course of events, the Commune opened a Central Correspondence Office for the Sections on 27 July 1792. This was simply an information bureau where no discussion whatsoever could take place, but it did mean that the Sections could now rapidly co-ordinate their policies. Following upon this move, the Section du Théâtre-Français, on 11 August 1792, named 'two civic messengers, authorized to go wherever necessary . . . with the purpose of giving and receiving the particulars, explanations and instructions which have any bearing

8 *A.P.P.*, AA/266.   9 *A.D.S.*, D 672.

upon public affairs and to report upon them to the Section'. However the Central Correspondence Office of the Commune did not survive the summer of 1792. On 10 February 1793, the Section de Quatre-Vingt-Douze complained about the delay involved in sending information by means of *commissaires*. The moderates for their part were not prepared for the Sections to exercise this liberty, and on 24 May 1793, the *Commission des Douze* adopted a resolution which regulated correspondence between the Sections. The following day the Section des Arcis, controlled by the moderates, asked that 'all kinds of correspondence' between popular societies should be forbidden. But such demands came a little late in the day, for on 4 June, the Section de la Halle-au-Blé, convinced that the unity of the Sections had been a factor in the victory of the popular movement, was already proposing the creation of a Central Committee composed of delegates from the *comités révolutionnaires* to maintain a 'permanent' correspondence with the Sections—'the only way of preventing treason'. On 1 Frimaire Year II, the same Section again appealed to the General Council of the Commune to set up a Central Committee of the Sections, 'in order to inform them of their decrees promptly'.[1] All these attempts were undermined by the hostile attitude of the Commune. The General Council, composed of representatives from the Sections, regarded itself as the real co-ordinating unit: a Central Committee, if only for correspondence, would have represented a rival authority.

At the height of the revolutionary crisis, and for the reasons outlined by the Section des Lombards as early as March 1791, communication between the Sections proved to be inadequate. The insurrectionary committees, such as those created on 10 August and 31 May, only came into being at the very moment when it was necessary to act, when the Sections delegated their sovereign powers. In order to prepare for these supreme moments in the history of the Revolution, and in the absence of an official central organization, the sans-culottes invented a new form of communication—fraternization.

For the sans-culottes there could be no unity without fraternity: in the texts of the Year II these two words were practically interchangeable. Fraternity means not only ties of affection between

[1] *Affiches*, 2 Frimaire Year II; *Journal de la Montagne*, 3 Frimaire Year II.

citizens; it signifies that these citizens are united in an indissoluble bond of friendship. Correspondence was simply an administrative procedure: fraternization was charged with an emotional signific-ance and a certain mystical quality. Its origins can be found in the federations of 1790, where we find the same fervent affirmation of unity, the same communion. But the federations had excited the interest of all classes in the nation: they were solemn affirmations of faith rather than manifestations of action. Frater-nization unites only those who associate themselves with the sans-culotterie; it is a weapon of action directed chiefly against the moderates. Correspondence between the Sections had been carried out with the help of *commissaires* provided with the necessary powers; whereas fraternization involved the sans-culotterie *en masse*. If one Section was threatened by the moderates, the entire general assembly of the neighbouring Section would move to the threatened assembly, and, in the name of fraternity, the two assemblies would be fused into one by the mysterious ties of the oath and the fraternal kiss, and decisions would then be taken in common. Fraternization was a pact of mutual assist-ance which, going beyond Sections and popular societies, united the sans-culotterie as a body.

In March 1793, the *société des Defenseurs-de-la-République* in-vited Sections and popular societies to assemble on 17 March in the place de la Réunion, 'to seal the union which should exist between all patriots with a fraternal kiss'. Fraternizations became far more general as the danger from the moderates increased. On 21 April 1793, a large deputation from the general assembly of the Section des Lombards visited the general assembly in the Section du Contrat-Social. Its speaker denounced 'the intrigues, anarchy, and endless disturbances caused by the royalist party of Dumouriez, and the bitter divisions which result in the assemblies'. He went on to invite the two Sections to swear a solemn oath 'to live and correspond with one another fraternally in a close and affectionate union, in perfect accord, and to crush the aristocratic monster under their feet'. The deputation and the general assembly then exchanged the fraternal kiss. On 23 April, the general assembly of the Section du Contrat-Social, led by its committee, returned the visit. On this occasion it was resolved that in future the two assemblies would meet as one assembly of 'brothers and friends'; the two committees were merged under the same president. Once again the oath of fraternity and union was taken, and the fraternal kiss ended the meeting. Henceforward, the two Sections were linked by a quasi-religious pact. On 14 May, a deputation from the Section des Lombards informed the general assembly of the Section du Contrat-Social that 'the aristocracy wish to overthrow the patriots'; immediately the president suspended the meeting and the whole assembly moved to the Section de Lombards so that assistance could be given to the sans-culottes who were in danger.[2]

Correspondence and fraternization both had the same aim—to unite, not only two neighbouring Sections, but all the forty-eight Parisian Sections. On 26 April 1793, after a citizen in the general assembly of the Section du Contrat-Social had announced that the Section des Gardes-Françaises was 'practically in a state of insurrection', it was immediately decided that a deputation of 'sans-culotte citizens' should be sent 'to restore order in a spirit of fraternization and cordiality'. On 27 April, a new resolution was passed stating that the general assembly, led by its committee, would join the general assembly of the Section des Gardes-Françaises on the following day, 'to fraternize and promise them their support, encouragement, aid, and assistance against those trouble-makers and disturbers of the peace who were attempting to overthrow the Republic'. On the next day, as planned, the two general assemblies joined in discussing the measures which had to be taken to restore order. Finally, on 29 April, a delegation from the Gardes-Françaises took an oath before the general assembly of the Section du Contrat-Social 'to unite and fraternize together in perfect harmony and understanding'. It was agreed that the two assemblies would fraternize 'once a week, in each Section alternately.'[3]

Fraternization enabled the Parisian sans-culottes to check the advance of the moderate movement in the Sections in May 1793, and later to assume control of the general assemblies. On 5 May, after violent scenes, the moderates succeeded in gaining control of the assembly of the Section de Bon-Conseil. Immediately, the sans-culottes appealed to the Section des Lombards for assistance, referring to 'the minutes of a reunion . . . by which the said two Sections promised and solemnly declared their union, fraternity,

---

[2] *A.N.*, C 355, pl. 1860, pp. 8, 9, 34.
[3] *A.N.*, C 355, pl. 1860, pp. 13, 14, 15, 16.

and assistance whenever the aristocracy sought to suppress freedom'. The sans-culottes from the Section des Lombards invaded the general assembly of Bon-Conseil, and were quickly joined by sans-culottes from the Section des Amis-de-la-Patrie. The moderates were expelled, and the three Sections linked themselves together by a 'fraternal decree', sending *commissaires* around the other Sections 'to seek the same fraternity and assistance from them all; to bestow the kiss of peace upon the president of each Section and swear an oath of allegiance and assistance to overthrow the disturbers of public order; and finally, to ask them to use every means within their power to prevent trouble-makers from lighting the flames of civil war in Paris.'[4]

The political import of sans-culotte fraternization is emphasized by the minutes of a meeting held in the Section du Contrat-Social on 12 May 1793. On this occasion, the Section de Bon-Conseil and the Section du Contrat-Social met as one assembly and decreed 'as a sans-culotte principle, one and indivisible, that in any place, and at any time, when one or more of the Sections of Paris find themselves united, the Sections thus joined together will act as a single assembly, and that the deliberations taken in this assembly will represent the will of them all'.[5] Fraternization clearly realized that unity of action which was so important to the more progressive Sections.

Towards the end of May, as the situation became more tense, fraternizations increased in number. On 18 May, after the moderates had again revealed their strength in the Section du Contrat-Social, a deputation 'of more than two hundred' proposed 'to fraternize with the sans-culottes of the Contrat-Social twice a week in order to separate the aristocrats from the sans-culottes'. This was followed by equally large deputations from the Section des Halles, des Gravilliers, and des Lombards. The five Sections then agreed to fraternize 'with their brothers the sans-culottes in other Sections if they are oppressed by the aristocracy'. First on their list came the Section de l'Arsenal, followed by the Section de la Butte-des-Moulins which were visited 'in order to drive out the aristocrats'. The next day there were new fraternizations in the general assembly of the Section du Contrat-Social. Delegations from the Droits-de-l'Homme, Marchés, Gravilliers, and the Bon-Conseil Sections crowded together and proposed 'to visit

---

[4] *B.V.C.*, MS. 117, f. 9.   [5] *B.V.C.*, MS. 119 f.

a few Sections where the aristocracy is said to be in control'.[6]

After 2 June, the threat from the moderates declined and the need to adopt fraternization as an offensive weapon gradually became less imperative. On 2 July, two *commissaires* from the Section de Bon-Conseil were sent to every Section to offer 'the fraternal kiss and promise of unity, indivisibility, and assistance in case of oppression, inviting them to show their own desire for unity by taking the same oath'. Two days later the Section de Luxembourg sent an appeal to the Section du Théâtre-Français 'for union in order to unmask the anarchic designs of the aristocracy'. The Section de l'Unité was satisfied with the dispatch of twenty-four *commissaires* to the Section de la Butte-des-Moulins to fraternize with the sans-culottes. On 11 June, the Section de Bondy launched an appeal for union with their fellow sans-culottes in the departments, adding that it would receive any deputation with the torch of truth and the olive-branch, symbol of peace. On 20 June, the *cannoniers* of the Parisian Sections appealed to their brothers-in-arms to fraternize in the Champs-Elysées and renew their oath to maintain the unity of the Republic. To seal this unity the Section des Tuileries on 4 August invited the *commissaires* of the departmental primary assemblies within the Section to participate in its deliberations: 'so that their wisdom might enlighten us fraternally on matters of common interest; for all Frenchmen are brothers'.

Once the moderates had been crushed in the Sections of Paris, the practice of fraternization as a popular political weapon fell into disuse, although there were still occasions when the sans-culottes felt that they should assert the necessity for union. On 6 and 10 Pluviôse Year II, the *société des Sans-Culottes Révolutionnaires* and the committee of the Section Chalier swore 'the most intimate union and fraternity' and declared 'eternal hatred towards anyone who would dare or attempt to separate them'.

In the spring of 1793, fraternization had been an effective weapon in the struggle against the moderates. In the absence of any organized party, and lacking a central organism which would have co-ordinated the political activity of all the popular forces, it was a means of uniting the sans-culotterie when circumstances demanded immediate action, and this unity in return tended to create an awareness of class differences. But once the sans-culottes

[6] *A.N.*, C 355, pl. 1860, pp. 36 and 37.

had gained control of the general assemblies and the Revolutionary Government had been strengthened, fraternization only retained a symbolic significance. In the altered circumstances, correspondence by means of *commissaires* seemed to be a satisfactory way, as it had been previously, of maintaining unity of action between the forty-eight Sections. A revealing aspect of the nature of the crisis in Ventôse Year II, as well as the incapacity of the Cordelier leaders, was that there seemed to be no move whatsoever to unite the sans-culotterie by means of fraternization—or even correspondence—although, one year before, it had undoubtedly played a significant part in their victory.

However, during the final insurrections of the Year III, the sans-culottes, conscious of their error, resorted to these tactics once again. On 10 Germinal, the Section de Guillaume-Tell decided that it would communicate all the measures it was taking to safeguard the lives and interests of the people with the other Sections: the passwords for this renewed correspondence would be 'Unity and Fraternity'. Two days later, the sans-culottes in the Section de Popincourt, after adhering to a decree issued by the Section de la Cité declaring itself to be *en permanence*, resolved that copies of their deliberations should be sent to 'their brothers' in the Arsenal, Maison-Commune, Arcis, and Homme-Armé Sections, adding that 'they will always be ready to fraternize with citizens from other Sections'. The political methods adopted by the sans-culotterie formed a coherent and unified programme— fraternization was unthinkable without the permanence of the Sections. But since the general assemblies were not in session following the suppression of permanence, the Section de Popincourt decided to send *commissaires* to alert the *comités civils*. One of these *commissaires* after his arrest at the place de Grève stated that he was on his way to the Section de la Cité 'to ask it not to depart from its customary friendship, as we were in the middle of a crisis'. Another stated that he was going to invite the other Sections to act together fraternally '. . . so that we do not begin to show signs of disunity, but that we might all be brothers'.[7]

The militant sans-culotte from the Section de Popincourt had emphasized the essential feature of the political behaviour of the sans-culotterie: it was based upon fraternity. This was not just an abstract conception, but the feeling, the inner conviction of

[7] *A.N.*, F 4774[37].

sans-culotte unity. The sans-culotte did not think of himself as an isolated individual: he thought and acted *en masse*.

Violence was adopted as a last resort by the sans-culotterie against anyone who refused to unite with them in their struggle: it became one of the most characteristic features of their political behaviour. Popular violence had enabled the bourgeoisie to launch their first attacks against the *ancien régime*, and there was never any question of the aristocracy being completely crushed without it. In 1793 and in the Year II, the sans-culotte adopted violent tactics, not only against the aristocracy, but against the moderates who refused to accept the idea of an egalitarian republic.

To understand this violence, and the feeling of exaltation which accompanied it, we would doubtless have to look sometimes for biological reasons: temperament often explains many reactions which would otherwise remain obscure. The reports of Prairial Year III on the terrorists of the previous year often stress the quick-tempered or violent sides of their nature. As one informer stated, a man with such a temperament was subject to fits of passion 'which might have led him to make exaggerated statements without foreseeing or even thinking about their consequences'. Reactions were more immediate and more extreme because the sans-culottes were often rough and crude, lacking any real education, their lives inflamed by misery.

In the Year III, terrorists were indiscriminately described as *buveurs de sang*, and although we must be careful not to generalize, or to take police reports and denunciations literally, it would be very difficult to deny that violence for some actually meant the spilling of blood. Arbulot, a cloth-shearer from the Section des Gardes-Françaises, arrested on 9 Prairial, was reputed to have been a very dangerous husband and neighbour, with a fierce and unyielding nature: it was said that he had taken great pleasure in the September massacres. Bunou from the Section des Champs-Elysées, arrested on 5 Prairial, was alleged to have asked for a guillotine for the Section in the Year II, 'and that if they could not find an executioner, he would take the job on himself'. Similar statements were supposed to have been made by Lesur from the Section du Luxembourg who was arrested on the following day. He was convinced 'that the guillotine was not doing its work quickly enough; that there should be a bit more blood-letting in

the prisons; and that if the executioner was tired, he would mount
the scaffold himself, even if it meant soaking the two-pound loaf
he had just bought with blood'. In the Section des Gardes-
Françaises, Jayet was arrested on 6 Prairial because he had said
in the Year II 'that he wanted to see streams of blood flowing
until they had reached ankle-height'. Another citizen on leaving
the general assembly of the Section de la République stated: 'The
guillotine is hungry; it has been fasting for too long.'[8]

Temperament alone, however, does not explain why practically
all the militant sans-culottes should have justified, if not exalted,
a recourse to violence and the use of the guillotine. For many,
brutal force appeared to be the only answer in times of acute crisis.
Yet these same men, who did not hesitate to spill blood on these
occasions, were quite peaceable citizens in the ordinary course of
their daily lives; good sons, husbands, and fathers. Duval, a shoemaker from the Section de l'Arsenal, was condemned to death on
11 Prairial Year III for his part in the rising of the first of the
month. His neighbours described him as a good father, a good
husband, and a good citizen—'a man of good morals'. The
awareness of the danger facing the nation, the belief in the
aristocratic plot, the atmosphere of the great insurrections, the
tocsin, the warning cannon-shot and the parade of arms all played
their part in lifting these men outside themselves, completely
altering their characters. According to the *comité civil* of the Section du Faubourg du Nord, Joseph Morlot, a house-painter
arrested on 5 Prairial, had two distinct natures: 'The one, when
governed by his natural disposition, is gentle, honest, and kind;
it presents a combination of all the social virtues which he prac-
tises discreetly in his everyday life. The other, awakened by
momentary dangers, produces the worst possible evils presented
in their most lurid form which he parades in the most indiscreet
manner.'[9]

But violence was not adopted simply for its own sake: it had a
political aim which was not devoid of a vague consciousness of
class differences, forced upon the sans-culotterie by the continued
resistance of the aristocracy. The *comité révolutionnaire* of the
Section Poissonnière was alleged to have planned the arrest in
Brumaire Year II of a citizen named Charvin, well known for

[8] *A.N.*, F⁷ 4581, pl. 1; 4627, d. 2; 4636, d. 2; 4749; 4774⁸⁶.
[9] *A.N.*, W 546; F⁷ 4774⁵³.

his moderation 'which weakens the people's confidence in revolutionary acts and leads to a deterioration of public morale in the Section'. Moussard, a teacher employed by the Executive Commission of Public Instruction, was arrested on 5 Prairial Year III. 'I was often over-enthusiastic', he wrote in his defence statement, 'What person does not go a little beyond himself in a revolution? . . . I am too exalted in my opinions, they say. Yes, the passion for good burns inside me; I respond to the joys of freedom, and my blood will always boil when I hear of the enemies of my country.'[1]

The guillotine was popular because the sans-culottes regarded it as the avenging arm of the nation, accounting for such expressions as 'national hatchet', and 'the people's axe'; the guillotine was also 'the scythe of equality'. Class hatred against the aristocracy was exacerbated by the widespread belief in the 'aristocratic plot' which, since 1789, had represented one of the motivating elements of popular violence. Foreign and civil war helped to strengthen the conviction of the sans-culotterie that the only way of crushing the aristocracy completely was by terror, and that the guillotine was necessary if the Republic was not to be overthrown. Becq, a clerk in the Admiralty who, according to the *comité civil* of the Section de la Butte-des-Moulins, a good husband and father and generally well thought of but extraordinarily exalted in his attitude towards the Revolution, directed his fanaticism against priests and nobles for whom he prescribed, as a rule, assassination. Jean-Baptiste Mallais, a shoemaker and *commissaire révolutionnaire* from the Section du Temple, sympathized wholeheartedly with these views. When he began one of his many arguments, the subject would inevitably be his hatred of priests and nobles whom he considered to be enemies of the people; and when he spoke of arming the wives of patriots, it was 'so that they, in their turn, could cut the throats of aristocrats' wives'. Barrayer from the Section de la Réunion was alleged to have stated in the Year II 'that they had to kill the young devil in the church' because if they did not, then 'one day he would massacre the people'. More significant still of the political significance which the sans-culottes attached to violence and the Terror were the remarks taken down by the police-agent Perrière on 6 Ventôse Year II: 'Are there any executions today? a small well-dressed moderate asked.—Without

[1] *A.N.*, F⁷ 4776; 4774⁵⁴.

any doubt, replied an honest patriot, since we are still surrounded by treason.'[2]

In the Year III, the recourse to violence had an even greater significance for the sans-culotterie. The Terror had also had an economic aspect: it had enabled the General Maximum to be applied which had guaranteed the people their daily bread. Reaction coincided with the end of price-fixing and the most acute food-shortage. Some sans-culottes naturally identified the Terror with a well-stocked larder, as they associated popular government with the Terror. The shoemaker Clément from the Section de la République was denounced on 2 Prairial for having said 'that they could not build the Republic without blood'. A citizen named Denis from the Section Brutus was arrested on 5 Prairial because in his opinion there were not so many 'good republicans to be found as when they used to guillotine people'. Chalandon, a wife from the Section de l'Homme-Armé used to say 'that things would never improve until they erect permanent guillotines on all the public thoroughfares of Paris'. The remarks made by Richer on 1 Prairial, a carpenter from the Section de la République, were more precise. Richer was convinced, 'that the only way to get bread is to spill a little blood', adding 'that during the Terror there was no shortage of it'.[3]

The Terror and popular violence played a major part in sweeping away the remains of feudalism and absolutism from the path of the bourgeoisie; although, when the sans-culottes resorted to these methods, they frequently had more particular objectives in mind. This violence exercised by the sans-culotterie nevertheless reflected a very different political behaviour from that accepted by the bourgeoisie, just as the actual practice of popular politics, characterized, above all, in 1793 and the Year II by the vote *par acclamation* and fraternization, reveals an entirely different conception of democracy from that of the bourgeoisie, even the jacobin bourgeoisie.

It is true that the revolutionary bourgeoisie did not recoil from the use of violence in the critical phases of their struggle with the aristocracy; nor did they disdain to adopt popular methods such as the procedure of voting aloud during the elections to the Convention in Paris. Circumstances, and a certain class interest,

[2] *A.N.*, W 112.   [3] *A.N.*, W 548.

justified this deviation from their customary practices. But these circumstances, and this same class interest, also determined that such methods could not be practised indefinitely once the Revolutionary Government was in power. For although they suited the temperament of the sans-culotterie well enough, they were incompatible with the political ideas and behaviour of the bourgeoisie: they threatened its superiority. They also undermined the revolutionary organization of the government and the dictatorship of the Committees. Here again, this contradiction aggravated the seriousness of the crisis.

V

POLITICAL ORGANIZATION

The force which the Parisian sans-culotterie placed at the disposal
of the bourgeois revolution, and which also commanded respect
for their own particular demands, would clearly have been less
effective had it not been organized. But, by adapting the legal
institutions created by the Constituent Assembly; by using the
revolutionary institutions forced upon the Convention; and
finally, by forging a new instrument of popular power in the
sociétés sectionnaires, the militants succeeded in bringing a flexible
and effective organization to the revolutionary movement. From
the spring to the autumn of 1793, this organization was thoroughly
tested in the struggle against the moderates, and played a major
part in bringing the Revolutionary Government to power. But
once the latter had been stabilized, it became increasingly apparent
that the duality of power between this government and the popular
movement could not in fact be reconciled.

The Sections, enjoying a very wide measure of autonomy,
directed by their committees and buttressed by the network of
societies which surrounded them, proved by the events of 5
September 1793 that they were capable of forcing their will upon
the Committees of the government and upon the Convention
itself. But this success also awakened the fear, particularly during
the critical days of the spring of 1794, that a new popular *journée*
would sweep the Revolutionary Government from power. From
the autumn of 1793 to the spring of the Year II, this problem,
presented in an increasingly acute and tragic form, determined the
relationship between the government and the democratic movement in the Sections which, by the institutions it had created,
appeared to represent an autonomous force within the Revolution
itself.[1]

In view of the elections to the States General, the royal

[1] For the whole of this chapter, see Ernest Mellié, *Les Sections de Paris
pendant la Révolution française (21 mai 1790–vendémiaire an IV)*, *Organ-
isation. Fonctionnement.*

ordonnance of 13 April 1789 had divided the city of Paris into sixty districts. But, after the elections were over, the districts had decided to continue their meetings and to deliberate in their permanent general assemblies, clearly resolved to administer their own affairs and to play an active part in political life. On 30 August, a municipal decree confided the administration of each district to a committee of seventeen to twenty-four members.

The Constituent Assembly, which had organized municipalities throughout France by the decree of 14 December 1789, could not allow Paris to retain a separate organization which favoured the autonomous tendencies of the capital. After lengthy deliberations, it passed the decree of 21 May–27 June 1790 which constituted the municipal charter of Paris. Forty-eight Sections were substituted for the sixty districts. The latter had been allowed to meet permanently, but this privilege was not extended to the Sections which were regarded primarily as electoral divisions, meeting in order to vote, and separating immediately the elections were over. But although the law restricted their freedom to meet, it did not suppress it altogether: if requested by fifty citizens, the Sections could meet—under certain conditions—other than for electoral purposes.

The supreme organ of the Section was the assembly: it was the 'embodiment of the people's sovereignty'. In the primary assemblies, citizens met in order to vote; they deliberated in the general assemblies.

Primary assemblies—the more important of the two according to the law which created them, and the very reason, in fact, for the existence of the Sections—were not held very frequently: there were only fifty meetings from 11 November 1791 to 11 February 1794. The decision of the Section du Théâtre-Français on 27 July 1792 to abolish the distinction between active and passive citizens, immediately imitated by all the other Parisian Sections, changed the character of these assemblies. After this date, they really did represent the organs of popular sovereignty. The decree issued by the Legislative Assembly on 10 August permitting everyone over the age of 25, if they had been resident in Paris for one year, to vote for the renewal of the *juges de paix*, and that passed on the following day stating that 'the division of Frenchmen into active and passive citizens was abolished', simply recognized an existing situation.

The conditions governing the meetings of the general assemblies were outlined in the law of 21 May 1790, which did not, however, define their duration, frequency, competence, or their aims. Although, in the beginning, meetings were held rather infrequently—the Section des Postes only met fifty times from 4 December 1790 to 25 July 1792 when meetings were declared permanent—the Sections gave a very wide interpretation to the law, taking a constant interest in public affairs and in politics generally. The Constituent Assembly restricted the application of the law on 18–22 May 1791 by decreeing that the general assemblies could only be convened for purposes of municipal administration: decisions taken on other matters would be unconstitutional, and therefore invalid. The activity of the Sections was seriously curtailed; they became simply administrative subdivisions of the capital. The Section des Postes held only six meetings from 30 May to 9 September 1791.

The Sections recovered their right to meet permanently as a result of the outbreak of war and the subsequent danger which threatened the nation. In theory at least, the general assemblies were given unlimited authority; and although the permanence of the Sections was abolished on 9 September 1793—the date when the government authorized the forty *sous* indemnity—the assemblies continued to take a keen interest in the political struggle, as well as in local affairs, until the spring of the Year II.

The municipal law of 1790 had been principally concerned with the organization of primary assemblies, making no reference to the holding or administrative regulations of general assemblies, apart from decreeing that their first task should be the nomination of a president and a secretary. The assemblies were left in complete control of their own organization. The lack of documentary evidence, particularly on internal regulations, makes it difficult for us to describe their organization in detail; although in 1793 and in the Year II, it appears to have been fairly straightforward. The assembly was controlled by a president, assisted by a committee and a *secrétaire-greffier* who took down the minutes. 'Tellers' were appointed for the purpose of voting, and 'censors' made sure that the rules governing the assembly were observed. The committee was usually renewed every month: the customary practice being to vote new members by rising to show approval, or *par acclamation*. The personnel of the assemblies changed little; a small number of militants sharing all the places. Some presidents, for example, were renewed in office throughout the Year II.

Meetings began with a reading of the minutes of the last assembly, after which members were informed of the laws, decrees, and departmental minutes issued by the Commune. This usually took a considerable time and delayed discussion on the main items of the agenda prepared, as a rule, by the president with the assistance of the committee. According to the law, meetings were supposed to begin at five o'clock and end at ten o'clock, but on many occasions discussion went on until much later. The meetings of the Section de la Montagne often continued until half-past eleven, which meant, according to the police-agent Hanriot, that many members 'could not get to work in time on the following day'. On 25 Ventôse Year II, one citizen made a spirited appeal for meetings to begin promptly at five o'clock so that the assembly could go on to discuss the agenda at six, and rise at ten o'clock precisely. As a rule, meetings appear to have been disorderly, with many heated arguments even when the sans-culottes were in complete control; frequently, no discussion at all was possible. When important questions were being debated, according to the report of Prévost on 30 Pluviôse, many citizens got up to speak on the most irrelevant subjects or shouted at the top of their voices making it impossible for the assembly to reach any decision. Such scenes were common in the Section de la République. In the Section Chalier, after the president had been seen drinking a glass of wine when he was still in the chair, several of his enemies in the assembly shouted: 'it's getting like a wine-stores here now; it will be a smoking-room next'. Other sans-culottes pointed out that many citizens had done the same thing in the past, and after an hour of argument and disorder, the meeting went on to discuss the agenda as if nothing had happened. It is true that the physical environment in which the general assemblies conducted their affairs was hardly conducive to good order. Churches and chapels forming part of the National Lands did not provide the right kind of atmosphere for these meetings, and the Sections were continually campaigning for alterations to be made, or for new buildings to be constructed. On 1 Germinal Year II, the Section de la Montagne—adhering to a petition from the Section de Bonne-Nouvelle—suggested that a meeting-hall should be built in each Section at the cost of the Republic, pointing out that 'many citizens were finding their way into the assembly by means of different entrances, which simply could not happen in a more enclosed building'.

It will help us to appreciate the exact role of the general assemblies in the organization and political activity of the Parisian sans-culotterie if we undertake two series of statistical analyses at this point. In the first place, how many citizens attended the meetings of the primary and general assemblies? And secondly, what proportion of citizens benefited from the 'forty *sous* indemnity'?

Unfortunately, since most of their minutes have disappeared, we cannot complete a chronological series and trace an attendance graph for the general assemblies up to the date of their suppression. The information at our disposal is further depleted by the fact that, as a rule, the minutes which still survive simply provide us with a rough estimate—usually taken during elections in the assemblies—instead of the exact number of members present. We can only arrive at an approximation; but we can make the best use of this approximation if we compare it with the number of active citizens taken from lists which were carefully drawn up in 1790, or with the numerous estimates of the population completed after 10 August 1792.

From the beginning of the Revolution—apart from periods of acute crisis and during the most important *journées*—only a minority of citizens participated in the political life of the Sections. During the censitary period, only a small number of active citizens attended the general assemblies, even when they were transformed into primary assemblies for electoral purposes. The percentage attendance seems to be remarkably low, varying according to the Section and the period, from 4 to 19. To make a really accurate assessment, we would, of course, need to take into account the social composition of the various Sections and the degree of political pressure exerted upon active citizens by the sans-culottes. From this point of view, it is significant to note that for the Faubourg-Montmartre, Fontaine-de-Grenelle, and Louvre Sections, which had a total population of approximately 12,000, attendance at the general assemblies in April–May 1792 was all the higher because they had fewer active citizens. The Section with the highest proportion of sans-culotte inhabitants—the

Section du Faubourg-Montmartre—had an attendance of 18 per cent. of the total number of active citizens, whilst the Section du Louvre—the most affluent of the three Sections—did not attract an attendance of over 5 per cent. From April to July 1792, the percentage of active citizens in the assemblies of the Section de la Fontaine-Grenelle remained steady at 7 per cent., whilst the Section du Louvre seems to have reflected the impending crisis more accurately—the figures rising from 5 per cent. at the beginning of May to 19 per cent. at the end of July when passive citizens succeeded in entering the assembly.

But, in order to judge the real significance of these attendances, we still need to take into account the agendas of the general assemblies: the election of a magistrate attracted more citizens than an ordinary debate. The great political debates towards the end of July 1792 aroused the interest of active and passive citizens, as the example taken from the assembly of the Section du Louvre shows. Therefore, for any given Section, we must follow attendances at the general assemblies for the whole of the censitary period. Despite the fact that much of the documentary evidence is incomplete, it is clear that attendances at the Section de l'Arsenal and the Section des Postes were extremely low. They rose a little when elections were being made to municipal offices, or when the assembly nominated magistrates for the Section. The lengthy and involved procedure of electing representatives to the Paris Commune often meant that citizens lost interest, as we can see from the low attendances at the general assemblies of the Section de l'Arsenal and the Section des Postes during the elections of February 1792. Just as indicative of this refusal on the part of the majority of active citizens to participate in the political life of the Sections was the 6 per cent. attendance at the general assembly of the latter on 23 June 1792, despite the importance of the agenda which included an inquiry into the conduct of the mayor and the municipality of Paris during the *journée* of 20 June. Was this the result of indifference or fear of popular pressure? The practice of abstaining from voting was a dominant feature of the political life of the Sections throughout the censitary period. It aroused frequent protests, such as those from the Section du Luxembourg on 21 November 1791 and the Section des Postes on 28 December.

Attendances increased for a short time after passive citizens had been admitted to the assemblies in July and August 1792, but it

was not long before they also began to lose interest. The figures for
the Section du Contrat-Social—formerly the Section des Postes—
again provide us with significant statistics. The total number of
citizens who attended the assemblies in October and November
1792 was the highest recorded throughout the censitary period.
The attraction, once again, was the election of the mayor of Paris.
But as soon as the assemblies went on to discuss more mundane
affairs, the attendance figures began to drop. They fell from 330 on
12 November, to 151 on the twenty-eighth, when the assembly
discussed the election of a *notable*. The complicated electoral
procedure and the numerous ballots were driving citizens, who
had been extremely faithful until this time, away from the assemblies; the more timorous or politically indifferent members withdrew when the political crisis became more acute. On 11 February
1793, there were only 194 voters in the primary assembly for the
election of Pache as mayor of Paris, and only 123 to elect a *notable*
on 18 January. Although the social composition of the assembly
had changed, actual attendances had fallen once again to the
average figure recorded during the censitary period. On 25
October 1792, the *Moniteur*, referring to a vote which had been
taken in the Section du Panthéon-Français, had emphasized the
apathy which marked the political life of the Sections: 'In theory,
each of the forty-eight Sections could attract at least 4,000 voters
. . . in practice, a deliberative assembly is often composed of only
150, 100 or even fewer citizens.' The anonymous reporter of the
Moniteur neglected to mention one important fact—the alteration
in the social composition of the general assemblies since 10 August.

After the sans-culottes had invaded the assemblies, many active
citizens withdrew from the political struggle altogether. As for the
passive citizens, only a minority of them continued to play any
part in public affairs once the immediate danger had passed.
Control of the assemblies simply passed from one group to another. The little statistical evidence provided by the minutes
indicates that the entry of the sans-culottes into political life did
not seriously affect the total number of citizens who frequented
the assemblies.

After 2 June, control of the political affairs of the Sections
passed into the hands of a minority of citizens increasingly
identifiable as a social group. The moderates were gradually
eliminated. Amongst the sans-culottes, only a minority attended

the assemblies regularly, and an even smaller number frequented the popular societies or *sociétés sectionnaires*. On 2 September 1793, there were only eighty-seven voters present in the general assembly of the Section du Pont-Neuf to elect four members to the *comité révolutionnaire*; 'a considerable number of citizens' having walked out of the assembly hall after delegations had arrived from other Sections 'in order to fraternize'. However, general assemblies were held more frequently than from 10 August to 31 May when they provided the arenas for the struggle between the sans-culottes and the moderates. After their victory the sans-culottes became more accustomed to the atmosphere and routine of the assemblies: for many, regular attendance was a proof of civism, and if the forty *sous* indemnity did not attract all the workers, it did, at least, attract quite a number of the poorest.

The documentary evidence available for the period 2 June–9 Thermidor shows that attendances at the general assemblies were particularly high during the second fortnight of June 1793 for the election of the Commander-in-Chief of the Parisian National Guard—a key post in the struggle between the sans-culottes and the moderates. Understandably, the greatest interest was shown in Hanriot's Section—the Section des Sans-Culottes—where, on 19 June, 678 voters were present, and in Raffet's—the Section de la Butte-des-Moulins—where, during the three votes taken on 16, 18, and 27 June, attendances rose from 780 to 824, and finally to 1,215. In the Year II, the highest recorded attendance of 900 in the general assembly of the Section de Bon-Conseil on 10 Ventôse can be explained by the importance of a political debate which excited the interest of the entire Section: Lullier was defending himself against a denunciation of his conduct by citizen Marchand. Only 100 voters were present in the general assembly of the Section Brutus on 15 Germinal for the renewal of the committee; but there were 430 on 15 Floréal for the nomination of the Section's commanding officer, The varying attendances in the Section de la Montagne—formerly the Butte-des-Moulins—from June 1793 to Pluviôse Year II, and for the Section des Invalides from Pluviôse to Messidor, emphasize the fact that when citizens were being elected to military posts, attendances increased noticeably, but fell again to the average level for the election of civil officials. Compelled to serve in the National Guard, but regarding their service as a right more than an obligation, the

MSFR

sans-culottes attached considerable importance to the election of their officers.

There is simply not enough statistical information relating to attendances at the general assemblies for us to measure the extent of the rupture between the sans-culotterie and the Revolutionary Government after Germinal and the execution of Hébert and Chaumette. The little evidence which still exists, gathered from many different sources, seems to indicate that the average attendance did not alter noticeably, the figures rising a little higher for elections to military posts, but falling correspondingly lower for the few nominations to civil offices which still lay within the competence of the assemblies. The attraction of elections, particularly to military positions, persisted. But to what extent were citizens attracted to the ordinary meetings of the assemblies?

After Thermidor, the social and political composition of the general assemblies changed yet again. As the sans-culottes were gradually eliminated, so attendances grew thinner: on 30 Frimaire Year III, there were only forty present in the general assembly of the Section de l'Unité, despite the fact that in 1791 this assembly had been composed of 2,653 active citizens. The Section des Invalides, which had 2,440 voters in the Year II, could only attract an attendance of sixty-nine for the election of the *comité de bienfaisance* on 20 Germinal. Although the *honnêtes gens*, no longer intimidated by the sans-culotterie, flocked back to the primary assemblies towards the end of the Year III after a long break in electoral operations, we must not overlook the conditions which governed electoral procedure at this time if we wish to appreciate the real significance of their return: in the Section des Arcis, the assemblies remained open from seven o'clock in the morning to ten o'clock in the evening and lasted three days. The reign of the *notables* had begun.

What proportion of the popular minority which regularly attended the general assemblies in the Year II benefited from the forty *sous* indemnity? In other words, to what extent did the workers participate in the political life of the Sections?

On 5 September 1793, Danton had proposed that the meetings of the general assemblies should be reduced to two a week, and 'that sans-culottes who attended these assemblies should be compensated for the loss of working-time involved'. As a result, the Convention decreed that 'poor citizens' would be entitled to an indemnity of forty *sous* for every assembly they attended. Four days later, Barère presented the decree which explained the practical application of this measure. Article II stated that 'citizens who had no means of livelihood other than that derived from their daily manual labour would be entitled to an indemnity of forty *sous* a meeting'. Article IV provided for the nomination, by the Sections, of *commissaires* authorized to ascertain 'the degree of want experienced by citizens included in article II', and to check on their attendances in the general assemblies.

This important measure was clothed with a certain ambiguity from the beginning. Did the Convention intend to indemnify salaried workers who attended the general assemblies for the wages they had lost? This was clearly the implication to be drawn from Danton's statement; but when the Convention accepted the principle of the indemnity on 5 September, only 'poor citizens' were mentioned. Was it, then, simply a question of paying sans-culottes who were destitute? Barère was certainly thinking along these lines when on 9 September he recalled the principle adopted four days earlier 'that every citizen who lives solely by the work of his hands would have the right, "in cases of proven need", to an indemnity'. The provision included in article IV— that the *commissaires* appointed by the Sections would be asked to determine the 'degree of want' suffered by sans-culottes entitled to the indemnity—seems to confirm this interpretation. Finally, article II was quite explicit on one point: the indemnity would not be paid automatically to citizens 'who have no other source of income but their daily manual labour'; it simply stated that they 'could' apply for it. The actual decree authorizing the payment of the indemnity was obviously far more limited in its scope than the measure proposed by Danton: it was intended for the destitute sans-culotte rather than the salaried worker. The disrepute heaped upon the indemnity, and upon those who benefited from it, by some of the Sections and the upper ranks of the sans-culotterie in general, narrowed this restrictive interpretation even further. On 14 Ventôse Year II, the police-agent Perrière noted that citizens in the Section des Sans-Culottes continually refused the indemnity 'because, they said, they did not want to be called "forty-*sous* patriots"'.[2]

[2] *A.N.*, W 112.

Numerous difficulties did in fact arise over the payment of the indemnity, giving the authorities in the Sections the pretext of interpreting it in many different ways—all of them restrictive. On 20 Brumaire, the Section de la Montagne decided that domestic servants would not be eligible for the indemnity, which was, strictly, a violation of the decree. The authorities in many of the Sections were clearly reluctant to put the decree into operation. Although, in the Section de Bon-Conseil, a citizen was placed on the list of persons to be paid the indemnity if he was prepared to state 'openly and conscientiously' that he was entitled to it, not one citizen in the Section de la République had received the indemnity by 25 Frimaire. Several citizens complained on this date that they had not been paid one penny by the *commissaires* authorized 'to register the names of those deserving sans-culottes who had been admitted to the general assembly'. There were renewed complaints on 8 and 9 Nivôse. 'Generally speaking, all those citizens who have been given official posts in this Section', wrote one police-agent, 'are just so many despots who do not like the thought of paying out money.' The police-agent Pourvoyeur, writing on 17 Nivôse, thought that the authorities in the Section des Lombards refused to pay the compensation awarded by law to 'destitute citizens', simply because they did not approve of the idea. On 5 Ventôse, during a debate in the general assembly of the Section de la Réunion on the class of citizen who was entitled to the indemnity, it was decided that the law only intended it 'for the really destitute citizen, and not for the workers who earn quite good wages'; a commission was appointed to advise the assembly on 'the best way of ensuring that it will be paid only to those actually in need of it'. On 9 Ventôse, the *comité révolutionnaire* confirmed this decision. In the Section de la Maison-Commune, a ruling on the payment of the indemnity had to wait until 30 Prairial, when a commission of twelve members was formed to determine 'the individual needs and morality of the claimants'; the general assembly was to deal with doubtful cases. Every head of a family who depended entirely upon his occupation for his living would be entitled to the indemnity—if he was a patriot. The commission, 'forced to take into account the disturbing economic situation of the Republic', would have to make inquiries concerning the conduct, financial obligations, the willingness to work, and any accusations made against unmarried workers before their names could be put on the list.[3] The decree of 9 September was being turned into a weapon of discrimination by the introduction of political and moral considerations.

Whatever importance we attach to the limitations imposed by the Sections, the indemnity was subjected to considerable criticism until Thermidor, and undoubtedly aggravated social antagonisms within the ranks of the sans-culotterie. Salaried workers obstinately demanded to be paid, even for extraordinary meetings of the assemblies, whilst the *possédants* continued to hold the opinion that by claiming the indemnity they had forfeited part of their civic rights. After the *commissaires de l'habillement* of the Section Poissonnière had been excluded from the popular society of the Section on 17 Germinal, one of them protested that since 'the assembly was not well-attended—only the *quarante sols* being present—its decision was not legal'. This remark is significant of the hostility between the *possédant* and the ordinary worker, but it also betrays the persistence of the old differentiation between 'active' and 'passive' citizens.

In many of the assemblies, citizens who claimed the indemnity —the *quarante sols*—soon formed a party to which radical patriots like Momoro in the Section Marat looked for support. In the Section de la Réunion, it was the patriot Didot who campaigned for their assistance in his quarrel with the *comité révolutionnaire* which controlled the assembly. On 5 Ventôse, he encouraged the workers who had been excluded from the payment of the indemnity to press the authorities for the forty *sous* which was rightfully theirs. Arrested four days later because, according to the *comité révolutionnaire*, he had tried to organize a party in the assembly, Didot offered his own interpretation 'that he had been arrested because he had championed the cause of the people and had given his support to citizens entitled to the forty *sous*'. The police-agent Jarousseau reported that the payment of the indemnity encouraged the formation of rival groups which struggled to win the allegiance of the *quarante sols* during elections. In the Section des Lombards, according to a report by Pourvoyeur on 17 Nivôse, the authorities frequently withheld payment of the indemnity to destitute citizens in order to reward their faithful supporters in the assembly. The *comité révolutionnaire* of the Section, obviously deciding that attack was the best method of

[3] *A.N.*, F⁷ 4775⁴⁴.

defence, accused a citizen named Rouy of having tried to organize a party amongst the *quarante sols*, for whom he had always 'shown considerable enthusiasm'. After Thermidor, the authorities in the Section des Lombards relentlessly pursued citizens who had benefited from the indemnity, such as the carpenter's apprentice, 'who did not show his face in the assemblies until the passing of the subversive decree which granted forty *sous* to each voter'. His accusers, revealing the bitterness of the *possédants* whose monopoly of power had been momentarily threatened, added that 'perhaps this citizen would never have emerged from the obscurity which nature had apparently intended for him, if the *gouvernement décemviral* had not made something out of him by paying him'.[4]

Taking advantage of the continual disputes and abuses which arose out of the payment of the indemnity, and stressing the financial strain involved, the *possédants* demanded its abolition. On 1 Nivôse, the police-agent Mercier wanted to know why the indemnity was paid on the tenth day of the revolutionary calendar when, in fact, wage-earners did not work on this day. On 14 Ventôse, Perrier remarked that 'a few citizens, apparently wishing to rid the assemblies of this interesting class who naturally favour the idea of a completely popular revolution, are doing everything they can to deprive these fairly poor citizens of the modest sum which the Convention—constantly witnessing its justice and humanity—intended as a compensation for the loss of a part of their valuable time'. Thus we can see how the incompatibility of ideas between the popular revolution and the bourgeois revolution crystallized around the question of the forty *sous* indemnity. It was not really humanitarian principles which had prompted the Convention to authorize its payment in the first place, but the belief that such a measure might weaken the opposition of the sans-culotterie to the suppression of permanence in the Sections. When it came to its actual application, the authorities—usually recruited from the highest ranks of the sans-culotterie—considerably restricted the original scope of the decree by their obvious reluctance to pay the forty *sous* to anyone. The government only intervened after Germinal when the advance of the popular movement had already been halted.

On 27 Floréal, the Section de l'Indivisiblité again presented the

---

[4] *A.N.*, F⁷ 3688³; 4775³; 4639. The term *gouvernement décemviral* being a Thermidorean reference to the Committee of Public Safety.

General Council of the Commune with a denunciation of the abuses arising from the payment of the indemnity, explaining 'that a salutary law does not benefit indifferent or covetous citizens'. These observations were referred to the Committee of Public Safety which decided to favour the restrictive interpretation of the law of 9 September already being practised by some of the Sections: in future, workers would not be compensated for the loss of wages involved in attending the assemblies; only destitute citizens would receive the forty *sous*. Here again, the ideas of jacobin dictatorship had triumphed over those of sans-culotte democracy. On 7 Messidor, the *Comité des secours*, instructed by the Committee of Public Safety, addressed a circular to the Sections of Paris which explained how 'many citizens abuse their right to attend the general assemblies by receiving the forty *sous* granted for that purpose without being entitled to it as destitute citizens, or without bothering to attend at all, or by making only a brief appearance in order to receive the indemnity'. The circular stressed the need for observing the restrictive interpretation of the law of 9 September—the indemnity should only be paid 'to patriots in difficult circumstances'; it was 'assistance which the nation devotes to the relief of poverty alone'.

The circular provided the Sections with the opportunity of revising their lists of citizens entitled to the indemnity. Many of the sans-culottes were eliminated, adding yet another grievance to the many which they already harboured against the Revolutionary Government. Unfortunately, there are not enough documents for us to calculate the precise number of victims of this purge and, consequently, the strength of the opposition it aroused. But on 5 Thermidor, a citizen named Rocherie was arrested in the Section de la Republique for having caused a disturbance in the general assembly—he had objected to his name being struck off the list of citizens entitled to the indemnity. The assembly of the Section de la Maison-Commune, which had adopted a very strict ruling on 30 Prairial, named twelve *commissaires* on 10 Messidor to see that the provisions of the circular issued three days earlier were observed. Their report, presented on 15 Thermidor, denounced the abuse 'which was leading to nothing less than the collapse of our glorious revolution by squandering part of our finances on indemnities which should really be given to our brave soldiers at the front, to their destitute families, and to republicans in straitened circumstances'. The report concluded: 'The Republic does not want salaried patriots.' The commission crossed off the names of 104 sans-culottes, which left a total of ninety-one citizens entitled to the indemnity, all of whom were, without any doubt, destitute.[5]

By this date, sans-culottes democracy had already been dealt a mortal blow. On 4 Fructidor, Bourdon de l'Oise denounced 'the disastrous forty *sous* indemnity', emphasizing that it was 'the intermediate class' (meaning the class between the aristocracy and the sans-culotterie, i.e. bourgeoisie) which had been responsible for the Convention's victory during the night of 9–10 Thermidor. Cambon then rose to protest against the abuses which had arisen out of the payment of the indemnity. The assembly agreed to its abolition.

Whatever the vicissitudes of the indemnity and the restrictions governing the application of the law of 9 September might have been, it would have been of great importance to know the number of beneficiaries in each Section in order to try and assess the influence of the workers upon the political life of the Sections as a whole. However, most of the relevant documents have disappeared. By the law of 13 Frimaire Year III, every authority was obliged to present an account of the money which had passed through its hands since the beginning of the Revolution. In Paris, *commissaires* were appointed for this purpose in each Section. Unfortunately, most of these financial statements are now missing— only those belonging to the Section du Théâtre-Français and the Section du Mont-Blanc have survived. Supplemented by one or two other documents, they emphasize the very small proportion of citizens who benefited from the indemnity in each Section when compared with the total population.

On 11 September in the Section du Temple, according to the police-agent Béraud, only 'just over fifty citizens' were present to receive their forty *sous*—a surprisingly low number when compared with the 1,662 active citizens in the Section on 6 June 1791, the 2,950 voters in the Year II, and the 1,340 destitute citizens receiving assistance (*indigents secourus*) in Germinal Year II. Generally speaking, all the Sections reflected the same proportion. Although 340 citizens were paid the indemnity on 5 Floréal in the Section des Arcis—a relatively high figure—only 99 were paid

[5] *A.N.*, F⁷ 4775⁴⁴.

in the Section de l'Indivisibilité on 25 Floréal. In the Section de la Montagne, the average number of citizens paid the indemnity from 3 October 1793 to 20 Ventôse was 95, although the Section had 2,395 active citizens in 1791, 5,031 voters and 1,008 *indigents secourus* in the Year II. In the Section de la Maison-Commune, 195 names were placed on the list of citizens entitled to the indemnity drawn up before the purge of 15 Thermidor, compared with 1,729 active citizens, 4,258 *indigents secourus*—a particularly high figure—and 3,347 voters.

The records kept by the *commissaires* of the Sections de l'Homme-Armé, Mont-Blanc and Théâtre-Français are more revealing since they cover longer periods. In the Section de l'Homme-Armé, 94 citizens benefited from the indemnity in Floréal, 98 in Prairial, 90 in Messidor and 87 in Thermidor, although this Section had been composed of 1,784 active citizens, 358 *indigents secourus*, and 10,481 inhabitants. From 1 Brumaire to 30 Thermidor the *commissaires* of the Section du Mont-Blanc paid out 8,352 *livres*, representing an average of 69 citizens receiving the indemnity at each meeting of the general assembly, compared with the Section's 856 active citizens, 1,031 *indigents secourus*, and a total population of 10,960. As for the Section du Théâtre-Français, 11,774 *livres* were paid out from 15 September 1793 to 30 Thermidor—an average of 84 citizens who received the indemnity for 1,736 active citizens, 846 *indigents secourus*, and 2,418 voters.

To complete our study, we would need to make an exact investigation of the social position of those sans-culottes who benefited from the indemnity; but the only detailed information we possess is the record of payments made by the *commissaires* of the Section de la Montagne during the general assembly of 20 Ventôse. Of the 105 persons who received the indemnity, 2 were disabled, 9 unemployed, 26 were odd-job men, 6 were operatives or day-labourers and 51 were artisans who were, in all probability, *compagnons*. The number of citizens in this list who were destitute as a result of illness or unemployment was hardly more than one-tenth of the total. But the odd-job men and day-labourers must have lived in rather poor and straitened circumstances. However, it is obvious that we are dealing mainly with sans-culottes whose only source of income was derived from their daily manual labour; although it is not clear whether this income enabled them to rise above the level of poverty.

Frequented in the Year II by a minority of politically active citizens, amongst whom the *quarante sols* were frequently regarded as citizens with diminished rights, the general assemblies—in theory, the sovereign organs of the Sections—would have been rendered powerless if it had not been for the executive organizations which assured them continuity of action.

The Sections, according to the law, were not simply electoral divisions. They represented administrative subdivisions of the Paris Commune, and as such, there were endowed with executive powers, officials, and elected committees. The law of 21 May 1790 placed a committee at the head of each Section which served as an intermediate link between the municipality and the general assembly: the same law provided the Sections with a *commissaire de police* assisted by a *secrétaire-greffier*. When the tribunals of the city of Paris were organized by the law of 25 August–29 September 1790, the Sections received a new official in the *juge de paix*, accompanied by several assessors. Committees with more specific powers, created whenever the necessity arose, were added to these basic political units—*comités militaires*, after the law of 19–21 August 1792 had legalized the new organization of the National Guard following the events of 10 August; *comités révolutionnaires*, created by the law of 21 March 1793; *comités de bienfaisance*, after the passing of the law of 28 March 1793; *commissions de salpêtres* in the Year II, and even *comités d'agriculture* in the spring of 1794. How far did these committees really enable the sans-culottes to exercise their autonomy in the Sections? And also, as a result of the creation of these committees, to what degree were the popular militants able to initiate administrative legislation and make a positive contribution to the political life of the Year II?

After the law of 21 May 1790, the *comités civils* functioned as executive organizations and information agencies within their respective *arrondissements*: they both supervised and assisted the work of the *commissaires de police*. Not only did they attend to the many orders, decrees, and decisions which they received, but they also supplied the municipal authorities, the General Council of the Commune, as well as the mayor and the *procureur*, or his deputies, with the information and advice demanded of them.

The day after the activities of the Commune of 10 August had been suspended, the *comités civils* were nominated according to the procedure adopted under the censitary régime. On 15 August, a new ruling was passed by which the committees were to be elected by the general assemblies. Composed of sixteen members, electing their own presidents and secretaries who were to be renewed every fortnight, the *comités civils* were reinvested with all the powers which had previously been attributed to them. But once the Sections declared themselves to be *en permanence*, the committees began to lose their importance, eventually to fall more or less completely under the control of the general assemblies, jealously guarding their sovereign rights. The assemblies drew up regulations which were designed to keep the committees strictly dependent upon their authority—those of the Section de la République on 30 September and the Section des Gravilliers on 13 October were clearly drafted for this purpose. According to the general assembly of the latter, the *commissaires civils* could be recalled at will—'as mandatories of the assembly, their duty is simply to carry out its orders'. The committee could not take action on any matter without referring it to the assembly which was the only body authorized to make decisions. It could not even issue provisional decrees; 'its function is to deal with all the details of police administration'. The ruling laid down precisely how the registers and records of the committee should be kept, and how they should be verified. Finally, the committee had to report to the general assembly every eight days. By such methods, the people could safeguard their sovereign rights and retain the autonomous authority of the Sections.

The *comités civils*, like all the executive bodies nominated by the Sections, were placed in an ambiguous situation. Elected by the general assemblies, they were their representatives and mandatories; but as administrators, they were dependent upon the Commune, authorized to carry out its instructions even when they contradicted the wishes of the assemblies. However, inundated with work, and wisely confining their activity to the administrative field alone, the *comités civils* did not come into open conflict with the assemblies. In 1793, as in the Year II, they played a very minor role in the general political struggle; and on 31 May in particular, they were careful to stay discreetly in the background. The fact

that the *comités révolutionnaires* had supplanted them in importance by this time made it all the easier for them to do so—until
7 Fructidor Year II, the *comités civils* only acted in a subsidiary
capacity, although, during periods of crisis such as 9 Thermidor,
the two committees deliberated together.

In the Year II, the *comités civils* devoted their energies mainly to
the problems of food supplies and relief work—a field in which
there was never any clear line of demarcation between their own
powers and those of the *comités de bienfaisance*. The distribution
of bread and meat called for a particularly active supervision on the
part of the *commissaires civils*: the regulations adopted by the
Section de la Maison-Commune and the Section du Mont-Blanc
on 27 July and 15 September respectively indicate the importance
which the *commissaires* attached to this aspect of their work. It
was frequently discovered that, despite their conscientiousness,
there were too few *commissaires* to carry out all the duties
assigned to them. On 25 Ventôse Year II, for example, the *comité
civil* of the Section des Invalides asked the general assembly for
six assistants.

The zeal shown by the *commissaires civils* was particularly
praiseworthy when we recall that until the spring of 1794 they
received no financial reward whatsoever for their work. It is true
that a municipal decree of 18 January 1791 had granted 1,200
livres to each committee—a sum which was far too small in the
opinion of the committees, and which was the subject of many
protests—but the intention was that this money should only be
used to defray expenses. When the Sections began to meet *en
permanence*, it was in fact realized that this figure was ridiculously
inadequate, and on 2 April 1793 the Commune granted the sum
of 3,000 *livres* to each Section so that the *comités civils* could pay
off the debts which they had contracted since 10 August. The figure
allocated to each committee was then raised to 1,500 *livres* a year
from 1 January, and to 1,900 *livres* from 25 April 1793 according
to a decree issued by the Commune which stipulated that this sum
would be paid 'as long as the Sections continued to meet *en
permanence*'. These measures did not satisfy the *commissaires civils*,
who naturally resented the fact that from 5 September 1792, the
members of the *comités révolutionnaires* had been paid three *livres*,
and from 8 November, five *livres* a day. The political significance
involved in this question of payment was emphasized by a member

of the General Council of the Commune on 11 September, who thought that 'in future, sans-culottes who are appointed to the *comités civils* should be compensated by the payment of a salary. Since a man cannot be expected to live off the air he breathes,' he explained, 'the failure to adopt such a measure would mean that the exclusive right of filling these positions would fall to our bewigged citizens; to former lawyers, notaries, and attorneys who, to say the least, are all suspected of a certain lack of civic responsibility.' On 22 Brumaire, the general assemblies, now controlled by the sans-culottes, entered the controversy. On the initiative of the Section de l'Observatoire, twenty-six Sections asked the Convention to pay the *commissaires civils* the same compensation as the *commissaires révolutionnaires*, convinced that the Convention did not 'want to see the committees filled only by merchants and the rich, to see poor but virtuous citizens excluded'. But since these petitions did not attract the unanimous support of the Sections, the Convention persuaded itself that it was all the more justified in postponing any decision. When the Section de l'Observatoire again tried to raise the issue on 10 Pluviôse, the Section de la Montagne refused to discuss it, pointing out that 'the true sans-culotte, if he devotes his time to public affairs, will always find the assistance and encouragement he needs amongst his brothers and in the good opinion of honest citizens': the social composition of the Section de la Montagne—formerly the Section de la Butte-des-Moulins—was one of the least popular in the capital. On 6 Floréal, however, the Convention finally gave way and granted the *commissaires civils* an indemnity of three *livres* a day 'for the time they are obliged to spend on matters of public interest'.[6]

This concession came too late, despite its retroactive nature, to alter the composition of the *comités civils*. Most of the *commissaires* employed at this time had been appointed in August or September 1792: there were very few sans-culottes who could have afforded the sacrifice of working without any financial reward. This explains why the members of the *comités civils* were chosen from the more affluent ranks of the lower bourgeoisie— many of them were retired tradesmen and artisans, small *rentiers* and citizens from the liberal professions. Of all the political organiza- tions in the Sections, the *comités civils* were the least popular.

[6] *Moniteur*, xx, 315.

The *comités civils* evolved in the same way as all the other institutions by which the Sections manifested their autonomy. Originally elected as mandatories of their fellow citizens, the status of the *commissaires civils* declined in importance as the authority of the Revolutionary Government increased; the appointment of *commissaires* soon depended upon the approval of the governmental Committees, and, ultimately, they became little more than the salaried officials of the municipality. This evolution, which was practically imperceptible to begin with, gathered momentum during the spring of 1794 and was completed after the fall of the Revolutionary Government. Although the law of 7 Fructidor Year II, which reduced the number of *comités révolutionnaires* to twelve, restored the *comités civils* to their former importance, and also conferred certain new powers upon them, the Convention decided on 28 Vendémiaire Year III that the number of *commissaires* in each Section would be reduced to twelve, four of them being renewed every three months by the *Comité de législation*. The *comités civils*, domesticated in this way by the government, survived for another year: they were finally abolished by the law of 19 Vendémiaire Year IV. With their suppression, the last vestige of the autonomy of the Sections disappeared.

The two most important officials in the municipal organization of the censitary period were the *commissaire de police* and the *juge de paix*, both attached to the *comité civil*. They remained in office throughout the Year II, but here again, the strengthening of the Revolutionary Government meant that the nature of their office changed.

According to the provisions of the municipal law of 21 May 1790, each Section could appoint a *commissaire de police* for a period of two years—with the possibility of re-election—from the citizens of the *arrondissement*. He was given important powers. He had the right to participate in the deliberations of the *comité civil*, and could proceed with the imprisonment of any citizen caught in the act of committing a crime, after receiving the signature of one of the *commissaires civils*. Subordinate to him, a *secrétaire-greffier*, also appointed for two years and eligible for re-election, recorded the minutes of the meetings of the *comité civil*, prepared the dispatches and correspondence, and kept the registers dealing with the affairs of both the committee and the commissariat. Suspended by the Commune of 10 August, re-elected by the decree of 19 September 1792, the *commissaires de police* emerged with their powers confirmed. After this date, they were recruited from amongst the more popular sections of the population: a salary of 3,000 *livres* a year—1,800 for the *secrétaires-greffier*— brought these offices within the reach of the sans-culotterie. In the autumn of 1793, however, their influence began to decline: they became simply the assistants of the *comités révolutionnaires*.

The *juges de paix* and their assessors were installed in office in the Sections following the law of 25 August–29 September 1790 which organized the tribunals of Paris. They were authorized to judge personal and property cases not exceeding the sum of fifty *livres*, and to handle appeal cases of up to 100 *livres*. It was also within their jurisdiction to deal with actions for damages, cases concerning the right of possession, repairs for which a tenant was liable, the payment of salaries and the honouring of agreements between employers and employees, and, finally, cases of slander and assault in which the parties involved had not been charged under the criminal law. Elected in the same way as the *commissaires de police* for a period of two years, and, eligible for re-election, it was on the advice of the *juges de paix* that the Legislative Assembly abolished the distinction between active and passive citizens on 10 August 1792. On 15 August, the Commune altered the procedure by which they were to be elected. In future, the *comités de section* were composed of eighteen members, and of the two candidates who were elected to the committee with the highest number of votes, the first was appointed as *juge de paix*, the second as the recorder. After the other sixteen members of the committee had been nominated as *commissaires*, the six candidates with the highest remaining number of votes were appointed as assessors.

The salaries of the *juges de paix* were fixed at 2,400 *livres* a year, to which was added their fees for affixing, witnessing, and the breaking of seals: his secretary, or recorder, only received 800 *livres*, plus a percentage of the fees. Despite the salary, the offices of the *juges de paix* became only slightly more democratic in 1793. They remained the appanage of the upper ranks of the lower bourgeoisie, offices for which one needed a certain legalistic frame of mind which the real sans-culotte never possessed. Consequently, the *juges de paix* were usually recruited from citizens who had been attached to some branch of the legal profession under the *ancien régime*, but who had since declared their sympathies for the popular cause. Once the Revolutionary Government had been organized, the Sections lost their right of appointing the *juges de paix* and their recorders—after the decrees of 8 Nivôse and 23 Floréal Year II, these officials were nominated by the General Council of the Commune.

These civil institutions were but one aspect of the autonomy of the Sections. Even more striking was the creation of an armed force in each Section which the sans-culottes invaded, from the lowest to the highest ranks, in the Year II.

In 1789, the bourgeois National Guard, spontaneously modelling its organization on the districts, had been divided into sixty battalions. This division was retained by the decree of 12–23 September 1791—which gave active citizens the exclusive right of serving in the Guard—despite the fact that the numerical agreement between battalion and district had been broken by the law of 21 May 1790 creating the forty-eight Sections. This anomaly was the subject of continual protests. The Section de la Croix-Rouge on 9 May 1792 announced that the whole plan had been 'treacherously conceived' in order to deprive the Sections of the free disposition of their armed forces. Whatever the justification for this charge, the anomaly did not survive the events of 10 August. On the thirteenth, in fact, the General Council of the Commune authorized the Sections to divide citizens into companies, and since the distinction between active and passive citizens had been abolished, everyone was to be armed. The government gave legal sanction for this measure by the law of 19–21 August, which slightly modified the original plan. The Parisian National Guard was divided into forty-eight 'armed Sections'; the number of companies in each Section being proportional to the population. At the head of each force came the Commander-in-Chief, followed by the acting commander, an adjutant and an ensign. Each company was to be composed of 126 men, and each Section would possess at least one company of artillery. Every citizen in the Section could participate in the election of commanders, officers, and non-commissioned officers. The Commander-General of the National Guard was to be chosen every three months by an assembly of all the Sections, with the possibility of re-election, although his tenure in office could not exceed one year.

Thus the Sections held complete control of their armed force. They carefully supervised the election of officers, and soon arrogated the right of dismissing those who failed to carry out their duties satisfactorily. In order to co-ordinate all the questions which arose between the different companies, military committees or *comités de guerre* were formed, which, if necessary, could be transformed into disciplinary councils. The Section du Théâtre-Français appointed a military committee after 10 August which was reconstituted as a disciplinary body in 1793. The *comité de guerre* of the Section des Lombards, composed of twenty-eight members elected by the general assembly, provides a similar example—it centralized the funds collected by the captains; distributed the assistance promised to volunteers, as well as to their parents, wives and children; corresponded with the administrative council of the battalion fighting on the frontiers, and provided its armament, clothing and equipment. All this work was subjected to the close scrutiny of the general assembly. Through these *comités de guerre*, the Sections were in constant touch with citizens serving in the armies, both encouraging them and surveilling their conduct. The numerous addresses sent to the armies, as well as the dispatch of *commissaires* to the front, prove how determined the Sections were that no gulf should separate the nation from its armies. On 14 May 1793, for example, the Section de la Halle-au-Blé appointed a *commissaire* to accompany volunteers from the Section to the Vendée, charging him to maintain an active correspondence with the general assembly.[7] The disciplinary councils—only slightly modified versions of the military committees—were composed of representatives from all ranks. Their specific task was to ensure the execution of the special regulations governing military service which were elaborated by the various Sections—the Section du Marais on 5 September 1792, Section du Panthéon-Français on 29 Pluviôse Year II and the Section de Popincourt on 10 Germinal. Yet another manifestation of sectionary autonomy.

After 9 Thermidor, the governmental Committees soon realized how this autonomous military force in the Sections could be employed against the central power: as early as 19 Thermidor,

_____
[7] *Moniteur*, xvi, 395.

the Commander-General and the staff of the Parisian National Guard were brought under the direct control of the Convention and its two Committees. During the Year III, the National Guard was remodelled several times with the intention of weakening its popular characteristics and strengthening the control exercised over it by the government. On 13 Frimaire, the Convention decided that citizens who served in the Guard had to be able to read and write, which meant that many sans-culottes were eliminated from the lower ranks. After the *journées* of Germinal, the law 28 Frimaire ended the association between the battalion and the Section and brought the National Guard under the direction of the *Comité militaire* of the Convention. Following the *journées* of Prairial, on the twentieth of the month, the Sections were forced to surrender the cannons which they had retained throughout this period, and to which they had attached such great importance. The final blow came on 16 Vendémiaire Year IV when the National Guard was placed under the orders of the Commander-in-Chief of the Army of the Interior. Events had proved that the para-military organizations of the Sections could not survive the collapse of the popular régime of the Year II.

Of all the popular institutions created by the Revolution which, in their evolution, accurately reflect its changing course, the *comités révolutionnaires* best symbolize, if not the autonomy, then certainly the exercise of popular power by the Sections.

After 10 August, certain Sections, either imitating the example or obeying the instructions of the Commune and its *comité de surveillance*, organized genuine *comités de surveillance révolutionnaire* which foreshadow those created by the law of 21 March 1793—the Section du Théâtre-Français on 11 August, for example, closely followed by the Section des Amis-de-la-Patrie which created a committee of fourteen members, and the Section des Postes on 21 August with a committee of twelve. Acting upon orders issued by the Commune, these committees were especially charged with the responsibility of examining and surveilling the conduct of suspects.

The crisis in March 1793 led to the creation of new committees. On the thirteenth, the general assembly of the Section de la Croix-Rouge organized a '*comité révolutionnaire*' to receive denunciations and search the homes of accused citizens, which replaced the *comité de sûreté générale* created after 10 August. The new committee was not dependent on the Commune for its instructions, but acted of its own authority. The evening before, the Section du Théâtre-Français had authorized its *comité de surveillance* to issue arrest warrants against citizens 'suspected of holding counter-revolutionary opinions'. The Convention decided to legalize the birth of an institution which was spreading through the Sections, and on 21 March 1793, a law was passed sanctioning the creation of committees of twelve members in each commune or Section of a commune. But the powers of these committees were singularly restricted—they could only supervise the conduct of strangers.

The new committees saw their competence widen rapidly. Elected at the end of March or the beginning of April in a general atmosphere of violence, composed mainly of proven sans-culottes, these committees were quickly organized as a striking-force against the moderates. From 1 April 1793, the general assembly of the Section du Panthéon-Français 'provisionally' granted its *comité révolutionnaire* 'all the necessary unlimited powers so that it can effectively preserve the nation from danger and protect the general safety of its citizens'. Having received a request from the Section du Luxembourg for more detailed information concerning the work of the committees, the Commune issued a circular on 4 April which aimed at co-ordinating their functions, but which also extended the scope of their activities. Apart from the surveillance of strangers, the circular authorized the committees to issue 'civic identity cards' (*cartes civiques*), examine the credentials of military personnel—imprisoning anyone whose papers were not in order—and arrest citizens who were not wearing cockades.[8] A singular increase in authority when compared with the powers conferred upon the committees by the law of 21 March.

The law of 17 September 1793 which authorized the committees to draw up lists of suspects, issue warrants for their arrest and affix the seals to their papers, simply legalized powers which the committees had, in fact, already conferred upon themselves. The comprehensive definition of the word 'suspicion' given by the Commune meant a corresponding increase in the competence of the committees, which, having shaken off the tutelage of the general assemblies, and already beginning to disregard even the

[8] *B.N.*, Lb[40] 1181.

authority of the Commune, now tended to control the entire political life of the Sections. Militating against the popular desire for autonomy, they became, in fact, the effective agents of revolutionary centralization.

One of the ways in which the governmental Committees could modify the *comités révolutionnaires*, and by which they eventually succeeded in bringing them completely under their control, was the indemnity granted to the *commissaires*. During the first few months of their existence, the *commissaires* had received no payment whatsoever, although the government had provided for the costs of the secretariat. On 27 April 1793, delegates from all the Sections met in the Section du Contrat-Social to press for an indemnity—an indispensable measure if the committees were to function smoothly and recruitment made more democratic. They received no satisfaction until after the events of 2 June. On 12 July, the departmental Committee of Public Safety agreed that the *commissaires révolutionnaires* should be paid a salary of three *livres* a day, and to meet the cost of this concession, the sum of 30,000 *livres* was placed at the disposal of the mayor of Paris. The Convention legalized these proceedings on 5 September. On 18 Brumaire Year II, the indemnity was raised to five *livres* a day.

The payment of the *commissaires révolutionnaires* transformed the nature of their office. Elected until this time by the general assemblies, the *commissaires* had been regarded as mandatories of the Sections, acting independently of the administrative authorities. They now became salaried officials placed under the control of the Commune; for on 5 September, immediately after granting the three *livres* indemnity, the Convention went on to decree that the *commissaires* would have to pass through the *scrutin épuratoire* of the General Council which had the powers to dismiss unsuitable officials and to make new appointments. The passing of the law of suspects on 17 September, stating that the committees would in future be required to correspond directly, and exclusively, with the Committee of General Security, increased the control exercised over the committees by the government, although they now escaped the surveillance of the Commune. The circular issued by Pache on 27 Brumaire Year II, in which he points out that if the committees now had to correspond only with the Committee of General Security in matters concerning the arrest of suspects, there was no reason why they should not keep the Commune informed of their work in other spheres, shows quite clearly that this last move by the government did not meet with the approval of the Commune. The municipal authorities tried hard to regain control of the powers which were gradually escaping them. All the members of the *comités révolutionnaires* were summoned by Chaumette to a meeting arranged for 14 Frimaire, but the Convention, encouraged by the acquiescent attitude of the committees themselves, succeeded in defeating the plans of Chaumette and the Commune before any real resistance could be organized.

On 6 Pluviôse Year II, a representative from the committee of the Section du Finistère was sent to the Committee of General Security to discover the correct procedure for replacing a *commissaire* who had been dismissed. The question was referred to the Committee of Public Safety which failed to offer any advice. The committee of the Section du Finistère then wrote to the latter authority to suggest that on no account should nominations be left in the hands of the general assemblies, where, all too often, the 'hypocrites of the Revolution' (*les tartuffes en révolution*) were in a position to influence decisions, but that they should be subjected to the shrewder judgement of the committees themselves, the Commune retaining its right of censure. This procedure was, in fact, adopted for a short time—on 22 Pluviôse, the Commune confirmed the nominations of two new *commissaires* chosen by the committee of the Section des Piques. But the responsibility of appointing new *commissaires* was soon left to the *comités révolutionnaires*, to pass finally, through them, into the hands of the governmental authorities. The Committee of Public Safety, which had remained silent in Pluviôse because it did not feel strong enough to encroach upon the attributions of the Committee of General Security, emerged with increased powers after the crisis of Ventôse: on 9 Germinal, the two Committees joined to nominate the purged *comité révolutionnaire* of the Section de Marat. In Pluviôse, the task of appointing *commissaires*—the subject of continual controversy between the two Committees— was entirely taken over by the Committee of Public Safety, leaving the general assemblies to protest in vain against this violation of their sovereign rights.

The *comités révolutionnaires*, which had constituted one of the cornerstones of jacobin dictatorship, did not survive the 9 Thermidor. The law of 7 Fructidor replaced them by twelve *comités de surveillance d'arrondissement*, each having four Sections within its sphere of jurisdiction. The Committee of General Security was given the responsibility of organizing the new committees which were to remain under its direct control. The provision that every member had to be able to read and write unquestionably excluded the humbler ranks of the sans-culotterie.

By virtue of their recruitment, particularly after the Commune had carried out its purge, the *comités révolutionnaires* had been the most democratic of all the political institutions organized in the Sections. Whilst the *comités civils*, which received no payment until 6 Floréal Year II, were recruited from the more affluent sections of the sans-culotterie, the *comités révolutionnaires*, salaried as early as July 1793 and playing essentially a political role, were chiefly composed of sans-culottes of modest, sometimes even humble, means. They saw in their office, not only the opportunity of devoting themselves to the Republic, but often a way of earning a better living and of rising in the social scale.

Both the civil and military institutions of the Sections can be traced back to the beginning of the Revolution; they had first taken shape during the censitary period. Originally influenced by the desire for local autonomy which characterized those citizens who benefited under the censitary system, then by the impact of popular forces struggling to share in the spoils of power, the nature of these institutions changed rapidly. These changes, however, only reflected the general direction of the Revolution itself which tended to become increasingly autonomous and popular in character. As instruments of revolutionary politics they were unquestionably effective; particularly when compared with the institutions of State and those of the central power— neither 10 August nor 31 May would have been possible without the organization and the striking-force which the Sections placed at the disposal of the insurrectionary committees. Created by the Revolution, these sectionary institutions devoted their energies to its success, and were rewarded in return with increased authority. But, tending to lose their adaptability, they eventually fell under the control of the Revolutionary Government which they had been instrumental in bringing to power.

There was also a double contradiction which undermined them and made their downfall inevitable. How could they reconcile the popular desire for local autonomy with the strengthening of the central power and the claims of jacobin dictatorship? And even more important, how could they win the support of the bourgeoisie —once the danger from the counter-revolution had passed—for institutions which only served to reflect the revolutionary enthusiasm of the sans-culotterie, and which remained undeniably popular in character? The sectionary institutions disappeared after 9 Thermidor, swept away by the wave of reaction, but it was the stabilization of the Revolutionary Government which had already determined their fate.

Once the permanence of the Sections had been abolished and the sectionary committees forced to submit to the will of the central power, the militant sans-culottes, fearing for the autonomy of their organizations and impatient with the control exercised over them by the Revolutionary Government, adapted an old institution to meet their new requirements—they transformed the popular societies into *sociétés sectionnaires*, or created the latter where no popular society existed. Since 1791, the Parisian popular societies had made a significant contribution towards the success of the Revolution: in the Year II, it was the *société sectionnaire* which represented the fundamental organization of the popular movement. Through these institutions, the militant sans-culottes directed the political thought of the Sections, controlled the administration, and exercised an influence on municipal and governmental authorities.

Whilst the moderates intended the societies to be simply educational in character, the patriots were determined from the beginning that they should play a political role. During the great debate in the Constituent Assembly in September 1791, which resulted in the societies being forbidden to participate in any political activity, Brissot and Robespierre joined forces to protest against this limitation. Brissot thought the societies should have three objectives: 'to discuss what laws should be passed; to explain laws which are passed; and to supervise the conduct of all public officials'. For Robespierre, their mission was to watch over and protect the rights of the nation. Marat, however, with his shrewd political insight, had predicted in *l'Ami du peuple* as early as 7

February 1791 the role which the *sociétés sectionnaires* would, and did, play most effectively in the Year II. He foresaw that the popular clubs would not be content simply with educating and informing citizens; the patriots in each Section would discuss the decrees submitted to the general assemblies, and, 'in this way, the members of the clubs will bring a considered judgement to the general assemblies of their respective Sections, and save good citizens from being deafened in future by the endless prattle of word-peddlars'. The popular societies would also keep a watch on the conduct of public officials, even those employed at government level.

Although on 10 August 1792, the oldest of the fraternal societies —meeting at the Bibliothèque des Jacobins Saint-Honoré— thought that the *sociétés sectionnaires* should devote their time to the instruction of citizens, the *société patriotique de la section du Pont-Neuf* on 6 June 1792 obviously meant to create an organ of control and surveillance—events were influencing the societies to participate actively in politics. From this point of view, the crisis of the spring of 1793 was decisive. According to their declaration on 18 April, the *société populaire et patriotique du Mail* was not only going 'to root out intrigue, combat malevolence, unmask guile, encourage civic zeal, and revive languishing patriotism'; it also intended to campaign tirelessly against 'royalism, fanaticism, *moderantisme*, and rolandism, which is the worst crime of all'. Its members would be active and indefatigable missionaries; its crusade would be devoted to the cause of freedom. The part played by the societies in the struggle against the moderates and federalism was such that the Convention, on 25 July 1793, passed a penal decree protecting them from any attack. On 22 August, denouncing the municipality of Nancy which had tried to dissolve its own society, the Jacobins demanded the death penalty 'against anyone who tried to suppress these patriotic retreats'.[9]

As long as danger threatened from within the nation, the Committees of the government deliberately encouraged the activities of the popular societies in order to give the revolutionary régime time to adjust itself, and to provide a greater impetus for the war effort. On 23 Brumaire Year II, the Committee of Public Safety asked the Parisian societies to draw up a list of citizens

[9] *Journal de la Montagne*, 23 August 1793; *Moniteur*, xvii, 459.

'best qualified to fill all kinds of public offices'. Although the organic decree of 14 Frimaire did not determine the place of the societies in the Revolutionary Government, and even prohibited them from sending *commissaires* or organizing any congress or central committee, the Committee of Public Safety thought it wise to assign a particular role to them by its circular of 16 Pluviôse. The societies were to be organs of surveillance and vigilance; they were to assist the *représéntants en mission* in their task of purging and organizing the constituted authorities; and collaborate with these authorities in nominating citizens to public office.

However important this role might have appeared to the Committee of Public Safety, it represented a comparatively minor one to that actually played by the popular societies. The circular of 16 Pluviôse can only be regarded as another abortive attempt in the tireless campaign waged by the governmental Committees to discipline the popular movement, to relegate it to a position of secondary importance. In fact, throughout the winter of the Year II, the societies—particularly the *sociétés sectionnaires*—far from being satisfied with this role, constituted the basic units of political life in the Sections.

From the autumn to the spring of the Year II, a vast network encompassed the capital. Whether they had already been founded when the permanence of the Sections was abolished or not, most of the popular societies tended to become societies of the Sections (*sociétés sectionnaires*).

Although it is sometimes difficult to discover the precise date of their foundation, it appears that two popular societies created in 1790, and three in 1791, had met continuously until the Year II. Of eight societies founded in 1792, four before 10 August and three created after this date, also met regularly until the Year II. The crisis of 1793 led to the formation of seven popular societies before the end of September. Finally, twenty-six were created in order to circumvent the provisions of the law abolishing the permanence of the general assemblies, and appear from the date of their foundation as *sociétés sectionnaires*. Occasionally, two rival societies met for a short time in the same Section. In the Section du Contrat-Social, for example, we find the *société des Amis-de-la-Patrie*, founded early in the Revolution, and the *société sectionnaire*, created on 26 September 1793; and in the Section des Gravilliers, the *société des Amis-de-la-Liberté, de l'Egalité-et-de-l'Humanité,* which met in the rue de Vert-Bois, as well as the *société section-naire*. Here, the old societies, favoured by the authorities and the Jacobins, managed to overcome the challenge from their new rivals which were forced to dissolve: an episode in the conflict between the 'patriots of 89' and the 'patriots of 93'—called 'the new brood'—a conflict in which social differences cannot be ignored. In the Section de la Réunion, however, the older but less flourishing fraternal society of the rue Saint-Avoye was absorbed by the new *société sectionnaire*, and the same process appears to have taken place in the Section de l'Unité.

Alongside these societies, old or new, which functioned at the base of the Section, a few founded at the beginning of the Revolution continued to meet in the Year II without becoming *sociétés sectionnaires*. In the Section du Montreuil we find the *société des Amis-des-Droits-de-l'Homme, Ennemis-du-despotisme*, founded in 1791; and the *Défenseurs-des-Droits-de-l'Homme-et-du-Citoyen* in the Section de la Maison-Commune. Apart from the respected *société fraternelle des Patriotes-des-deux-sexes* meeting at the Jacobin club, perhaps we should mention of the most important remaining societies—the *société des Hommes-du-14-Juillet* (formerly the *société des Gardes-Françaises*); the *société des Défenseurs-de-la-République-une-et-indivisible* which met at the café Chrétien in the former place des Italiens; the *société des Hommes-Révolution-naires-du-Dix-août* meeting where the *société des Filles-Dieu* had once met in the rue Saint-Denis; the *club électoral de l'Evêché*, and the *société populaire et républicaine des Arts*. These societies were usually frequented by militants, who, in different ways and at different times, had played an important part in the memorable events of the Revolution—14 July, 10 August, 31 May. It is not surprising, therefore, that we frequently find them as leading organizations of revolutionary activity in the Year II. The Cordelier club, although it stood on a high plane, fell into much the same category. As for the Jacobin club, it is true that the sans-culottes—women in particular—faithfully attended its meetings, but their practical influence was negligible. The militant in the Sections felt more at ease in their own societies which formed a protective ring around the popular movement from the autumn of 1793 to the spring of the Year II.

Following the example of the Jacobins, the popular societies compiled a list of regulations defining their aims, conditions of membership. and the procedure to be adopted at their meetings. The older societies had drawn up similar regulations as early as 1790–1, which had served as the inspiration for those adopted by the societies founded in 1792. A year later, these societies decided to revise their rules in the light of the changed political situation, modifying statements of principle, rephrasing the form of their oaths, and altering the conditions of membership. Finally, in the autumn or the beginning of the winter of the Year II, the *sociétés sectionnaires* decided upon their own regulations which were often copied from those of the older societies.

The rules begin with a statement of the aims of the society. The *société du Luxembourg*, which revised its rules on 19 February 1793, wanted to establish 'frequent communication between citizens which will widen and increase their knowledge and their patriotism by uniting them for a common purpose'. During the discussion on the part to be played by the societies, one of the members, anxious to separate their role from that of the general assemblies, referred to them as schools of republicanism and morality. The *société des Hommes-Libres* in the Section du Pont-Neuf stated unequivocally on 28 August 1793 that its main aim would be the instruction of its members—each meeting would be devoted to the reading and discussion of matters of public interest, talks on the Constitution, the Rights of Man, their obligation as citizens, and on an appreciation of the laws. In its plan of organization on 5 October, the *société fraternelle des Amis-de-la-Patrie* placed the accent on surveillance rather than instruction: 'Everyone of us must supervise the conduct of those charged with the government of the Republic', referring, of course, to public officials, but also to contractors who supplied the armies—'those leeches of the State'. The *société des Amis-de-la-République* in the Section des Piques intended to concern itself mainly with instruction. In its ruling of 19 October, it outlined its aims as 'the study and understanding of the laws, the discussion of topics of public interest, the protection of the oppressed, the surveillance of traitors, the denunciation of their plots, and correspondence with all true friends of liberty and equality'. The last to issue its regulations, the *société de la rue Montreuil* announced in Germinal Year II that apart from surveillance and instruction, its members would be called upon to provide mutual assistance. The *société de*

Belleville stated its aims quite simply as 'the surveillance of those who govern us, the instruction of the public and the propagation of good morals and patriotism'. Finally, the *société populaire de Sceaux* intended 'to supervise the conduct of the constituted authorities—the only means of keeping them to the path of duty— to enlighten our brothers as to their rights; to accord protection and assistance to the oppressed'.[1]

Having stated their aims, the regulations then go on to define the conditions of admission. Usually, if a citizen had proved his patriotism during the great events of the Revolution, he was admitted without question. The *société patriotique du Luxembourg* admitted 'all citizens attracted by their patriotism who, judged by their sense of civic duty, are considered worthy of joining this association'. The *société républicaine des Marchés* welcomed 'every patriotic citizen' in the Section; the *société des Amis-de-la-Patrie*, 'all citizens recognized as being good patriots and true republicans'; whilst the *société des Amis-de-la-République* in the Section des Piques simply invited 'patriots'. According to the rules of the *société de la Halle-au-Blé*—reproduced from those of the *société des Gardes-Françaises*—no citizen would be admitted 'if he cannot prove his constant and universally accepted patriotism, and if he does not personally complete his military service'. As far as the *société des Vertus-Républicaines* in the Section de l'Observatoire was concerned, every 'honest French citizen' qualified for admission; for the *société de la Section de Montreuil*, it was necessary to have 'the qualities required of a good republican' which are not defined; whilst for the *société des Amis-des-Droits-de-l'Homme* in the same Section, a member had only to be an honest citizen 'believing in virtue and good morals'.

These rather general conditions, however, would not have guaranteed the smooth functioning of the popular societies without certain added precautions. Most of the societies were careful to exclude, in advance, all those citizens who were members of monarchical clubs, the feuillant club or the *club de la Sainte-Chapelle*, as well as the signatories of anti-civic petitions. In addition, the *société des Gardes-Françaises* and the *société de la Halle-au-Blé* refused to admit citizens who had contributed 'to the depravation of morals, whether by accepting prostitutes as tenants, or by engaging in similar dealings which offend the

[1] *A.D.S.*, 4 AZ 590; 3 AZ 159[2].

integrity and austere life of the true republican'. The *société des Amis-de-la-Patrie* also proscribed notaries; whilst the *société de la Maison-Commune* refused admission to any supporter of Lafayette. The *société de la Section Poissonnière* required every prospective member to mount the *tribune* and state 'what he had done for the Revolution since it began': every citizen who criticized the *journées* of 20 June and 10 August 1792, 31 May and 2 June 1793 would be rejected. The *société de l'Unité* prepared a list of citizens who would be ineligible for admission which included, priests, nobles, attorneys, lawyers, 'and, as a rule, every public official who has not proved his attachment to the Revolution, apart from carrying out his official duties', as well as citizens who frequented 'the company of notorious suspects and aristocrats', 'every egoist who makes speculative gains out of the misery of the people', and 'finally, every citizen who refuses to comply with the regulations of the law on basic commodities'. The *société section-naire de la République* confronted its candidates with a series of questions: 'What did you do before the Revolution? What have you done since the Revolution? What have you done for the Revolution? Have you ever been a noble, a banker or a stock-broker?'[2]

The candidates were generally presented by members of the society who were prepared to guarantee their good conduct. A list of candidates was then drawn up by the admittance committee, and the prospective members asked to submit to an interrogation before the assembled society—in some societies, candidates were publicly examined on three consecutive occasions. The *société Poissonnière* adopted the practice of leaving the names of candidates pinned to the door of the assembly hall for a period of eight days. The minimum age for admission, when specified, was seventeen, and the candidate's first act on being admitted was to take the oath. These precautions did not satisfy the *société des Marchés* which sent its list of prospective members to the *comité révolution-naire* 'for it to be purged, inviting the committee to single out those members whose patriotism and morals might be open to suspicion'. Most of the regulations provide for a periodic purge of the membership as a guarantee against any lapse of civic responsibility or patriotism. The *société du Luxembourg* announced 'that there will be a civic revision at the end of every quarter'. In fact, these strict conditions did not immunize the popular societies,

[2] *A.D.S.*, D 989.

and particularly the *sociétés sectionnaires*, from accusations of unpatriotic behaviour. Subjected to these criticisms, and the sly attacks of the Jacobins, the societies replied with more purges, becoming increasingly frequent during the winter of the Year II when the Revolutionary Government had reason to suspect that they might provide the necessary support for another popular movement. When the Jacobins, in an attempt to discredit them, refused the societies their affiliation, they purged themselves in order to prove their patriotism. The *société de la section des Piques*, for example, adopted a ruling for a purge of its membership on 22 Pluviôse Year II. The work had been prepared by a committee of twenty members, appointed as early as 14 Nivôse; it was submitted to the *comité révolutionnaire* which gave the ruling its approval. The increased authority of the Revolutionary Government had forced the societies to make a substantial withdrawal from the positions which they held during the autumn.

As a rule, the payment of a subscription—low enough even for the poorest sans-culotte to afford—acknowledged that a citizen was a member of a society. When the *sociétés des Hommes-Libres* in the Section du Pont-Neuf planned to fix its subscription rate at four *livres*, one speaker pointed out on 1 September 1793 'that he would have to lower the entrance-fee if we wished to give every true sans-culotte the opportunity of swelling the numbers of the society, which only stands to gain by admitting the purest section of the population'. On the eighteenth, the membership fee was lowered to three *livres*, and the quarterly subscription at thirty *sous*. The *société des Amis-de-la-Patrie* asked for a maximum subscription of three *livres* and a minimum of thirty *sous*, without indicating when members were expected to pay—citizens 'of modest means' were not expected to pay anything at all. In the *société de l'Unité*, the rate was three *livres* for the first three months, and two *livres* every subsequent quarter. The *société de la Halle-au-Blé* required the sum of two *livres* when issuing its membership card, and a subscription fee of one *livre* every quarter. On 17 September, the *société Lepeletier* had fixed its membership fee at 100 *sous*, but 'if any true sans-culotte who could not afford to pay 100 *sous* presented himself, he would be received just the same'. The *société Poissonnière*, which adopted a subscription fee of forty *sous*, also admitted sans-culottes who were not in a position to contribute towards the expenses of the society, if their names had been forwarded by the admittance committee. The members of the *société de la Maison-Commune* paid ten *sous* a month; those of the *société de la République*, twenty-five *sous* a quarter. The *club républicain de la section de l'Homme-Armé* rejected 'all pecuniary conditions', and 'extended a welcoming hand to every patriot in the Section, regardless of his means': a box was left in the assembly hall so that members could donate what they wished. These different rates reflect the social composition of the Sections: the subscription fees generally being higher in the older societies than in the *sociétés sectionnaires*.

The committee of any society was also formed according to the regulations. The usual composition was a president, a vice-president, one or two secretaries—sometimes even three or four—elected for one month, but eligible for re-election after this period; a treasurer and an archivist who were nearly always elected permanently. 'Inspectors' supervised the entrances, whilst 'censors' maintained order in the assembly hall. Sub-committees or commissions assisted the officials of the society in administering its affairs—admittance or examination committees, administrative committees, and correspondence committees according to the different societies. The *société des Amis-de-la-Patrie* also had a relief committee, and the *société de la Halle-au-Blé*, a committee of surveillance to receive denunciations.

The older societies usually met twice a week. Those created in 1793—the *société de la Butte-des-Moulins*, for example—seem to have followed the example of the general assemblies in meeting *en permanence*, at least after 2 June. It was in these societies that the real struggle against the moderates was fought. After the general assemblies had been forbidden to meet permanently, the *sociétés sectionnaires*, created simply to evade the law, arranged to meet on those days which would not coincide with the meetings of the assemblies, which meant, in fact, every day of the *décade*, except the fifth and the tenth. The militant *sectionnaire* was given very little time for leisure. Amongst the societies to adopt this procedure were the *société des Marchés*, the *société des Amis-de-la-Patrie* and the *société de la Maison-Commune*. Some societies, like the *société des Vertus-Republicaines*, the *société de l'Unité*, and the *société de la Halle-au-Blé*, confined their meetings to four a week—the second, fourth, seventh, and ninth days of the *décade*. Others met on only three days—the second, the fourth, and the seventh:

amongst the latter we find the *société de la République*, the *société de la Section Poissonnière* and the *société des Amis-de-la-République* in the Section des Piques. The old societies, generally affiliated to the Jacobin club and anxious not to interfere with the assemblies of the mother-society, only met two or three times in each *décade*.

The assembly hall was open from five o'clock in the evening, although the meeting did not begin until an hour later—in summer it began at seven o'clock. The members of the committee sat behind a long table on a raised platform, each wearing his red cap. A rostrum (*tribune*), raised a little higher, was reserved for speakers. Conspicuously placed above or around the committee were the busts of liberty—sometimes one of Brutus or the 'statue of freedom'—the walls being decorated with the tricolour, a red cap, the emblem of the society, and a few republican mottos or symbols. Meetings were open to all citizens in the Section, and in order to accommodate the public, a wooden enclosure about four feet high divided the hall into two sections. At the entrances, '*tribuns*' often welcomed citizens to the society; women being shown to one side, men to the other.

The meeting began with a reading of the minutes and any correspondence. The names of candidates for admission were then announced, and the sub-committee nominated for the purpose presented its observations. This was followed by a discussion of the various reports received by the society. The *société sectionnaire de la République* began to discuss the main items of the agenda at seven o'clock. The hour between eight and nine was devoted to a reading of the *Journal du soir* and the *Bulletin de la Convention*. The *société des Vertus-Républicaines* in the Section de l'Observatoire began its meetings by reading the minutes at seven o'clock, any communications received by the committee and the *Bulletin des Lois*; at eight o'clock it went on to discuss 'the main agenda'. The *société de la rue de Montreuil* followed the same procedure. From eight o'clock to nine, the *société Poissonnière* preferred to devote its attention to various 'dissertations on morality and patriotic works'. The *société des Amis-de-la-République* in the Section des Piques reserved one day a week 'for the reading of short patriotic addresses which could be understood by every member'.

Members were asked to speak from the *tribune* and to wear the *bonnet rouge*; the regulations, frequently ignored, also stated that no member was allowed to interrupt or question a speaker. In the *société des Amis-de-la-Patrie*, the ruling was that 'every member who makes personal comments or insults any other member' should be called to order. The *société patriotique du Luxembourg* proscribed 'every rehearsed or complimentary speech': as in every other society, citizens were asked to adopt 'the republican manner of speaking, commonly called *tutoiement*'. The members of these societies were not all born orators. A regulation passed by the *société de la République* stated that 'if a speaker strays from the point or becomes boring, his listeners will stand'; when seven citizens had shown their disapproval in this way, it was the duty of the president to ask the society whether or not the speaker should be allowed to continue. Voting took place aloud, by the raising of hands, or by standing to show approval. Sometimes voting slips were used, in which case the slips had to be signed— the sans-culotte was always suspicious of the secret ballot, fearing that it might be used to perpetrate some intrigue or plot. In spite of all the regulations, and the censors who were present to maintain order, meetings were often noisy, sometimes disorderly: quarrels between individuals were frequent. But the sans-culotte, easily provoked, was equally ready to forgive, and, more often than not, these disputes were settled with the fraternal kiss in the midst of general applause. The members of the societies, as well as the public, were extremely sensitive and emotional in their response, allowing themselves to be easily moved by the speakers —a whole assembly might be swept by a wave of enthusiasm, by 'republican ecstasies'. Everyone would rise and repeat the oath of living as free citizens or dying. One member would begin to sing 'a song to the favourite tune of the Carmagnole', and 'the universal choir' would take up the strain before launching into the hymn of the 'Marseillais'. Moments of intense emotion, of patriotic fervour, when the humblest citizen forgot his station in life and joined in the worship of freedom and the Republic.

The popular societies sought to increase the force of their impact on political events by affiliation in much the same way as the general assemblies had adopted the method of correspondence. Robespierre, in his speech of 29 September 1791, defined affiliation as 'the relation between one legitimate society and another which leads to a mutual correspondence on matters of public interest': it was natural, if not inevitable, therefore, that societies who were affiliated should wish to correspond with each other. This dual process tended to draw these political organizations into one vast network which immeasurably augmented their strength. A circular issued by the *société populaire de Belleville* in the Year II suggested that 'this intimate and desirable union' could be formed 'by the realization of our rights and our obligations; by watching and working together. . . . In order to do this, citizens throughout the nation must unite with the central or mother-society which will constantly be receiving and imparting those traits of enlightenment and experience which will inform, animate, and invigorate our patriotism.'[3]

The right of the societies to engage in affiliation and correspondence aroused considerable controversy. The Constituent Assembly discussed the question on 29 September 1791, and although it passed a decree prohibiting the presentation of collective petitions, it was afraid to take any action at this time against the right of affiliation. The matter was raised again in the spring of 1792 when the clubs affiliated to the Jacobins threatened to become an effective instrument of the revolutionary movement. In an anonymous pamphlet, 'a friend of the Constitution' declared that 'the clubs must be isolated and independent of one another; they must not correspond with each other in any way'. In 1793, the links of affiliation and correspondence between the Parisian popular societies partly explain the success of the popular offensive against the moderates. One girondist orator was alleged to have urged the authorities to 'cut the thread of correspondence between the popular societies'. 'For our part', replied a deputation from the Section de l'Arsénal, 'we say let these salutary threads remain. They will join all the points at the circumference to the centre; they alone will guarantee the lasting solidarity' of the Constitution which was being prepared.[4]

The societies founded at the beginning of the Revolution, and those created in the spring of 1792, either renewed or requested their affiliation to the Jacobin club after 2 June—the *société de l'Homme-Armé*, for example, on the sixteenth, and the *société des Hommes-Libres* in the Section Révolutionnaire, already affiliated to the Cordelier club and the *société fraternelle de deux sexes* on

[3] *A.D.S.*, 4 AZ 590.   [4] *A.N.*, C 256, d. 489, p. 4.

12 September. The foundation of the *sociétés sectionnaires* tended to disrupt the accepted procedure of affiliation and correspondence. The older societies, affiliated to each other and to the Jacobin club, allowed the mother-society to direct their activities; whilst the *sociétés sectionnaires*, recruited on a more popular and purely local basis, rarely solicited the affiliation of the Jacobins, although they joined with each other. The *sociétés sectionnaires* threatened to become an autonomous movement. This explains the animosity which developed in government and jacobin circles from the autumn of 1793 and, eventually, the general offensive aimed at their destruction. The societies tried to save themselves by requesting their affiliation, but when they were refused—as was usually the case—this belated move only served to discredit them even further. After they had finally been dissolved in the spring of the Year II, the right of affiliation and correspondence exclusively favoured the Jacobins: it was used simply as a means of governmental centralization.

Once the Revolutionary Government itself had been overthrown, however, the authorities quickly realized the inherent danger of affiliation. As early as 24 Fructidor Year II, Durand de Maillane drew the attention of the Convention to 'the threat to liberty' in the affiliation of the popular societies to the Jacobin club. On 25 Vendémiaire Year III, a decree was passed which prohibited the societies from participating in 'any affiliation, aggregation, federation, or correspondence'.

During periods of crisis, affiliation and correspondence did not provide the societies with the complete answer to the problem of concerted action, with the result that the more far-sighted militants tried to create an organism which would both co-ordinate and direct their activity. But their early endeavours to organize a central committee of the popular societies aroused the same opposition as the proposed plan for a central bureau of correspondence by the general assemblies. The initiative was eventually taken up by the *société fraternelle des deux sexes* which met at the Jacobin club. On 25 April 1793, the society 'recognizing the dangers which confront the nation, and convinced that the citizens who can save it are to be found in the popular societies', invited the latter to send *commissaires* to co-operate in the task of forming a Central Committee. The *société fraternelle* naturally encountered many difficulties, not the least of them being the hostility of the

Jacobins. The Committee had originally intended to meet at the salle de la Fraternité—formerly the headquarters of the *société des Jacobins Saint-Honoré*—but was finally obliged to meet at the Evêché; the regulations governing the work of the Central Committee were not approved until 30 October 1793. The Parisian societies were represented directly on the Committee, two delegates being chosen from each society. Its objective was 'to maintain an active correspondence with all the popular societies in the Republic; to provide them with a point of contact; and to present for their discussion, problems raised during the meetings of the Central Committee—or those sent to it by any of the societies—which appeared to be of vital concern to the Republic'. On 12 Brumaire Year II, the General Council of the Commune formally recognized the creation of the Committee, which reminded the municipal authorities of its existence on the eighteenth by presenting them with a petition 'aimed at extirpating the evils caused by fanaticism and error'. The new Committee was placing itself at the head of the popular movement.

Its activities provoked immediate reaction. One of the first organizations to protest was the *Club électorale* or *Club central du département du Paris*, also meeting at the Evêché, which had been reconstituted since 21 September 1793. Aspiring after the same role, the club denounced the work of the new Committee on 27 Brumaire Year II; its suspicions having been confirmed by the Committee's decision to hold its meetings behind closed doors. The matter was referred to the department of Police Administration. Confronted with this move, the Central Committee must have decided that it had little alternative but to dissolve, since we find no further mention of its activities. A contributory factor was the increased momentum of the jacobin offensive against the *sociétés sectionnaires*. Article 17, section III of the law of 14 Frimaire was soon to prohibit any congress or central reunion of the popular societies. In the organization of the Revolutionary Government there was room for just one 'forum of public opinion' —the mother-society of the Jacobins.

The duties of instruction and surveillance as laid down by their regulations did not, in fact, completely satisfy the ambitions of the popular societies. They gradually widened the scope of their activities until, in the majority of the Sections, they had substituted themselves for the general assemblies and secured the allegiance of sectionary officials. To a certain extent, the popular societies were duplicating the political system of the government, depriving it of its coactive force.

If it did not claim the undivided attention of the societies, instruction always played an important role in their meetings, particularly when, in the Year II, they fell under the control of the jacobin and governmental authorities. Most of the societies opened their meetings with the reading of patriotic newspapers, speeches delivered in the Convention or the Jacobin club, decrees and laws, civic or moral addresses by the militants, and on many occasions, with the recitation of the Constitutional Act or the Declaration of Rights by children. Members of the *société section-naire de la République* listened to the reading of the *Journal du soir*, the *Bulletin de la Convention*, decrees issued by the Commune, and the daily orders of the National Guard at every meeting. On 27 Pluviôse, a child of 7 recited the Declaration of Rights; on 4 Ventôse, there was an address on the planting of a tree of liberty; three days later, a small child of 8 read a speech written to commemorate the death of Chalier; Saint-Just's report on incarcerated citizens evoked loud applause on 22 Pluviôse; Robespierre's on the principle of the Revolutionary Government —already a little outdated—was read on 17 Germinal; five days later, Saint-Just's account of the arrest of Danton, and on 7 Floréal, his report on police administration; on 22 Floréal, the society listened to Robespierre's discourse on religious and moral ideas. These examples are typical of the kind of instruction received by members of the various societies. Some of them, like the *société Lepeletier*, began to hold extraordinary sessions devoted to the recitation by children of the Declaration of Rights, the Constitution, or similar appropriate addresses.

Surveillance, in the broadest sense of the word, also figured prominently amongst the activities of the societies. During the great purges of the autumn of 1793, the government naturally turned to the popular societies for information. On 13 September, they were invited to present the Committee of Public Safety with 'a list of unworthy officials suspected for their lack of patriotism'; on 9 October, they were asked to keep a close watch on the administration of food supplies and military clothing; on the fifteenth, to supply information on all administrative decisions concerning the *émigrés* and the confiscation of their property. In fact, the societies had anticipated these invitations. On 5 September, the *société des Hommes-Libres* had already decided to discuss all appointments to public offices. A member of the *société Lepeletier* was given the responsibility of discovering what posts were about to become vacant and what citizens had forwarded applications for these posts. In return, departmental heads adopted the practice of discussing candidatures with the popular societies before taking any decisions. The registrar of births and deaths asked the *société sectionnaire des Droits de l'Homme* in Brumaire Year II whether it thought a certain Jean Liard worthy of a place in his offices: 'the time has come', he wrote, 'when patriots must be everywhere; it is the best way of ensuring that the aristocracy appear nowhere'. The fact that the societies were usually in charge of the issue of *certificats de civisme* meant that they could exercise an effective measure of control over public officials: on 2 Brumaire, the *société des Hommes-Libres* decreed that all administrative civil servants living in the Section Révolutionnaire would be obliged to renew their certificates within a period of one month.[5]

The militant members of the societies were particularly anxious to extend their vigilance beyond the surveillance of officials to the control of the military equipment and war supplies. The *société des Amis-de-l'Egalité* in the Section de la Réunion appointed *commissaires* on 2 Brumaire to check the quality of shoes and sheets stored in a barracks—their subsequent report was unfavourable. Three days later, the society asked the general assembly to appoint *commissaires* to work alongside its own so that their inspections would carry more authority. On 8 Brumaire, it secured the evidence of a captain and several soldiers who complained from the *tribune* about the quality of the equipment which had been allocated to them. The inspectors authorized to receive and distribute these supplies were immediately denounced; the *comité révolutionnaire* was asked to proceed with their arrest and place the incriminating evidence before the public prosecutor. In Nivôse, the *société des Hommes-Libres* in the Section Révolutionnaire named three *commissaires* to inspect the activity of armament workshops situated in Paris, and 'to report on the various obstacles impeding the work of these

[5] *B.N.*, MSS. new acq. fr. 2713, f. 51.

establishments which are so vital to the success of the Republic'. The *commissaires* carried out their task conscientiously, visiting the three workshops in the Section, making inquiries about the patriotism of the overseers and the zeal of the workers, interesting themselves in every aspect of the process of manufacture and suggesting possible improvements. On 9 Germinal, the *Commission des armes et des poudres* congratulated the society on its 'invigorating surveillance'.

By an almost inevitable process, the societies used their powers of surveillance to exert an influence upon, and finally to control, the entire political life of the Sections. According to the *société de la section Poissonnière*, the popular societies represented nothing less than 'the purged Sections': as such, they gradually began to substitute themselves for the general assemblies. The pace of this evolution naturally quickened when the latter were prohibited from meeting *en permanence*—the *sociétés sectionnaires* were founded to evade the law and to reconstitute, under a different name, the assemblies which had been forbidden to meet on certain days. Guaranteeing continuity of action and meeting permanently, the reality of power in many of the Sections centred around the *société sectionnaire*, reducing the role of the general assembly to that of registration.

On 15 September 1793, a citizen in the assembly of the Section des Champs-Elysées proposed 'that on those days when the law prohibits any discussion, republican sans-culottes should constitute themselves as a popular society to maintain a continuous and active surveillance'; its most important task would be the preparation of 'all discussions intended for the general assemblies'. On 21 September, the *société de la section de Brutus* invited the president and the secretary of the general assembly to send them, the day before their meetings, 'a list of the questions which, in their opinion, merited particular attention and which needed to be discussed in advance'. A few days later, the society decided that it had the right to draft measures which it thought the assembly ought to adopt. These same preoccupations inspired the foundation of the *société de la Maison-Commune*: 'Intriguers would be able to use the time which elapsed between one general assembly and another to co-ordinate their plans and hinder the work of the general assemblies'; the society would maintain a continuous surveillance. Above all, 'since the time at the disposal of the assemblies is limited, it is important to prepare the questions submitted for their discussion so that their work can be carried out successfully'. One of the aims of the society, therefore, would be 'to accelerate the proceedings' of the assembly. On 24 Brumaire, the *société sectionnaire de la Réunion* stated quite simply 'that it would be chiefly concerned with discussing and clarifying problems before they were presented to the general assembly'.[6]

These plans, often executed in a rather conspiratorial manner, help to explain the animosity which the *sociétés sectionnaires* created amongst the moderates in the autumn of 1793 who were quick to accuse them of organizing 'cliques'. The main criticism levelled against the societies in the Year III was that they had usurped the rights of the general assemblies. On 20 and 30 Pluviôse, the *société de la Fontaine-Grenelle*, reduced to a 'select circle', was reproached for having monopolized all civil and military appointments, and 'all the acts of sovereignty which belong by law to the people united in the primary assembly of the commune or Section'—the assembly had been forbidden to issue decrees or certificates recognizing citizens as *indigents*, testifying to their civic character, or even registering their address unless it had previously received a report and the consent of the society.[7]

The complaint was not without foundation. For some months, from the autumn of 1793 to the spring of the following year, the assemblies, and sometimes even the sectionary authorities, seem to have abdicated their rights in favour of the popular societies. In many of the Sections, the general assemblies were content simply to ratify their decisions. On 15 Brumaire Year II, the assembly of the Section des Invalides authorized the society to receive a petition concerning food supplies from the Section de la Maison-Commune, 'and to give or refuse the adherence requested, on its behalf'. On the same day, the assembly of the Section des Droits-de-l'Homme announced that, in future, it did not intend to participate in the worship of any cult other than that of Reason: it delegated the responsibility of informing the General Council of the Commune of its decision to the society. On 30 Brumaire, the Section de la Montagne asked the popular society to deal with a circular from the Committee of Public Safety requesting the names of citizens to fill various offices. On the same day, the *comité révolutionnaire* of the Section de l'Observatoire, 'seeking to put

[6] *A.N.*, F[7] 2495.   [7] *A.N.*, D iii, 256[4], d. 5, p. 32.

an end to the many complaints and rumours occasioned by the disarmament which had been carried out in order to foil the plans of the aristocracy', decreed that citizens who had been disarmed should address any queries they had to the popular society which would make final decisions. The assemblies, from which the moderates and all other opposition groups had been excluded, made no attempt to resist: on 10 Brumaire, the assembly of the Section de Beaurepaire allowed the *société des Sans-Culottes-Révolutionnaires-du-31-mai* to use its headquarters on the days when it was forbidden to meet 'in view of the importance of the popular society's work'.[8]

As a rule, the societies were even more interested in making appointments than in influencing the decisions of the general assemblies. In the autumn of 1793—acting for once with the approval of the government—they began to censure and purge officials employed in the Sections. The vote of censure, according to a denunciation made in the Year III against the *société de Brutus*, presented 'a wonderful opportunity of pursuing and persecuting patriots', referring of course, to the moderates. On 20 October 1793, the society passed a vote of censure on the conduct of the *comité révolutionnaire*, the *juge de paix* and his *secrétaire-greffier*, the *commissaire de police* and the *commissaire aux accapare-ments*. From criticizing the conduct of officials, the societies went on to intervene in their election. Accused of having acted 'tyranni-cally, in order to influence the general assembly when making appointments, and of presenting the assembly with a list of candidates which had already been discussed', the *société fraternelle du Panthéon-Français* replied on 25 August 1793 that it had never denied discussing candidates: 'we pride ourselves all the more for submitting them to a second censure, and for the fact that our choice has always been accepted'. On 17 Brumaire, the *société Lepeletier* chose three *commissaires* to levy forced loans, then invited its members to retire to the general assembly to participate in their official election. On 5 Nivôse, the assembly of the Section de Beaurepaire accepted a citizen named Ricordon as a member of the *comité civil*, on the recommendation of the society. Choosing candidates for public office was a regular feature of the work of the *société Poissonnière*. On 19 Nivôse, it prepared a list of candidates for places on the *comité civil* which was presented for the assembly's

[8] *B.V.C.*, MS. 119, f. 47.

approval the next day; three days later, it nominated a *commissaire aux accaparements*, and on the twenty-fourth, several candidates to complete the *comité révolutionnaire*; on 7 Ventôse, the society named a *secrétaire-greffier*, and a week later, prepared a list of citizens for the *comité de bienfaisance* who were all appointed by the assembly on the following day. When the *commission des salpêtres* in the Section de Brutus wished to enrol new commissioners on 28 Pluviôse, it turned to the popular society which duly presented the commission with suitable candidates. On 4 Ventôse, the *société Lepeletier* named four of its members to sit on the committee of the general assembly which was to be renewed on the following day.[9]

Finally, the societies decided to take over the responsibility of issuing *certificats de civisme* from the general assemblies, and, in some cases, from the *comités révolutionnaires*. As a rule, both the assemblies and the committees referred applicants to the societies, or demanded that they obtained their endorsement. On 11 September 1793, the *société de la section de Beaurepaire* suggested to the General Council of the Commune that, in future, requests for these certificates should be addressed to the popular society so that they could be carefully examined. In the end, the general assembly itself abdicated its rights in the matter—on 5 Germinal, it decided that all *certificats de civisme* would be issued by a commission of twelve members chosen from the society. Thus, already influencing the decisions of the general assemblies in making nominations as well as in drafting addresses and petitions, the societies succeeded in controlling practically every aspect of political life in the Sections—a citizen who failed to obtain his *certificat de civisme* from a society found himself deprived of every civic right.

To make an accurate assessment of the part played by the popular societies, we would have to know the number of their adherents and their social composition, although we should not attach too much importance to the total number of members who adhered to a society, but confine our attention to those who attended regularly—the real strength of the societies lay in the number of militants, not in their total membership. The solution to these problems has been complicated by the fragmentary nature of the documentation, either because the records of the

[9] *B.N.*, MSS. new acq. fr. 2662, f. 63.

societies have been badly kept, or because, as a precautionary measure, they were destroyed after Thermidor.

The total membership of any one society appears to have varied according to the period and the Section concerned, although this variation was never very pronounced. According to a deputation visiting the Jacobin club on 14 June 1793, the *societe de l'Homme-Armé* was composed of '200 sans-culottes, devoted to the montagnard cause'. At approximately the same time, the Section had 2,000 citizens who qualified for armed service—about a tenth of the active citizens of the Section, therefore, attended the popular society. Only 37 members were left in the old *société Lepeletier* after it had carried out its purge in September 1793; although by the time the society planned to conduct another purge in Ventôse, this figure had risen to 89. In July 1793, the armed force of the Section included 3,231 men. Apparently, therefore, only one or two citizens in every hundred joined the popular society from the autumn of 1793 to the following spring. The *société des Amis-de-l'Egalité* in the Section de la Réunion conducted its purge from 23 September 1793 to 7 Frimaire Year II, reducing the membership to 148, or, since the Section had 4,378 voters, a proportion of three or four members out of every hundred citizens. Two hundred and eighty citizens belonged to the *société républicaine de l'Unité* on 23 Nivôse Year II, which represented a membership of 9 per cent. of the total population of the Section which was approximately 4,000. According to the report of the *commission d'épuration*, the *société de la section des Piques* had a membership of 400 in Pluviôse Year II, and since the Section was issued with 3,538 *cartes de sûreté*, it would appear that the percentage rose in this case to 11 per cent. At the end of its purge on 22 Ventôse Year II, the *société républicaine de Mont-Blanc* was reduced to 112 members: in July 1793, the armed force of the Section had been composed of 2,378 citizens, giving us a membership of about four out of every hundred citizens. The *société de la section de Brutus* at the time of its dissolution on 30 Germinal had 208 members out of 2,670 voters, a figure of approximately 7 per cent. The proportion of members adhering to a society when compared with the total population of a Section rarely appears, therefore, to have risen above 10 per cent.

If we trace the evolution of just one society—as far as the documents will allow—we find that attendances, swollen for a short time during the spring of 1793, tended to fall during the winter of the Year II as the Revolutionary Government grew stronger. In June 1792, the *société des Hommes-Libres* in the Section du Pont-Neuf was composed of 44 members, four of whom had not paid their subscriptions. During the summer, it is impossible to give an exact date, the membership rose to 72—*messieurs les récipiendaires* of June had thrown open their ranks to the sans-culotterie. The conflict between the Girondins and the Montagnards, sans-culottes, and moderates, led to a few defections and towards the end of the winter of 1793, the society was composed of 69 members. There was a noticeable increase during the period of intense political activity immediately following the events of 2 June, when the sans-culottes and the moderates disputed control of the general assemblies and popular societies, and by the beginning of August the membership had risen to 100. It continued to rise after the societies had registered their victory, either because the latter had strengthened their organization, or because the moderates had decided to adhere to the societies as a precautionary measure. The purge completed on 2 Frimaire Year II reduced the membership again to 85; 17 members having been excluded and a decision on 22 others deferred because they had signed anti-civic petitions or were 'comparatively unknown'. The decreased momentum of political life in the Sections, the discredit thrown upon the societies at the beginning of the spring, and the fear which had seized many of the militants, clearly had their effect on the membership: on 14 Prairial, the day of its dissolution, the *société des Hommes-Libres* was composed of only 53 citizens. A similar decrease was noticeable in the *société sectionnaire de la République* after Germinal, although the proportions differ. Founded on 5 Nivôse by 62 citizens, the total membership had risen to 264 on 2 Ventôse; but a drastic purge carried out from 22 Germinal to 17 Floréal again reduced this figure, this time to 154.[1]

If the effective membership varied, the social composition of the societies appears to have been more stable, although there was a marked tendency towards democratization in the Year II. Founded for the purposes of instruction, particularly for passive citizens deprived of the vote, they attracted citizens of modest means from the beginning: 'local fruit and vegetable sellers' according to the

[1] *A.N.*, D III, 256[7], d. 7, p. 1.

Chronique de Paris for 3 November 1790; 'water-carriers and other reliable citizens' according to *le Babillard* on 25 June 1791. However, merchants and master-craftsmen seem to have dominated the societies in the early stages of the Revolution. After 10 August, tradesmen, artisans, and shopkeepers formed the bulk of the membership. It was only in the autumn of 1793 that *compagnons*, operatives, and the lower-grade workers began to enter the societies and to play an active part in their deliberations. Finally, citizens attached to the liberal professions, but of average means—artists, lower-grade civil servants and public officials, not to mention those who escape classification—adhered to the societies from the beginning. As we might expect, the social composition varies from Section to Section: the *société patriotique de la section de la Bibliothèque* enjoyed a more bourgeois recruitment for a considerable time. Active citizens, who were given the exclusive right of participating in extraordinary meetings where problems affecting the Sections were discussed, enjoyed privileged treatment in the societies at first; passive citizens only playing a secondary role. But these distinctions disappeared in the summer of 1792, although active citizens retained their influence for almost a year. In the autumn of 1793 it was the sans-culotte who dominated the societies. Here again, we need to distinguish between the societies founded at the beginning of the Revolution composed of 'the patriots of '89' and the more popular *sociétés sectionnaires* frequented, according to their enemies, by 'the new brood of patriots' —those of 1792 or even 1793. Police-agents frequently noted the popular character of the meetings of the *sociétés sectionnaires* in the Year II. On II Ventôse, Bacon remarked on the number of 'citizens in shirt-sleeves', operatives and bricklayers in the *société des Arcis*; but he does not tell us whether they were members of the society or of the public. On 20 Germinal, the *société de la Maison-Commune* announced that its members were all 'totally deprived of wealth'. The *société de la rue du Vert-Bois* in the Section des Gravilliers was denounced on 24 Pluviôse Year III because it had been composed 'almost entirely of workers and comparatively uneducated citizens who were all too easily led astray'.[2] However, it is difficult to make a really accurate assessment of the social composition of the popular societies without a more complete documentation—only a few of the membership

[2] *A.N.*, F⁷ 4774³⁷.

lists which still survive contain any reference to professions. Of the twenty members belonging to the *société des Hommes-Libres* in the Section du Pont-Neuf in June 1792 whose professions we do know, we find that craftsmen and merchants of a certain social category predominate—nine clockmakers, three jewellers, and two engravers, in addition to 'one *bourgeois* from Paris'. During the summer, the effective membership rose to seventy-two. The professions of sixty of these citizens are given—two were wholesale merchants, three were civil servants, and four belonged to the liberal professions. The majority of the other members were either tradesmen or artisans connected with some branch of the art and luxury trade—thirteen jewellers, twelve clockmakers, six engravers or carvers, two sword-cutlers, one smelter, one fan-maker, one dealer in fancy-turnery, and one upholsterer. Of the remaining artisans or traders, there were three haberdashers, two tailors, two shoemakers, one hosier, one joiner, one locksmith, one painter, one brush-maker, and one café-owner. The social composition altered slightly in the beginning of August 1793. Out of seventy-one members, we find fourteen clockmakers, fourteen jewellers, and seven engraver-carvers, who always headed the list; but there were now seven minor civil servants, two mechanics, and one cook. Unfortunately, owing to the lack of information concerning the social status of members for the Year II, we are unable to discover to what extent the lowest stratum of society in the Section du Pont-Neuf succeeded in entering the *société des Hommes-Libres*.

Amongst the 125 members admitted to the *société de la section de la Réunion* from 23 September 1793 to 12 Frimaire Year II whose professions we know, the seventeen office clerks and lower-grade civil servants form the largest group. These were followed by the fourteen jewellers and the twelve craftsmen attached to some branch of the luxury trade. Three wholesale traders and eleven merchants—generally no specific trade is mentioned, three *rentiers* and five retired artisans or tradesmen living off their income represent the more affluent ranks of the middle bourgeoisie. Amongst the ordinary craftsmen, the eight shoemakers are the most numerous. The lowest stratum of the sans-culotterie is represented by four small shopkeepers, two workers—again, no indication as to their precise trade—two cleaners, one bricklayer, one woodcutter, one pedlar, one dealer in second-hand goods, one dealer in old clothes, and one odd-job man. Finally, the liberal professions account for three surgeons and an apothecary, two sculptors, two ushers, two solicitors, two public scriveners, one schoolmaster, to which we can add the former canon, and the curate of Saint-Méry.[3]

On 23 Nivôse Year II, the *société républicaine de l'Unité* had a membership of 280. Although there were thirty-six merchants, wholesaler traders, or manufacturers, twenty-eight civil servants and only sixteen workers and others in the lower income group, the bulk of the society was composed of 181 craftsmen and shop-keepers whose social status cannot accurately be defined.[4]

Once again, confronted with the imprecise nature of the documentation and vocabulary of the period, we are forced to realize how any study of the societies—as of the sans-culotterie in general—must, in the last resort, be hedged with uncertainties. It is clear that the popular societies became more democratic during the autumn of 1793, the *sociétés sectionnaires* admitting even the humblest sans-culotte; but in the old and the new societies it was the artisan and shopkeeper element of the *petite bourgeoisie* which predominated—a category wide enough to include citizens from very different social backgrounds, and which extended, by a series of almost imperceptible gradations, from the lowest rank of *le peuple* to that of the middle bourgeoisie.

We must also remember that, from a political standpoint, the mass of citizens who adhered to the societies were of less import-ance than the small number of militants who regulated their activities. Whatever the total memberships might have been, the societies were only regularly frequented by a minority of active sans-culottes, representing the *cadres* of the popular movement, and consolidating it from within.

Some of the documents can be misleading in this respect. The *sociétés sectionnaires*, like the general assemblies, admitted the public to their meetings, and in the spring of 1793, the *société des Hommes-Libres* provided places for 200 citizens when arranging the seating accommodation of their meeting hall, although it is quite certain that their actual membership was only half this number. At first, women usually attended in large numbers, but it was not long before those who had adhered to the popular societies shared in the disgrace of the *société des Femmes*

<hr/>

[3] *A.N.*, F⁷ 2495.   [4] *British Museum*, F.R. 827 (5).

Républicaines-Révolutionnaires and had to be content simply with the role of spectators. The same was true of the children and youths who came 'to be instructed, and imbued with revolutionary principles'. This explains the large attendances recorded by police-agents like Bacon on II Ventôse in the societies of the Section des Arcis and the Section de l'Indivisibilité, and in the society of the Section des Lombards where he noted, in particular the large proportion of women present; and on 13 Ventôse in the societies of the Section de Bon-Conseil and the Section des Droits-de-l'Homme. On 22 Ventôse, the *société sectionnaire de la République* discovered that its assembly hall was too small to accommodate the number of citizens who wished to attend its meetings, and five days later decided to move the temple of Reason. But although the meetings of the *sociétés sectionnaires* attracted fairly high attendances until the spring of the Year II, the number of members actually participating in their deliberations was quite small, and this was particularly true of the older societies. The militants in the societies, and indeed in the general assemblies, were continually exhorting their colleagues to be more assiduous in their attendance. On 25 May 1793, the president of the *société patriotique de la Butte-des-Moulins* launched such an appeal; and on 24 Pluviôse Year II, a member of the *société de la section Poissonnière* announced his intention of reporting any members who missed three consecutive meetings to the presentation committee. These appeals elicited no response.

In the autumn of 1793, according to a denunciation sent to the Convention, only fourteen members attended the meetings of the *société des Défenseurs-de-la-République*, four of them being women. At the end of its purge on 7 Frimaire Year II, the *société des Amis-de-l'Egalité* in the Section de la Réunion was composed of 148 members—at the meeting held on 9 October, only 43 of them were present; 42 on the fourteenth, and 37 on 19 Brumaire. On 5 Nivôse, 62 members attended the inaugural meeting of the *société sectionnaire de la République*. The petition presented to the Convention on 28 Ventôse by the *société de Mutius-Scaevola* was signed by 95 members; but it is not at all certain that all these signatures were collected in the course of one meeting. The average attendance at the *société fraternelle des deux sexes*, according to a denunciation on II Prairial, was only 120, the numbers being divided fairly equally between men and women.[5]

The conclusions to be drawn from these few statistics are confirmed by the rare collections of minutes which have survived. Those for the *société patriotique de la section de la Bibliothèque*—in 1793 it changed its name to the *société populaire Lepeletier*—for example, tell us that on 14 November 1790, eighty voters participated in the election of the president. On 24 April 1792, the society failed to reach a quorum when only nine members were present. On 17 September 1793, the society was forced to remind members of an earlier decree stating that at least eleven of them had to be present before discussions could begin: a week later the society failed to reach this figure. On 1 October, seventeen members were present, but the society again failed to reach a quorum on the fifteenth. On 19 October, after one member had protested against these continually low attendances, the society decided to exclude any adherent who missed six consecutive meetings. This threat appears to have had relatively little effect: on 7 Brumaire, the society was forced to announce that no new candidates would be received unless there were at least twenty-five members present; and on the twenty-second, only forty-two adherents signed a petition to the Convention.[6]

Attendances were particularly low in the *société de la section Poissonnière* where, on 14 Frimaire, there were not enough members present to open the meeting. On the twenty-fourth, the committee was elected by just twenty-five voters; three days later, this figure had risen slightly to thirty-nine for the election of the presentation committee. On 2 Nivôse, forty-two members chose the president, but on the seventeenth, only twenty-seven were present to elect the presentation committee. A week later, we find that there were thirty-seven participants in a first vote, and forty-five in a second. On 2 Pluviôse, the president was elected by forty-three voters, and the secretaries by fifty-three. Attendances during the critical days of the spring swelled to seventy-eight on 2 Ventôse, seventy-seven on 2 Germinal, but then dropped once again to forty-eight on 2 Floréal.[7]

The same low attendances characterized the meetings of the *société des Hommes-Libres:* the attendance-sheets rarely carry more than twenty signatures for the month of August 1793,

[5] *A.N.*, F[7] 4774[42].   [6] *A.N.*, C 280, pl. 769, p. 8.
[7] *A.D.S.*, D 989.

although the total membership of the society stood at 100. The crisis which mobilized the sans-culotterie towards the end of the winter of the Year II led to a noticeable increase—an average attendance of over fifty on the last days of Pluviôse, reaching its highest figure of fifty-eight at the height of the crisis on 19 Ventôse. The confusion which reigned amongst the sans-culotterie following the execution of Hébert had its inevitable effect upon attendances: forty-five present on 4 Germinal, thirty-four on the twenty-second and less than thirty in Floréal. The campaign against the popular societies appears to have aroused some response, for there were thirty-six members present on 4 Prairial. But the *société des Hommes-Libres* was finally forced to dissolve ten days later—the fifty-three signatures on the attendance-sheet represent a vote of protest on the part of the members as well as a sign of their attachment.

In 1793, the popular societies had organized themselves into a striking-force against the moderates, a fact which explains the protection afforded them by the Revolutionary Government—as yet in the early stages of its development—during the course of the summer. In the autumn, the proliferation of the *sociétés sectionnaires* manifested the determination of the militants to retain their influence over the political affairs of the Sections. From this time, the hostility between the *sociétés sectionnaires* and the political organizations of the government became increasingly apparent, reflecting the fundamental antagonism between popular power and sans-culotte democracy on the one hand, and jacobin dictatorship and the Revolutionary Government on the other.

Disposing of their own armed force and nominating their officers, administering their own affairs, electing their officials and their committees, the Sections had transformed themselves into forty-eight autonomous organizations within the heart of the capital. Through correspondence in normal times, by fraternization in periods of crisis, the political institutions of the Sections—assemblies, committees, and societies—were duplicating the work of the municipality of Paris; their powers threatened to surpass even the competence of the Committees, and to weigh down the scales of the delicate social equilibrium upon which the Revolutionary Government rested heavily in favour of the sans-culotterie. Created to safeguard the interests of the bourgeois revolution, the Committees could not tolerate the prolonged existence of a separate popular organization which escaped their control: they deprived the Sections of their right to nominate *commissaires* who, paid and, therefore, subject to dismissal by the government, were transformed into ordinary public officials; they disciplined the general assemblies and suppressed the *sociétés sectionnaires*. But in so doing, they forfeited the confidence of the sans-culottes from whom they derived their support—nothing but the shell of their organizations remained, devoid of all popular content. Jacobin centralization had triumphed over the autonomy of the Sections. But, faced with the impatient forces of reaction, how long would the Jacobins remain in control deprived of the support of the sans-culotterie?

VI

DAILY LIFE OF THE MILITANT
SANS-CULOTTE

WITH so many popular organizations claiming his attention, the militant sans-culotte devoted an important part of his leisure time to political affairs, even when he occupied no official post in his Section. Only an occasional visitor to the Jacobin club—apart from the inconvenience of attending, the social environment of the club was not one to which he was really accustomed—he divided most of his evenings between the *société sectionnaire* and the general assembly. To help him dispose of his time, the societies published a pamphlet entitled *The Political and Patriotic use of the Décade*, closely modelled on the one issued by the Jacobin club itself. Five evenings a week were reserved for the mother-society which was always regarded as 'the unique centre of public opinion'. The popular societies and *sociétés sectionnaires* usually met on the second, fifth, and seventh days of the revolutionary week, in addition to which they often held a civic ceremony at eleven o'clock on the *décadi*. The general assemblies held their meetings on the fifth and tenth days. 'In the evenings, after a hard day's work,' Hébert wrote in the *Père Duchesne*, 'the sans-culotte goes to relax in the Section; and when he is surrounded by his brothers . . . someone will shake him by the hand, another will clap him on the shoulder, asking how life was treating him.'

Wearing his *bonnet rouge* and, if the situation was critical, armed with his pike, the militant sans-culotte arrived at his Section dressed in a manner which immediately placed him in his social category.

The *bonnet rouge*, even more than the short jacket (*la carmagnole*), was the most distinctive part of the costume: worn by slaves after they had been freed, it was also adopted in 1789 as a symbol of liberty. Chateau-vieux's Swiss had worn it after their release from the galleys,[1] and from this time, although it was never

---

[1] Translator's note: forty-one Swiss soldiers of Chateau-vieux's regiment had been condemned to the galleys after mutinying in Nancy over a legitimate request to be paid their share of the regimental fund. General

adopted by the revolutionary bourgeoisie, it became part of the costume of the people: 'The sight of a woollen *bonnet rouge* fills the sans-culotte with joy, and let no one mock him for it,' warned the *Revolutions de Paris* in March 1792. 'His enthusiasm is both praiseworthy and well founded. He has been told that in Greece and Rome this woollen cap was the symbol of freedom and the rallying-sign for all those who hated despotism. With this in mind, his first desire is to become the owner of a *bonnet rouge*.' An attempt to force it upon the Jacobins around this time, however, proved unsuccessful. On 19 March 1792, Petion and Robespierre joined forces to oppose a motion that it should be worn by speakers and the members of the committee: the latter was convinced that it would only 'detract from the powerful impression' of the one national emblem—the tricolour *cocarde*.

Despite the reticence of the Jacobins, the custom of wearing the *bonnet rouge* spread slowly amongst the authorities of the different Sections after 10 August. On 8 December 1792, the general assembly of the Section des Droits-de-l'Homme decreed that the president would be obliged to wear one during meetings; and on the following day, the Section des Sans-Culottes imposed the same obligation on every one of its officials. The *bonnet rouge* had already become the symbol of the political power of the sans-culotterie, and as such the object of sarcastic comment or attacks from the moderates. On 17 April 1793, after the general assembly of the Section du Pont-Neuf had passed a resolution stating that no one would be allowed to speak from the *tribune* unless he was wearing the *bonnet rouge*, one of the members, Dubaton, decided to ignore the ruling in order to voice his protest, 'sparing no adjectives to disparage this sign of the people's freedom'. He was reported to the department of Police Administration and excluded from the general assembly for one year. On 21 April, recognizing that in most of the assemblies the president and secretaries were 'covered with the cap of freedom', the Section du Contrat-Social decreed that its president would present an address to the Convention on the following day *en bonnet rouge et pantalon*.

The victory of the popular movement also meant a victory for the *bonnet rouge*. In the Section de Beaurepaire, Lambin, a medical

Bouillé quelled the mutiny on 31 August 1790. These same soldiers had made themselves popular with the people after refusing to fire on the crowd which had stormed the Bastille. They were released in April 1792.

practitioner and a militant, was 'one of the first to substitute the jacobin costume and, above all, the *bonnet rouge* for his elegant hair-style and professional attire'. On 16 Brumaire, prompted by Chaumette, the General Council of the Commune decreed that the cap would be worn in future by every one of its members; three days later, the treasurer of the *société des Amis-de-la-Patrie* was instructed to buy four *bonnets rouges* for the committee. In the autumn of 1793, a satirical pamphlet appeared depicting the militant sans-culotte with 'a *bonnet rouge* on his head, a sabre at his side, and a large moustache under his nose'. Any citizen imprudent enough to criticize the woollen cap in public was immediately marked down as a suspect. The *société des Républicaines-Révolutionnaires*, however, tried unsuccessfully to impose it upon women. The society was denounced to the General Council of the Commune on 7 Brumaire, and on the following day to the Convention which had already decreed that citizens should be allowed to decide for themselves. When a deputation of women appeared before the General Council of the Commune complete with *bonnets rouges*, it was greeted with cries of 'No *bonnets rouges* for women'. Chaumette was applauded for a rather tendentious speech in which he pointed out that a woman's place was in the home. The anti-feminist reaction was gathering momentum.

The *bonnet rouge* began to disappear with the collapse of the popular movement; we find fewer references to it in the documents after Germinal. On 17 Messidor, the General Council of the Commune heard Payan denounce citizens who thought that they had reached the 'acme' of patriotism by wearing one. As we might expect, the *bonnet rouge* fell into even greater disfavour after Thermidor: Armonville created an uproar in the Convention on 9 Nivôse Year II when he wore one to speak from the *tribune*; and on 30 Pluviôse, after the general assembly of the Section des Lombards had 'expressed its disapproval of the *bonnet rouge*', the secretary carefully detached the national *cocarde* from the cap decorating the wall of the assembly hall.

In any accurate depiction of the militant sans-culotte, the pike claims at least as important a place as the *bonnet rouge*. Symbol of the people in arms, it recalled the great revolutionary *journées* and manifested the exercise of popular sovereignty by means of insurrection. Petitioners appeared at the bar of the Convention or the Jacobin club wearing the *bonnet rouge* and armed with the pike—a telling reminder of popular power. When Jacques Roux summoned the Convention to proscribe speculation and decree the death penalty for hoarding on 25 June 1793, he added: 'The sans-culottes will execute your decrees with their pikes.' According to Hébert, 'when aristocrats hatch some foul plot to undermine freedom, (the sans-culotte) reaches for his sabre and his pike and rushes to his Section'.[2]

Throughout the Revolution, the pike was considered to be the popular weapon *par excellence*. When, at first, the sans-culottes were excluded from the National Guard, patriots demanded that they should be armed with the pike. After war had been declared, they even envisaged the formation of a company of *piquiers*. On 25 July 1792, the Legislative Assembly having been presented with a *Manual of Citizens Armed with the Pike*, Carnot proceeded to demonstrate its many advantages, and proposed that the assembly should organize the manufacture of pikes on a large scale so that they could be supplied to the armies. On 1 August, the Assembly authorized the municipalities to make special arrangements for their manufacture—the cost to be met by the Treasury —and to distribute them amongst citizens who had not been issued with rifles but who were still authorized to bear arms. In the summer of 1793, whilst the sans-culottes were pressing for mass conscription and the government was doing everything possible to encourage the production of war supplies, the pike again seemed to be the only answer to the problem of combating tyranny. On 14 August, the Convention listened to an address praising its many attributes—'the most feared of all weapons . . . this terrible and invincible arm'. On 21 September, the deputy Lejeune told the Jacobins that 'we should turn our pikes to good account . . . this dreaded weapon has been neglected for far too long, the aristocracy having purposely discredited them; but it is only by taking hold of the pike that the French nation was reborn; we have only come to realize the true value of liberty through the sans-culotte pike'.[3] However, this weapon was not used against the enemy on the frontiers, but exclusively in 1793 and the Year II to combat tyranny within the nation. As such, it became the object of lavish praise and was even referred to as something 'sacred' to the sans-culotte cause. The symbol of popular power, it

[2] *Père Duchesne*, No. 335, n.d. (Pluviôse Year II).
[3] *Moniteur*, xvii, 745.

distinguished the 'pike-carrier' sans-culotte. The word itself evolved in much the same way as the word *carmagnole*, ultimately being used to describe the sans-culottes themselves. The pastry-cook Dubois was arrested on 12 September by the *comité révolutionnaire* of the Section des Lombards for shouting *A bas les piques!*[4]

During the Terror, many of the moderates and aristocrats masked their inner convictions beneath the sans-culotte costume and the peculiarities of the militant. In Frimaire Year II, the *Père Duchesne* fulminated against 'the new instructions given by the *porte-esprit* of the king, Jacques Ninny' for the aristocrats to ape the patriots by presenting the following caricature: 'long trousers, a short jacket, a black wig and *bonnet rouge* to hide a fair head of hair, a false moustache, a pipe stuck in the mouth in place of a tooth-pick, a heavy old stick to give the impression of being something of a character, and to swear no more and no less than the *Père Duchesne* instead of tripping words delicately off the tongue'.

The militant sans-culotte could indeed be identified just as readily by his language and behaviour as by his dress, his *bonnet rouge* and his pike. One of the essential features of this behaviour, one which expressed a certain idea of social relationships, was the use of the intimate manner of speech or *tutoiement*—the *Père Duchesne* would also have liked a certain number of oaths to be adopted (the popular tongue having lost none of its vigour at this time).

The democratization of the Revolution was reflected in the change of social habits and customs. The fraternal societies made a significant contribution in this respect by adopting the use of 'citizen' for 'monsieur'—an example which was immediately copied by the Convention. But this did not satisfy those citizens who wished to sweep away all prejudice and inequality, and make their language a vehicle of expression for the sentiments of fraternity which filled their hearts. As early as 14 December 1790, the *Mercure national* had passed its verdict in favour of *tutoiement* in an article *On the Influence of Words and the Power of Speech*. There were renewed appeals in 1791. But its adoption was delayed until the arrival of the sans-culotterie upon the political scene during the summer of 1792 when it was imposed upon at

4 *A.N.*, F⁷ 4682.

least a section of the population. Once again, the decisive factor proved to be the influence of the general assemblies and popular societies. On 4 December 1792, after one speaker had observed 'that the word *vous* militated against the right of equality; that it had only been used in association with feudal rights and obligations; and that *toi* was the most suitable word for free men to adopt', the general assembly of the Section des Sans-Culottes decided to forbid the use of *vous*—'a relic of feudalism'—and substitute *toi* in its place. On 8 December, the assembly of the Section des Droits-de-l'Homme instructed its committee to use *tutoiement*; whilst the *société populaire de Sceaux*, which issued its regulations about this time, announced that 'Members will treat one another as brothers; they will adopt the intimate or familiar manner of speech and address one another as "citizen", completely renouncing the use of the word "monsieur".'[5] As the *Chronique de Paris* had written on 3 October: '*Toi* suits citizen, just as *vous* suits monsieur . . . under the auspicious reign of equality, familiarity is nothing but the reflection of the philanthropic virtues which we carry in our hearts.' The Girondins, however, declared themselves against the popular use of *tutoiement*: Brissot denounced the futility of 'this breach of good manners'; Robespierre shared the latter's views on the question.

The sans-culotte triumph in 1793 brought *tutoiement* into general usage, despite the misgivings of a few Montagnards. Encouraged by their success, the sans-culottes sought to make it compulsory. On 10 Brumaire Year II, a deputation of all the Parisian popular societies protested at the bar of the Convention against the use of *vous*: 'This word is still the cause of much evil; it is a barrier to the social intercourse of the sans-culotterie; it encourages flattery and the conceit of perverse citizens; it contradicts the principles of fraternal virtues.' The popular societies asked for a law 'to reform these vices . . . as a result of which, there will be less pride, less discrimination, less social reserve, more open familiarity, a stronger leaning towards fraternity and, therefore, more equality'. Ignoring the possibility that they might be deceived by this verbal fraternity, the sans-culottes asked that citizens who refused to adopt *tutoiement* should be declared suspect 'as flatterers, encouraging conceit which is simply another word for inequality'. Although Basire wanted the assembly to

[5] *A.D.S.*, AZ 159[2].

issue a decree, the deputation had to be content with an honourable mention. On 21 Brumaire, Basire brought the question up once again and asked for a formal law to be passed. The Convention, having already refused to issue a decree compelling citizens to wear the *bonnet rouge*, again ignored Basire's request and went on to discuss the agenda for the day after Thuriot had asked 'if it was not contrary to the very principle of liberty to tell citizens how they should express themselves'.[6] Obviously opposed to this interpretation, the Directory of the department of Paris, following the lead of the Franciade district, decreed on 22 Brumaire that *tutoiement* would be employed in its offices and in its correspondence: 'in future, only the language of fraternity will satisfy French republicans'. *Tutoiement* was used by every sectionary organization throughout the Year II, as well as by the municipal and national administrations. As for personal relationships, the change was not effected without offending old-established customs. On 5 Nivôse, two citizens entered into an argument with an elderly waiter at the café Procope who had not adopted *tutoiement* when serving them. The informer reporting the incident noted that 'they called him a slave', obliging the waiter to make an apology. 'It must be remembered', the report continued, 'that there is no law forcing anyone to use *tutoiement*, and that no citizen can be allowed to criticize another for not adopting something which is absolutely voluntary.'[7]

After Germinal, when the fortunes of the popular movement had begun to recede, criticism of *tutoiement* became more frequent —the prelude to an imminent reaction. In his *Reflexions on the Abuse of Authority by the comité révolutionnaire of the Section du Temple*, a citizen named Bouin outlined his particular objections to it, especially when adopted by women: 'Used as it is at present', he explained, 'it produces a bad effect by giving the impression that the Revolution is leading us back to a state of coarse and unmannerly behaviour . . . since there are many officials who use it in a tactless and surly way which offends, humiliates, and loses us the sympathy of the very people we should be trying to win over to our present situation; and this pernicious effect is particularly the case with women for whom *tutoiement* lacks, in every respect, a certain propriety, dignity, and sense of moral decency.'

[6] *Journal de la Montagne*, 22 Brumaire Year II; *Moniteur*, xviii, 402.
[7] *A.N.*, F⁷ 3688³: the first of Pourvoyeur's reports.

On 17 Messidor, the General Council of the Commune heard Payan denounce those who, in order to acquire the reputation of good citizens, were making a determined effort 'to use *tutoiement* gracefully'.[8]

The reaction quickened considerably after 9 Thermidor, *tutoiement* gradually disappearing altogether as popular influence declined. On 11 Nivôse Year III, the *Vedette ou gazette du jour* announced that '*tu* and *toi* are disappearing from ordinary conversation and . . . they do not figure as frequently as they did in epistolary style'. There was a disturbance in the café de Foy on 21 Ventôse after an ordinary citizen had adopted the familiar manner of speech when addressing a general. The *journées* of Prairial dealt the final blow. After the latter insurrection, *tutoiement* disappeared as rapidly, and at the same time, as the ardent desire for equality.

Egalitarianism had been widespread after 10 August 1792, particularly in the National Guard. The General Council of the Commune had ordered on 13 August that all ranks were to be supplied with woollen epaulettes, which immediately attracted ironic comment from the sans-culottes. During the *journées* of Prairial Year III, shouts of '*A bas les épaulettes, A bas les épaulettiers!*' frequently marked the signal for revolt. The sans-culotte did everything he could to proscribe the wearing of any distinctive uniform, protesting strongly against attempts to reintroduce special uniforms for privileged units like the grenadiers and chasseurs. One of the favourite themes of the militants and popular journalists was the recognition of 'practical' equality in the various military units. In *l'Ami du peuple* on 14 August 1793, Leclerc suggested that the Revolutionary Army should provide a salutary example: 'let commanders, officers, and soldiers receive the same pay and eat the same bread, so that differences of rank do not become the object of a vain parade, but serve a useful purpose'. In Brumaire, Hébert devoted part of No. 311 of the *Père Duchesne* 'to a buxom wench named Tulip' who had written from the Moselle to ask him 'Why generals and their aides-de-camps do not also wear the national uniform? Why are they covered in gold braid? Perhaps you will say that it is necessary to have some distinction between the ranks so that the ordinary soldier can recognize his officer; but is it really necessary

[8] *Moniteur*, xxi, 237.

for republicans to distinguish themselves by their fine clothes? . . . If we are all equal, . . . we must put an end to the aristocracy of dress, particularly in the army.' The general assemblies did everything possible to maintain an outward show of military equality in the Parisian National Guard. On 15 April 1792, the assembly of the Section de Quatre-Vingts-Douze invited the Commander-in-Chief 'never to forget that he received his authority from free men, and that free men must never be ordered about like slaves'.[9] The Section de la Cité decreed on 1 Nivôse Year II that each *décadi* officers and non-commissioned officers would eat in the same mess as the lower ranks.

The demand for personal service in the National Guard was the most striking manifestation of this desire for military equality— the sans-culottes launched a determined campaign for the abolition of the system of replacements. On 30 October 1792, the armed Section des Droits-de-l'Homme asked for the passing of 'a severe law against any citizen who refused to serve personally in the Guard, seeing that in a Republic every citizen is a soldier'. The time spent in the National Guard would provide citizens with a preparatory course in equality: 'The obligation of personal service will lead to the complete abolition of the class distinctions which used to exist.' The Section de l'Homme-Armé stated on 25 November 1792 'that the guard-room is the only crucible where we can continue the work of amalgamating hard-working poverty with wealth'.[1] The Sections persisted in their campaign. In July 1793, after the initiative had been taken by the Section des Lombards, they adopted a petition which emphasized the contradiction between the egalitarian principles enshrined in the Declaration of Rights and the system of replacement: 'Legislators, we ask you to decide if equality can possibly exist in a country where the rich are always able to send the poor out to die for them.' The Convention refused to be swayed: an assembly of bourgeois composition, it could not abolish what was, in fact, a privilege of wealth.

The meetings of the general assemblies and *sociétés sectionnaires*, service in the National Guard and patriotic missions did not completely absorb the time which the militant sans-culotte

[9] *A.D.S.*, D 777 2, printed in-8, 2 pp.
[1] *A.P.P.*, AA/266, p. 134.

devoted to social activities. According to the *Journal d'un employé*,[2] he could often be found conversing with his friends in some *cabaret*, passing an evening in one of the many cafés, or perhaps dining out in an inn. Over the glasses of wine, the topic of conversation usually turned to politics and there were many renderings of patriotic hymns. On the days when there was no work (it was some time before the *décadi* supplanted Sunday as a day of rest, but the militant never wavered in his strict observance of the former) the sans-culottes crowded into the nearest suburban *cabaret*. Hébert's pen often lingered over the description of la Courteille with its vine-gardens, its little taverns and its carefree atmosphere. 'The last *décade*', he wrote in the *Père Duchesne* which appeared in Ventôse, 'after I had celebrated republican mass in the temple of Reason in the morning, in other words f . . . having listened to the most patriotic addresses and sung hymns in honour of liberty at the top of my voice, I set out happily in the evening with some fine youngsters to go to vespers in dear old Courteille.' Police-agents were unanimous in their opinion that the people were generally in fine spirits during these days, even when the political situation was critical. 'The streets of la Courteille', reported Perrière on 21 Ventôse Year II, 'overflowed with crowds of happy neatly-dressed citizens; the sounds of dancing and music could be heard everywhere . . . the people observe civic Lent by singing the Carmagnole and all the dearly-loved refrains of liberty.' The sans-culottes did not confine themselves to the taverns of Courteille for long; they soon began to frequent the squares and boulevards which had previously been reserved for the more affluent section of the population. Perrière noted on 15 Ventôse, 'that the boulevards were crowded with people from one end to the other', and that 'there were many more *coeffes*[3] than hats'. But what particularly pleased Perrière was the fact that 'outwardly poor citizens who, in the old days, would never have dared to show themselves in these places reserved for the *élite* of society, were now walking side by side with the rich, holding their heads just as high . . . there was an air of contentment about it all, and a stranger would never have guessed that

---

[2] *A.D.S.*, 4 AZ 425. A manuscript diary of the civil servant Girbal, Year II–Year VI.

[3] Popular style of head-dress as opposed to that worn by the bourgeoisie.

these same people were forced to make so many sacrifices on account of their present situation'.

Lacking the statistical documentation to complement the numerous descriptive passages which are available, it is difficult to present an accurate picture of the day-to-day existence and, particularly, the standard of living of the average sans-culotte. However, judging from the literary sources and the occasional document which enables us to make a more detailed examination, it was extremely modest.

The dossiers dealing with individual cases of bankruptcy provide us with a few figures for the craftsmen and shopkeeper class.[4] It is true that some of these sans-culottes bordered on the middle bourgeoisie. André Guettier, a merchant-currier living in the little rue Taranne, Section des Quatre-Nations, announced his bankruptcy on 28 January 1793, valuing his assets in furniture and household goods at 6,000 *livres*. Jacques Antoine Courbin, a master locksmith in the rue de Bondy who declared himself bankrupt on 25 March, owned furniture, personal belongings, linen, and clothes amounting to 5,000 *livres*. But the majority of these tradesmen and shopkeepers lived in far less comfortable style. The wine-merchant Morville, living in the rue Guérin Boisseau, declared bankrupt on 14 February 1793, only possessed furniture and linen to the value of 850 *livres*; Charles Guendré, who went bankrupt a fortnight later, similar belongings worth 830 *livres*. The assets of Charles-François Madeline, a painter from the rue Saint-Martin, amounted to 600 *livres* in furniture, clothes, and linen. Arnal, a grocer in the rue de Murier Saint-Victor, Section des Sans-Culottes, must have lived on the verge of destitution—his furniture and household goods were valued on 18 February 1793 at just 353 *livres*.

The living conditions of one or two of the sectionary militants, as far as we can judge from the official reports of searches or investigations carried out in the Year III, give this same impression of want or deprivation on an even greater scale. Claude Desmarets, a porter at the wheat quai, appointed as a member of the *comité révolutionnaire* of the Section de la Maison-Commune on 16 October 1793, was soon obliged to tender his resignation—

[4] *A.D.S.*, D 11, U³ 1 and 2, *Tribunal de commerce*, dossiers of bankruptcy 1–72 and 73–163, 14 May–24 December 1792, and 14 January 1793–8 Fructidor Year V.

his salary of 1,800 *livres* a year was not enough for him to provide for his wife and three children. The family lived in one room, furnished only with the bare necessities: two tables, three beds, and a cradle, one chest of drawers, one cupboard, one sideboard 'containing just a few articles of crockery' and 'other small objects which are hardly worth mentioning'. The value of the furniture and household goods belonging to Descombes, Section des Droits-de-l'Homme, executed at the same time as Hébert, did not amount to more than 400 *livres*. Ducroquet, *commissaire aux accaparements* in the Section de Marat, lived with his family in conditions which bordered on misery. When he was arrested in Ventôse—already 700 *livres* in debt—his wife was left penniless; she wrote to him to say that she would borrow money, and save every penny in order 'to make ends meet'. In a letter which Ducroquet wrote to his wife on 1 Germinal, he recalled the difficulties they had faced in order to raise their two children; as for clothing the third child which his wife was expecting, he suggested that his worn shorts or perhaps parcel of old clothes which his mother had promised to send from Amiens might serve the purpose.[5]

Even if he held a minor post as a civil servant or was employed as a *commissaire* by his Section, the sans-culotte could only draw on very limited resources. A *commissaire révolutionnaire* received a salary of 5 *livres* a day, or 1,800 a year; a committee secretary, 1,200, and an office-clerk, 800. The sans-culotte Girbal, a copying-clerk in the office of the *Administration des biens des émigrés*, earned 150 *livres* a month: on 30 Ventôse Year II, he spent 11 *sous* on wine in a *cabaret*; on 4 Germinal, he dined with friends at a cost of 5 *livres*, 2 *sous* per head; when he ate in an inn —not having the time to go home—his meal cost him 32 *sous*; on 10 Messidor, he spent the evening with his wife in Montmartre, paying 4 *livres*, 15 *sous* for a 'poor dinner'. After he had paid for his food, he was obviously left with very little else to meet his other expenses.

It is difficult to decide exactly what proportion of the family budget had to be set aside for rent, but, faced with the increased cost of living due to the depreciation in the value of money, the problem clearly caused the sans-culotte much anxiety. As early as 1789, a *Particular and local cahier of the Third Estate* had

[5] *A.N.*, W 77, pl. 1, p. 51.

asked for 'a limit to the prohibitive cost of rents so that the *petit bourgeois* is not forced to spend half his income just to provide a roof over his head'. The contrast between the residential quarters in the west, and those in the east and centre of Paris was already beginning to provoke comment. Nobles, financiers and the bourgeois *nouveaux riches* were comfortably installed in their splendid town houses, complete with forecourt and garden, stretching from the *faubourg* Saint-Germain to the Chaussée d'Antin and le Roule districts. The popular classes—lower bourgeoisie, shopkeepers, craftsmen, and *compagnons*, lived in overcrowded conditions in the narrow gloomy streets of the old quarters. This social segregation, however, was not complete; the same old buildings often housed the most diverse social categories, from bourgeoisie to *compagnons*—the poorest living on the top floors, wealthier tenants on the lower floors. The *Père Duchesne* tells us that 'we must not expect to find the sans-culottes in palaces, or in the stores of wealthy merchants and dealers, but in the attics where they live. . . . If you want to meet the cream of the sans-culotterie, you must visit the garrets of the workers.'[6] Boutry, a shoe-maker and *commissaire révolutionnaire* in the Section de Mutius-Scaevola, married with two children, occupied only one room on the fifth floor. The shoe-maker Potel, another *commissaire*, lived with his wife and three children on the fourth floor at No. 106 rue Tiquetonne. Again, just one room for the Desmaret's family of five in the Section de la Maison-Commune. These were not exceptional cases, but the living conditions of the majority of the popular militants. The less fortunate, *compagnons*, labourers and odd-job men, continually on the move from one address to another, found accommodation in the many houses offering furnished rooms (*maisons garnies*).

During the early years of the Revolution, and particularly in 1791, landlords experienced great difficulty in finding tenants, although there were certain brief periods favourable to the letting of furnished rooms. Emigration, economic stagnation, foreign and civil war, as well as the repressive measures which were introduced, all contributed towards the large-scale exodus of Parisians from every class of society, reaching its peak in the spring of the Year II after the law of 27 Germinal had forced nobles and foreigners to

[6] No. 339, n.d. (Pluviôse, Year II).

leave the capital within ten days. However, there were compensating factors: an incoming stream of refugees fleeing from the war in Europe and civil discord within France itself—Belgians, Alsacians, Rhénans, Lyonnais, &c. Finally, the development of the administrative machine and the organization of industry on a war basis attracted a considerable number of minor civil servants and workers into the various Parisian offices and workshops.

Despite the shortage of tenants, however, the sans-culottes, who found that the value of their money was depreciating from day to day, still thought the price of rents excessive. The popular campaign for price-fixing even covered this question of high rents—we find several petitions demanding reductions, and a few suggesting a maximum rental charge corresponding to that imposed on basic commodities of food. Greater stress was laid on this aspect of the campaign towards the end of the summer of 1793, although there does not appear to have been any particular deterioration in the problem of accommodation; it was simply that the success of the popular campaign had encouraged the sans-culottes to make further claims. On 5 September 1793, Barbot, a retail haberdasher living at No. 17 rue Transnonain in the Section des Gravilliers, urged that 'a general law to curb the covetousness of landlords' should be passed. On 16 October, the Section de la Cité presented a draft petition for the approval of the general assemblies which sought to reduce the cost of leasing property. Adopted by all the Sections, it was presented to the Convention on 10 Brumaire Year II. Admitting that 'The law of the maximum has proved to be a singular blessing for the people', the petition went on to suggest that 'this notable act of justice would appear to be incomplete'. What was needed, in the opinion of the Sections, was a reduction in the cost of leasing and renting property so that prices corresponded once again to their 1760 level, 'because it was in 1764 that the tyrant Louis XV and his perfidious ministers began to speculate on the living conditions of the people; it was from this time that the sudden rise in the cost of leasing property followed closely upon a similar rise in the cost of food'.[7] On 17 Brumaire, the Section de l'Observatoire asked the General Council of the Commune to allow the wives of volunteers to occupy houses requisitioned by the nation and *émigré* property

---

[7] *A.N.*, D III, 251–2, d. 1; *Journal de la Montagne*, 11 Brumaire Year II.

which was still vacant, doubtless with no charge for the title-deeds. The Convention, which had already agreed to the maximum on basic commodities of food much against its will, refused to fix the price of rents which would have been a direct infringement of the rights of landlords.

This same conservative approach to the social structure created many difficulties for principal tenants as well as those who let furnished rooms. Landlords usually let a house *en bloc* to one principal tenant, more often than not a trader, shopkeeper, or craftsman who used the ground floor for business purposes or workshop, occupied one apartment for himself, and then sub-let the remainder. Responsible to the landlord for the payment of rents and the general upkeep of the building, the sub-tenants addressed all their problems to him. In the Year II, this main tenant, his own business already suffering from the effects of price-fixing, particularly if he was a trader, found it extremely difficult to collect all the rents from his sub-tenants on the appointed date—a problem which the landlord, solely concerned with receiving an exact account, refused to take into consideration. On 28 Floréal Year II, nine principal tenants, all of them butchers whose businesses were on the verge of bankruptcy, urged the Convention to authorize the annulment of their leases. The *Comité de législation* opposed the measure on the grounds that if it did agree, it would not be long before every principal tenant would be asking for the same concession, in particular 'those who keep furnished rooms'.

The situation in which the latter found themselves was indeed just as critical. At first, the attraction of the Revolution in Paris had brought visitors from abroad and the provinces searching for accommodation which enabled them to enjoy a period of comparative prosperity—the number of leases taken out from 1789 to 1791 show this quite clearly. But once the Revolution reached a more critical stage, when war had been declared and the Terror organized, people who let furnished rooms began to lose their tenants; the price of furnished sub-let rooms fell by a half. Harassed by their landlords, forced in some cases to sell their furniture which meant an irreparable blow to their business, they also began to ask for the cancellation of their leases. On 8 Brumaire Year II, managers of *maisons garnies* from the *faubourg* Saint-Antoine told the Convention that 'Everyone knows the business of letting furnished rooms in Paris is, if not completely finished, then quite definitely at a standstill until the end of the war'; the measures of general security, they explained, had deprived them of lodgers: 'Legislators, is it your wish that we should hand over to our landlords the money which we do not even receive ourselves?' The refusal of the Convention and its *Comité de législation* to reply to these complaints soon led to the presentation of more petitions: 'In all its decrees, the Convention has done everything possible to assist the sans-culotterie and ensure a fairer distribution of wealth'; surely, it would not force citizens with families to sell their furniture 'so that their losses can enrich wealthy landlords, the majority of whom show very little sympathy for the Revolution?' On 15 Brumaire, yet another protest presenting similar arguments, this time from managers of furnished rooms in the *faubourg* Saint-Honoré. Complaints continued to pour in throughout the Year II; many sectionary officials were themselves sub-letting furnished rooms. In Floréal, a citizen named Bazin vehemently attacked landlords whose incomes 'had not fallen by one *sou*', and who had loaded the full weight of their greed on the backs 'of the most useful and industrious section of the population'. In Prairial, on 4 Thermidor, and again on 17 Fructidor, the managers of *maisons garnies* repeated their grievances. However, in a memorandum issued at the end of Prairial, the *Comité de législation* explained that 'the observation of principles' made it impossible for such petitions to be welcomed and for leases to be annulled. The possibility of an indemnity could not be entertained without laying an additional burden on public finances.

The problem was practically insoluble. The government was trapped between popular demands on the one hand, and the principle of social conservation on the other. Once it had decided that they could not attack the rights of ownership, it was inevitable that the former would be rejected. The Thermidorean reaction, by making it possible for *émigrés* and suspects to return to Paris, finally resolved the problem of furnished rooms; but it also provoked a serious accommodation crisis from which the sans-culottes were the first to suffer.

The question of accommodation and high rents was of secondary importance to the sans-culottes when compared with the problem which absorbed most of their wages or salaries—that of providing enough food for themselves and their families.

Unquestionably, bread was the principal item in the sans-culotte diet. For the lower classes, it represented practically the exclusive source of nourishment; their daily wages being usually too low for them to afford any other major commodity. The *Père Duchesne* was fond of repeating that 'Our principal possession is bread.' On 26 February 1793, the Section des Invalides drew the attention of the Convention to the high cost of food by pointing out that 'the men of 14 July and 10 August live on bread. . . . What is going to happen in homes where ten *livres* of bread are eaten every day if bread remains at the present high level fixed by monopolists.'[8] A pamphlet entitled *The Last Word of the Sans-Culottes asking for Bread*, which appeared about this time, is a lengthy statement of their grievances illustrating its importance in the lives of the people. The daily ration of the average adult worker was estimated to have been three *livres*; that of a child. one and a half *livres*. At the height of the famine on 25 Ventôse Year III, the Convention decided that one and a half *livres* was the minimum ration which could be given to manual workers, the remainder of the population receiving only one *livre*.[9] In normal times, this amount was doubled. The importance of bread as a source of nourishment forced the sans-culotte to be more exacting than he might otherwise have been; not only did he want sufficient bread for his needs, but he wanted it to be of good quality—this helps to explain the campaign for the maximum and for strict regulations, the continual recriminations about alleged infringements, the demand for bread to be made from pure flour in the same way as that baked for the rich. Hébert found that these topics lent themselves particularly well to the diatribes of the *Père Duchesne*. We can derive some idea of the difficulties which faced lower-class families if we look at the case of one workman in the Panthéon timber-yards: in Ventôse Year II, his daily wage was three *livres*; the price of bread at this time was three *sous* a *livre*, and the daily consumption of one family of four to five persons was as high as twelve *livres*. The amount deducted from the family budget for bread appears to have remained at a dangerously high level throughout the Year II; but unfortunately, lacking the necessary statistical documentation, it is impossible to offer any precise figures.[1]

[8] *A.N.*, F¹⁰ 227.   [9] *Moniteur*, xxiii, 701.
[1] C. E. Labrousse in his *Esquisse du mouvement des prix et des revenus en France au XVIIIᵉ siècle* reaches the following conclusions: bread claimed

Despite the efforts of the government and the Commune, there was very little demand for the potato, a vegetable which, according to one militant belonging to the *société populaire des Amis-de-la-Patrie*, few sans-culottes found to their liking. Meat, on the other hand, figured fairly prominently in the diet of the Parisian lower classes. We find numerous indications of this; in particular, the large number of butchers in the capital, and the widespread discontent when meat became scarce towards the end of the winter of the Year II. When the Section de l'Indivisibilité decided that it was necessary to ration the supply of meat on 30 Pluviôse, it fixed the daily amount for each person at half a *livre*. The sans-culottes appear to have taken reasonable advantage of this allocation: Girbal, a civil servant living in the Section de Guillaume-Tell, received two *livres* for himself and his wife on 11 Ventôse; two *livres* again on the sixteenth; and three *livres* of veal on the eighteenth. However, when the municipal authorities passed a regulation on the distribution of meat on 29 Germinal, the individual ration was fixed at half a *livre* every five days.

Finally, an appreciable proportion of the family budget was spent on the purchase of wine. Taverns for the poorest citizen, cafés and *cabarets* for the more affluent, the sale of drinks played a significant part in the daily lives of the sans-culotterie, emphasizing the importance of the large number of wine-merchants in the Parisian popular movement, and the relatively high proportion of official posts which they occupied in the Sections. Girbal regularly frequented the *cabarets* with his colleagues, carefully recording every item of expenditure. He paid particular attention to his personal store of wine, going as far as the villages on the southern outskirts of the capital—Clamart or Ivry—to choose his supply, and then bottling it himself. The countless complaints about the mixing of wines—the *boissons mixtionnées* as they were called by the *commissaires* appointed as wine-tasters—prove that the sans-culotte had a high regard for his wine and its quality.

over half the family budget of the worker; vegetables, fat, and wine, 16 per cent. (which would seem to be too low); clothing, 15 per cent., heat, 5 per cent., and light, 1 per cent. On the eve of 1789, following the general rise in the cost of living, bread had accounted for 58 per cent.; it rose as high as 88 per cent. in 1789, leaving only 12 per cent. for other expenses. In the Year II, as a result of the fixing of prices, the figure for bread must have fallen, but would still have claimed over half the budget of the lower-class family.

The worst possible crime in the eyes of the *Père Duchesne* was to be caught drinking water. There can be no doubt whatsoever that on this subject at least, Hébert accurately reflected the feelings of the lower classes. If the authorities did not put an end to the intrigues of monopolists, he wrote in Pluviôse, 'we will all be drinking water like ducks, which, in my opinion, is a punishment which should be reserved for moderates, aristocrats, royalists, and followers of Philip Egalité'.[2]

The literary sources also give us some idea of the sort of life which the average sans-culotte led. Hébert often used the *Père Duchesne* to paint a vivid picture—not completely devoid of emotional content—of the sans-culotte who was forced to live 'from day to day by the work of his hands. But as long as he has a large loaf in his bread-bin and a drop of brandy (*rogome*) in his glass, he is happy.'[3] If the *Père Duchesne* shows us the sans-culotte content to live with his wife and children in his garret, provided that he has enough bread, 'a drop of stew', and 'the patriotic glass to buck them up when they are exhausted by fatigue',[4] Chaumette, more emotionally inclined, sees the wretched man 'bent in two by the crushing weight of a hard day's work; struggling against misfortune from one day to the next, and forced to return in the evening to his attic where he moistens his crust of dry bread with his tears'. The diatribes against luxury, the definition of the ideal life, simple and frugal, which we meet occasionally in the texts are not just empty echoes of Rousseau: they describe a certain way of life, a certain popular conception of existence. In his *Interviews with a Citizen from Philadelphia . . . and a Republican Frenchman*, the civil servant Maurin finds that happiness is dependent upon 'natural virtues'—'Let us look in at the home of a patriot. . . . We find simple customs, a frugal table, a mother feeding her baby. . . .'

Owing to the lack of documentary evidence, it is equally difficult to be certain of the standard of education reached by the average sans-culotte as it is to reconstruct the material conditions of his daily life.

There were many militants occupying important posts in the Sections who could neither read nor write. Motivated by hunger

[2] No. 341, n.d. (Pluviôse Year II).
[3] No. 313, n.d. (end of Brumaire Year II). [4] No. 341.

and misery during periods of crisis they were, however, conscious of a certain number of ideas which had filtered down from the more cultivated social categories to the least educated: as a result, citizens who had never even read the *Social Contract* could begin to grasp Rousseau's ideas on popular sovereignty. The popular societies, by bringing the sans-culottes into direct contact with the work of the Jacobin club, played a major role in this respect; their contribution to the political education of the sans-culotterie was of the greatest importance. This helps to explain the high regard in which they were held by the Montagnards as well as the hatred with which they were pursued after Thermidor.

The popular press exercized a far greater influence than its actual circulation might lead us to suppose: the number of citizens whose opinions were shaped by the patriotic papers was greatly increased by the fact that they were read regularly in the evening meetings of the popular societies and general assemblies. There were also numerous occasions when workmen or passers-by gathered round to listen to readings of these papers on building sites or in the public squares. Varlet was not the only militant to use the speaker's rostrum for purposes of propaganda. On 15 October 1793, a large crowd gathered on the pont-au-Change to listen to two orators, standing on wooden platforms, reading patriotic news-sheets.[5] A citizen named Collignon described himself as 'the public reader of the sans-culottes': from the beginning of the Revolution, he had been reading a republican catechism which he had composed himself to crowds assembled in public squares and places of entertainment. In October 1793, the general assembly and the popular society of the Section de l'Arsenal, having decided 'that there were not enough presses to meet the demand for instructing the people', asked for 'the organization of a campaign of "vocal publicity", by means of a paper printed expressly for the people and read, even in the villages, by officials and trained public readers'. Although this petition was not accepted by the authorities, who were inclined to distrust all popular orators, the reading of patriotic news-sheets in the streets, on building sites and timber-yards, continued to be a regular feature of political life in Paris until the Year III. On 1 Prairial at ten o'clock in the morning, the stone-cutter Closmesnil, perched precariously on some scaffolding, read a news-sheet

[5] *Journal de la Montagne*, 26th day, 1st month Year II.

to more than 100 workers at the Panthéon yards which was judged to be subversive, and which led to his prompt arrest. Petitioning in his favour, his work-mates explained that they had chosen him 'because of his voice and his willingness, to read a paper called the *Auditeur national* every day at meal-times, which we buy collectively so that we can all be informed of events in a fraternal spirit'. The case of the workers on the Panthéon site was certainly not an isolated one.

In the streets, occasionally at work or during the course of an evening's stroll, the sans-culotte had many opportunities, not only to listen to the reading of current political writings, but also to read them for himself. Some of the militants used to post up manuscript sheets in public. In the Section Chalier, Montain-Lambin could be found twice every *décade* nailing his manuscript sheet to the door of the Section's guard-room which, according to the police-agents, attracted a considerable number of readers. Printed posters were of even greater interest: until Germinal, the different factions indulged in an absolute riot of placarding. During the first few days of Nivôse, the walls of Paris were covered with posters issued by Vincent, Ronsin, Manuel, and Maillard. Passers-by would gather in small groups to discuss the different points of view, thus ensuring that even the most ignorant sans-culotte participated in the political education of the people.

It seems most unlikely that the militants who had received a little education would have taken much advantage of it to read at home. Occupied with their work during the day, and with the meetings of the popular society or general assembly in the evening, there was very little time left for them to cultivate the habit. Hébert describes how the sans-culotte rose at dawn, 'sweated blood and tears' during the day to feed his family, then returned to his garret in the evening after spending a few hours at his Section—'He eats with the appetite of a horse, and after his meal, he keeps his family amused by reading to them of the "great anger" or the "great joy" of the *Père Duchesne*.'[6] But the average sans-culotte found it extremely difficult to find enough time to read even the popular news-sheets regularly. Official reports of searches carried out in the homes of the militants in the Year II, and in Year III, rarely establish the presence of any books or collections of newspapers; the most we find is an occasional

[6] No. 313, n.d. (end of Brumaire).

reference to a few odd news-sheets by Marat or Hébert, or one or two patriotic writings. The reading of the majority of the militants went no further than these current commentaries on political events. Even the most informed militant does not appear to have been directly acquainted with the philosophical thought of the century: usually, he had only an indirect knowledge through the press or the speeches of the Jacobins and Cordeliers acquired, more often than not, in the meetings of the popular societies. In all probability, it was through these channels that Rousseau's ideas finally succeeded in influencing the most active and the most politically conscious militants.

As for more serious works of literature, the reading of the most educated sans-culotte did not extend any further than the books sold by *colporteurs*. Despite the fact that it has now disappeared completely, the literature sold by these travelling booksellers has played an important part in the formation of popular sensibility and national culture. Malesherbes, in his *Mémoire sur la librairie* of 1759, tells us that the peddling of books increased considerably during the course of the eighteenth century, despite a series of particularly repressive laws. The Revolution gave a tremendous incentive to the trade by abolishing this legislation, by relaxing all forms of censorship, and by interesting the sans-culotterie in political affairs. In the Year II, works on piety and particularly the lives of the saints, which had been one of the traditional features of this popular literature, disappeared from the *colporteur*'s box. On the other hand, works on magic appear to have attracted just as much interest judging from the continued success of *The Explanation of Dreams and the Art of Fortune-Telling with Cards*. Romantic works were still much in demand, and there was a great increase in the number of printed works on contemporary political events. At the beginning of Pluviôse Year II, the *comité révolution-naire* of the Section de la Montagne seized possession of the box belonging to the *colporteur* Buy during the course of a search, and drew up the following inventory of its contents.[7] Serious literature is represented by the *Œuvres* of Racine, the *Pucelle d'Orléans*, the *Liaisons dangereuses* and *Tom Jones ou l'enfant trouvé*—these works were intended for a more cultivated clientele, one which can already be classed as bourgeois. *The Cavern of Mathilde*, and the *Tale of a Tub* satisfied the romantic or satirical demands of truly

[7] *A.N.*, F⁷ 4627.

popular taste. *Ways of Making Ends Meet* can be classified along with the various writings on how to overcome poverty and the sayings of *le bonhomme Richard* which figures so prominently in popular *colportage* at the end of the eighteenth century. Contemporary political writings were represented by a *Poem for the Revolution*, and two pamphlets without titles. This wide range of subject-matter proves clearly enough that the literature sold by *colporteurs* was intended to meet the demands of every section of the sans-culotterie, from the lower bourgeoisie, endowed with a certain degree of culture, to the really popular levels.

The sans-culottes idealized the simplicity of their daily existence, transforming it into a particular pattern of behaviour, and condemning those who failed to conduct themselves in accordance with its principles. The militant sans-culotte was a born moralizer, quick to identify his own way of life with the practice of republican virtues. According to the militants, public virtues could only be founded upon personal qualities, and both found their expression in the sentiment of patriotism: 'To be a good citizen', explained the French republican to the citizen from Philadelphia, 'one must be a good son, a good husband and a good father; one must unite in a single word every private and public virtue . . . only then will you have a true definition of the word patriotism.'

The militants did not confine themselves to these Rousseauist considerations. Chaumette stormed against the General Council of the Commune for its moral failings, and undertook to purge the entire capital. On 16 September 1793, the *société des Républicaines-Révolutionnaires* petitioned for prostitutes to be detained in national institutions where the environment would be conducive to clean living, and where they could be given work befitting their sex. The society also suggested that lectures might be given twice a week on patriotism, and 'that finally we should attend to their physical and moral purification'.[8] In an address to the Convention, the Section des Tuileries asked for a law to be passed suppressing all houses of immorality and gambling. 'Without morals, there can be no law and order; without law and order, no personal safety; without personal safety, no liberty.' Throughout the Terror, citizens 'lacking morals' were frequently classed as

[8] *Procès-verbaux*, imp. xxi, 23: *Moniteur*, xvii, 661; *Archives parlementaires*, lxxv, 284.

suspects; a denunciation in September 1793 stated that morals were 'the main foundation' of the Republic. On 28 Ventôse, the *comité révolutionnaire* of the Section du Faubourg-Montmartre decided upon the arrest of a citizen named Hautevoine because he 'lacked moral principles, lacked any sense of decency—in fact, an immoral citizen who makes his living partly out of his daughters who lead a scandalous life'. In his manuscript news-sheet, Montain-Lambin stated that his objective was 'to instruct citizens in their duty': he was particularly severe with drunkards—'the man who seeks to lose his sense of reason is not worthy of being a republican'—and prostitutes. His news-sheet was a great success. These pronouncements on morals and virtue do not reflect a state of general corruption so much as the simplicity and dignity of the sans-culotte life as regulated by the militants. There are many brief depictions in Hébert's writings of the kind of family life which must have been enjoyed by the majority of the sans-culottes: 'When he enters his garret in the evening, his wife throws her arms around his neck, his little ones run to kiss him.'[9] Ducroquet's simple letters to his wife bear witness to a family relationship full of tenderness and dignity, even in its extreme poverty.

A sense of dignity, but without social prejudice. There were frequent cases of sans-culotte couples living together without having gone through the formality of a marriage ceremony; some of these free unions were regulated after the birth of a child; but there must have been many which were never officially solemnized. The number of illegitimate children recorded in the registers of the Humanité alms-house—formerly the Hôtel-Dieu—in the Year II is revealing in this respect. On 13 October 1792, Etienne Pascal, a *compagnon* farrier of 26 years of age, and Marie-Louise Buffin, one year older, presented themselves before the general assembly of the Section de Bondy 'united eighteen months ago by the tenderest bonds of affection, and having a child baptized under their respective names, born of the free union in which they had lived since this time'. They had come to attest 'the authenticity of their love', having no other proof than the 'free, reciprocal, and express wish which binds them one to the other'. The general assembly 'out of respect for good morals and the most respectable of natural emotions', ordered that this declaration should be

[9] *Le Père Duchesne*, No. 313, n.d. (end of Brumaire).

transcribed into its registers.[1] This was, however, an exceptional case: this simple declaration before their fellow citizens was regarded as being just as superfluous as the legal ties of marriage. Petitioning for the recognition of equality between legitimate and illegitimate children on the question of succession, a sans-culotte 'master-bricklayer' described himself—not without ostentation—as 'an illegitimate son, father of six children whose mother has never been to a marriage ceremony, which does not prevent the household from getting on like a house on fire and the children from growing up just as if the notary and the curé had paid us a visit'.[2]

The persistence with which the sans-culottes demanded equal rights for illegitimate children and unmarried mothers reflects the importance of free union amongst the lower classes. The Section de Bon-Conseil complained to the Convention that the law which provided assistance to the families of soldiers 'makes no reference to those interesting souls who, victims of a cruel prejudice, used to be called illegitimate. It is equally silent on women who, out of a sincere feeling of affection, have given birth to children before fulfilling their legal obligations; that is, by omitting the formality which authorizes their union in the eyes of the law.'[3] In practice, however, the sectionary authorities made no distinction between unmarried mothers or illegitimate children during the Year II. On 20 Messidor Year III, a member of the commission providing relief for the families of soldiers in the Section de la Maison-Commune noted that different decrees of the assembly granted assistance 'to women who are not bound to citizens serving on the frontiers by the legitimate ties of marriage'—honnêtes gens were regaining control, and re-establishing the ideas of traditional morality; the assembly decreed that in future its commission would not grant assistance to women 'who cannot furnish proof of being legally married'.

The absence of social prejudice amongst the sans-culotterie helped to strengthen their social solidarity. The word itself does not do justice to all which this entailed, but there are numerous examples of this civic virtue which, according to the sans-culottes, was nothing but the outward expression of their fraternity. If

---

[1] B.V.C., MS. 120.
[2] 'Letter of a sans-culotte . . . to the Père Duchesne', imp., n.d., in-8°, 4 p. (B.N., Lb⁴¹ 3431; Tourneux, No. 20194).
[3] A.N., W 174, n.d.

there were certain individuals who practised social relief work, the contemporary form of charity—Jacques Roux in the Section des Gravilliers and Montain-Lambin in the Section de Beaurepaire, who described himself as 'the dispenser of good works'—the sans-culottes as a group were conscious of their mutual responsibility and interdependence. In the frequent collections levied—not all of them used for purely patriotic purposes—the sans-culottes gave proportionally more than citizens with better means: yet another grievance against the rich. The adoption of children was one way by which they manifested their practical solidarity. On 16 October 1793, the Section de la Montagne adopted an orphan whose father had left with the armies; one woman immediately offered to look after him, and the assembly confidently placed the child in her care. On 30 Frimaire Year II, the Section des Droits-de-l'Homme adopted the child of a captain killed in the Vendée, whose mother had recently died. Françoise Ravinet, an inn-keeper, well known for her participation in all the revolutionary *journées* up to Prairial Year III, herself the mother of four young children, did not hesitate to take charge of a fifth 'through adoption and humanity'. We can discern in these examples the glimmerings of a new moral code.

In their everyday behaviour and mentality, their social and political aspirations, as well as by their organizations, the section-ary militants undoubtedly represented an autonomous force in the revolutionary movement. The crisis occasioned by the shortage of food supplies immeasurably strengthened their power by mobilizing the sans-culotterie. As a result, the Revolutionary Government and the ascendancy of the bourgeoisie were threat-ened. It is true that certain characteristics tend to identify the sans-culotte with the Jacobin—like the latter, he could be fanatical in his political convictions, finding in his sectarianism the heroism needed to face, if necessary, the ultimate sacrifice. His passion for unity was just as great, and if his behaviour occasionally appeared to be leading him in the direction of anarchy, he had no sympathy whatsoever for individualism. Within the heart of a Revolution which had destroyed social orders, institutions, and communities, the sans-culotte, like the Jacobin, restores the spirit of party and endows it with a certain human warmth; his familiar horizons were bounded by his 'brothers and friends' in the popular societies and general assemblies. The militant sans-culotte lived as one of a group and acted *en masse*.

In the final analysis, it is the passion for equality which distinguishes the sans-culotte: 'practical equality' (*l'égalité de fait*) was the necessary complement to equality of rights.[4] It is, above all, this passion which fired his revolutionary enthusiasm and mobilized him against the aristocracy, then the bourgeoisie. Not only does it set him apart from the Girondin and the moderate; it also distinguishes him from the Jacobin and the Montagnard, both equally preoccupied with the social hierarchy. By this same passion for equality, the sans-culotte recalls the leveller (*niveleur*) and anticipates the social democrat (*partageux*).

But was the time ripe for a social democracy?

[4] Babeuf uses this expression in *le tribun du peuple*, No. 35, 9 Frimaire Year IV.

CONCLUSION:

THE POPULAR MOVEMENT AND BOURGEOIS REVOLUTION

In the final analysis, the 9 Thermidor constitutes a tragic episode in the conflict of classes within the former Third Estate. But, to place it in the right perspective, we need to remember that the Revolution was fundamentally a struggle between the European aristocracy and the Third Estate as a whole. In this struggle, it is hardly surprising that the French bourgeoisie should have played the leading role. The Revolutionary Government, founded upon an alliance between the montagnard bourgeoisie and the Parisian sans-culotterie, had been given the task of defending the Revolution against the aristocracy both within France and beyond her frontiers. As far as the Montagnards were concerned, it was perfectly natural that the Revolution should have placed the bourgeoisie in control of the nation's destiny; but, in any case, this was not the immediate problem. Solely concerned with victory, the Montagnards—particularly the Robespierrists—realized that the Third Estate would have to remain united as it had been in 1789. This explains the alliance with the sans-culotterie which made possible the installation of the Revolutionary Government during the summer of 1793. It also explains why this government —at least until the spring of 1794—should have been so anxious to arbitrate between the interests of the bourgeoisie and the popular movement; to share the necessary sacrifices between them; and to intervene immediately either of them threatened to undermine the policy of national defence. It was a question of directing the entire resources of the nation for war.

On the basic issues—hatred of the aristocracy and the will for victory—the Parisian sans-culottes wholeheartedly supported the Revolutionary Government: the measure of this support can be judged from the fact that on 13 Vendémiaire and 18 Fructidor, setting aside their own legitimate grievances, many of them assisted the Thermidorean bourgeoisie to crush the counter-revolution. But differences of opinion on other vital issues rapidly alienated the sympathy of the Parisian sans-culotterie; and although these differences can be traced to the consequences of the war, they nevertheless reveal, quite clearly, the incompatible interests of two distinct social categories.

On the political level, the war created the need for an authoritarian régime. The sans-culottes showed that they were fully conscious of this by playing an important part in the creation of such a government. But it soon became apparent that the democratic ideas favoured by the Montagnards and the sans-culotterie were not designed to meet the particular problems which arose: this was especially true of the kind of democracy practised by the sans-culotterie which, moving spontaneously towards the exercise of direct government, was incompatible with the conduct of a war. The sans-culottes had asked for a strong government to crush the aristocracy; they never considered the possibility that, in order to do this, it would be forced to discipline the popular movement.

In addition, the political ideals of the sans-culotterie, vaguely defined during the revolutionary insurrections, did not tend to further the interests of liberal democracy as interpreted by the bourgeoisie, but those of popular democracy. Control over their elected representatives, the right of the people to revoke their mandate, certain procedures such as those of voting aloud or *par acclamation*, proved that the sectionary militants had no intention of accepting an empty and formal type of democracy. Their struggle succeeded in giving practical expression to what had originally been only an idea; they saw the Republic as the embodiment of the democratic ideal. For the really politically-minded sans-culotte, liberty and equality had not been offered to the people once and for all in 1789; they were principles which had to be reconquered from day to day—liberty becomes liberation, equality, social acquisition. This was the only way in which the happiness of every citizen (*le bonheur commun*), universally recognized as the aim of society, could be realized. This process cannot be explained simply by the unfolding of events during the Year II: it was a fundamental contradiction between the Parisian sans-culotterie and the bourgeoisie, between sectionary militants and the Revolutionary Government.

From an economic and social point of view, the contradiction was equally insurmountable. Robespierre and many other Montagnards had repeated that the country could not be governed in time of war as in peace, a statement which was not only politically, but economically valid. The Revolutionary Government, equally dependent upon both sides, was forced to arbitrate between the conflicting interests of the *possédants*, prepared to support the government, and the wage-earners, instrumental in bringing it to power.

It was only with considerable reluctance that the members of the Committee of Public Safety—firm adherents of a liberal economic system—agreed to pursue a policy of controls and fixed prices. It was only the realization that they could not harness the resources of the nation for war without a controlled economy that finally convinced them of its necessity as a temporary measure to be discarded once the war had ended. The revolution which they controlled was still, despite its increasingly democratic character, a bourgeois revolution. As such, it would have been absurd to fix the price of manufactured goods without fixing wages which ultimately decided what their cost price would be. The government found that it had to maintain a certain balance between the owners of business and manufacturing concerns, whose support was indispensable, and the wage-earners.

A controlled economy was also necessary if a complete collapse in the intrinsic value of money was to be avoided. In order to prevent the *assignat* from becoming absolutely worthless, despite the inevitable inflation (the possibility of a complete devaluation of money in the middle of a war was not seriously considered), the government was forced to impose a maximum on wages as well as on manufactured goods. If it had agreed to a rise in wages, this would inevitably have led to a rise in the price of supplies vital to the war effort, since the government had decided not to interfere in private ownership or profits—a policy which can only be explained in the light of a bourgeois revolution. The Committee of Public Safety accepted price-fixing as a means of realizing a policy of national defence financed by the State without releasing an 'infernal' spiral in prices, profits and wages which would, in turn, have resulted in uncontrollable inflation—the *assignat* would have been ruined and the Revolutionary Government swept from power.

This policy depended upon the continuation of the alliance between the Montagnards and the sans-culotterie, and, although it adversely affected the interests of the bourgeoisie—even the jacobin bourgeoisie—by restricting economic freedom and placing a ceiling on profits, the latter, at least, were prepared to play their part in the defence of the Revolution and accepted the dictatorship of the Committees. But, apart from war supplies bought by the State and fodder requisitioned from the peasantry, craftsmen and shopkeepers—Jacobins included—evaded the provisions of the maximum. A conflict with the wage-earners was inevitable.

The sans-culottes, suffering from the effects of inflation and the shortage of food supplies, still looked at the problem from the standpoint of a relationship between wages and prices as they had done under the *ancien régime*. Their campaign for price-controls and requisitioning does not reflect their concern for national defence so much as their interest in providing themselves and their families with sufficient food. As for the workers, they were naturally anxious to take advantage of the relative shortage of labour to demand higher wages without bothering to consider the effect upon prices. From the autumn to the spring of the Year II, when the sans-culottes were in control of the capital, or, at least, feared by the Convention, they were successful in these demands: the Hébertist Commune, disregarding the law, refused to intervene. The government decided that it was time to act.

After Germinal, the Revolutionary Government reviewed the problem of the declining profits of manufacturing concerns, caught between the maximum on the one hand and an illegal rise in wages on the other. Numerous decrees by the Committee of Public Safety authorized a rise in the price of goods compared with the scale fixed by the maximum of Ventôse, despite the law. But these higher prices would have had no real effect if wages had continued to rise. The result was the decree of the Robespierrist Commune on 5 Thermidor enforcing the *maximum des salaires*. Although this decree was only to be introduced in the capital, the Committee of Public Safety—in view of the approaching harvest—had asked the districts to decree what amounted to a similar drop in wages for agricultural workers as early as Prairial. By depriving the wage-earners of the advantages which they had so recently acquired, the Commune appeared to be departing from the mediatory policy which had previously been adopted by the government. The controlled economy of the Year II, which was not based upon class differences, became unbalanced: after Thermidor, the whole structure collapsed.

It is clear that in a fundamentally bourgeois society the system of arbitration introduced by the Committee of Public Safety would be bound to favour the *possédant* class more than the wage-earners; the former being in a position to compensate for losses sustained as a result of price-fixing by producing for a private market. If it had been at all possible, the Robespierrists would probably have been only too happy to redress the balance. There can be little doubt that artisans and shopkeepers would have been less hard on the consumer if, assured of an adequate supply of raw material and food supplies, their sales guaranteed them a reasonable profit. *Compagnons* and artisans had always maintained that, in order to safeguard their right to live, prices should bear a direct relationship to wages: they might well have resigned themselves to the maximum if only they could have been sure of receiving the basic necessities of life.

But the Revolutionary Government simply did not have the means of regulating the law of supply and demand for manufactured goods and vital food supplies: production methods and transport facilities had not yet been modernized by the capitalist concentration, rationalization, and mechanization of industry. The government had to work within the framework of an outmoded economic structure; war further aggravated the problem of keeping the nation supplied. Insurmountable difficulties arose when the economic system of the Year II was introduced to meet the demand for livestock and farm produce. The interests of the peasantry had also to be taken into consideration. Even the regular supply of bread was affected by inadequate means of transport, coupled with the absence of any form of concentration in the milling trade—one of the problems which capitalism would eventually solve.

The Revolutionary Government decided, therefore, that the best it could do in these circumstances was to keep the population of Paris supplied with bread, without going so far as to organize rationing on a national basis. As for the rest, local authorities and consumers had to make what arrangements they could to see that producers and merchants observed the provisions of the maximum. Requisitioning was reserved solely for the benefit of the army. The Parisian sans-culottes, discovering that this arrangement did not appear to be working in their favour, demanded a rise in wages and resorted to strike action: the Committees, faithful to the tradition of the *ancien régime*, declared such action to be illegal. Thus, at the root of the fundamental contradiction which had arisen between the Revolutionary Government and the popular movement responsible for bringing it to power, lay the failure of an artisanat economy to adapt itself to the demands of a full-scale national war.

The contradictions peculiar to the Parisian sans-culotterie were equally as important in explaining the collapse of the system of the Year II as the conflicts which divided the Revolutionary Government and the popular movement.

There was a social contradiction between the Jacobins, drawn almost exclusively from the ranks of the lower, middle, and even the upper bourgeoisie, and the sans-culottes, if we accept Petion's description of the latter as day-labourers and *compagnons de métiers*. But it would be wrong to identify the sans-culotte with the wage-earner, despite the fact that wage-earners formed the largest section of the sans-culotterie. The reality is far more complex. The sans-culotterie did not constitute a class, nor was the sans-culotte movement based on class differences. Craftsmen, shopkeepers and merchants, *compagnons* and day-labourers joined with a bourgeois minority to form a coalition but there was still an underlying conflict between craftsmen and merchants, enjoying a profit derived from the private ownership of the means of production, and *compagnons* and day-labourers, entirely dependent upon their wages.

The application of the maximum brought this contradiction into the open. Craftsmen and shopkeepers agreed that it was a sound and reasonable policy to force the peasantry to feed the population of the towns; but they protested immediately the provisions of the maximum began to affect their own interests. *Compagnons* reacted in much the same way. By creating a shortage of labour, the *levée en masse* and the civil war led to a rise in wages: if producers and 'middlemen' refused to observe price-fixing, why should the workers offer themselves as victims? The demands of the revolutionary struggle had welded the unity of the Parisian sans-culotterie and momentarily pushed the conflict of interests into the background: there was no question, however, of suppressing them altogether.

Differences in social outlook complicated the problem even

further. The contradictions within the ranks of the sans-culotterie were not simply those which separated the *possédants* and producers from the salaried workers. Amongst the latter we find, in particular, those who belonged to the clerical and teaching professions, who, because of their way of life, regarded themselves as bourgeois, not to be identified with the *bas-peuple*, even if they embraced the same cause. On the other hand, many citizens recognized as being members of the bourgeoisie described themselves as 'sans-culotte' and acted as such.

The sans-culottes, recruited from so many different levels of society, could not, therefore, have been really conscious of belonging to a certain class. Although they were generally hostile to the new methods of production, it was not always from the same motives—the craftsman was afraid of being reduced to the status of a wage-earner; the *compagnon* detested the monopolist because he held him responsible for the rising cost of living. As for the *compagnons* alone, it would be anachronistic to speak of them as being class-conscious, since their mentality was still conditioned by the world of the craftsman in which they lived and worked. The capitalist concentration of industry, by bringing them into daily contact through the factory, had not yet created the mentality which would awaken the feeling of class solidarity.

However, if class-consciousness cannot be attributed to the sans-culotterie as a body, it is possible to detect a certain awareness of class amongst the wage-earners. Entirely dependent upon their employers, they regarded themselves as a distinct social group, not only because of the manual nature of their work and their place in the system of production, but also on account of the clothes which they wore, the food they ate, their pastimes, social habits and, in particular, their living accommodation. The fact that they were mostly uneducated—education being reserved solely for citizens privileged by birth and wealth—also tended to distinguish them from their fellow citizens, creating a feeling of inferiority and, sometimes, of powerlessness amongst the lower classes. Militant sans-culottes frequently reveal their hostility towards *hommes-à-talent*, but, by raising themselves to the same level, longed to play a decisive part in controlling their destiny.

Composed of diverse elements, not constituting a class and, therefore, devoid of class-consciousness, the Parisian sans-culotterie, despite a few hesitant attempts to co-ordinate their activity, lacked a really effective weapon of political action—a strictly disciplined party which could only have been created by a drastic purge followed by recruitment on a class basis. This was equally true of the Revolutionary Government, since the Jacobins themselves were not representative of any one social class. The entire régime of the Year II rested upon an abstract conception of political democracy which largely explains its weakness. The consequences of this were particularly disastrous for the popular movement.

Although there were many militants who tried to discipline the general assemblies and popular societies, leading figures in a number of the Sections aggravated the situation by disputing power amongst themselves, occasionally by abusing it when they eventually succeeded in gaining control. As for the mass of the sans-culotterie, apart from hatred of the aristocracy and the summary methods envisaged for dealing with the problem— chiefly massacre—they do not appear to have been gifted with any degree of political insight: they were simply waiting to receive the benefits which the Revolution would inevitably bring. They campaigned for the maximum, not so much in order to defend the *assignat* and guarantee the production of war supplies, but because they believed that price-controls would help to maintain their standard of living. When they realized that, in many respects, a controlled economy did not meet this requirement, they abandoned it in favour of a new policy. Would the sans-culottes have agreed to drop their demand for higher wages if—an untenable hypothesis—*possédants* and producers had agreed to respect the provisions of the maximum by accepting a margin of profit which the Revolutionary Government considered to be reasonable. The possibility appears to be extremely remote. The war made certain sacrifices inevitable—one of them was that no section of the community should try and profit from the circumstances it created in order to further its own particular interests.

From this point of view, the 9 Thermidor was, indeed, a *journée de dupes* for the sans-culottes. Disillusioned by the effect of the maximum, discontented with the Revolutionary Government, they failed to realize that its collapse would also involve their own ruin. Ten months later, their resistance weakened by the effects of famine and the high cost of living, realizing at last what they had lost, they demanded a return to a controlled economy, rose in insurrection for the last time only to be completely crushed and swept from the stage of history.

The internal contradictions of the sans-culotterie, however, do not entirely explain the collapse of the popular movement: its gradual disintegration was inscribed in the dialectical march of history itself. The indirect attacks of the Committees and the consolidation of the Revolutionary Government, the drama of Germinal and the feeling of deception which followed, only partly explain its weakness. It was, in fact, inevitable that the popular movement should have lost momentum: its development, its very success, only strengthened those factors which finally contributed to its defeat.

There was, in the first place, a reason of a biological nature. Most of the militants had been actively engaged in the revolutionary struggle since 14 July 1789; they had participated in every insurrection. Since 10 August 1792, they had redoubled their activity. But the enthusiasm and excitement of the great *journées* involved a certain expenditure of nervous energy which, after the victory, increased the tension and strain involved in the daily life of the militant. Five years of revolution had drained the physical resources of the sectionary personnel who provided the cadres of the popular movement. It was only natural that this physical exhaustion which, at different times, forced many of the leading figures of the Revolution—Robespierre himself in Messidor—to retire momentarily from the political scene, should not also have affected the militants always in the thick of the battle. Robespierre had predicted that as the war dragged on, the people would begin to 'show signs of apathy'. This apathy communicated itself to the popular movement, depriving it of its vigour and initial enthusiasm.

There was also a psychological reason arising out of the events of the Year II. The end of the civil war, the halt to the invasion, and, finally, the realization of victory, led to an understandable relaxation of tension. This was true of the population as a whole, although the relief felt by the bourgeoisie cannot be explained by the end of the Terror alone—there was also the prospect of an end to the economic policy of controls and fixed prices, as well as the return of administrative and governmental authority into the hands of the *notables*. The people were anxious to reap the benefits of all their effort. The opening of a register in the Section de la Montagne for new adherents to the Constitution cannot be regarded simply as a political manœuvre: in the eyes of the militants, the *Acte constitutionnel* of June 1793 was the symbol of social democracy; they had continuously campaigned for the right to receive public relief and the right to instruction. But the majority of the people were primarily concerned with their right to subsist. Since victory was at last in sight, they expected, if not exactly abundance, then, at least, less difficulty in being provided with food as well as a guaranteed daily supply of bread. In fact, victory led to the demobilization of the popular movement.

The Parisian sans-culotterie were also weakened from month to month by the dialectical effect of the war effort. The conscription of 300,000 men, the recruitment for the Vendée, then for the Eure, the *levée en masse* and the creation of the Revolutionary Army, deprived the Sections of a considerable number of the youngest, most active, often the most conscientious and enthusiastic patriots who regarded the defence of the nation as their first civic duty. In order to assess the vitality of the popular movement, an exact calculation of the number of men who enlisted for the various campaigns would clearly be of the greatest possible advantage. But, if we cannot attempt a general study, we can, at least, gain some idea of the significance of the loss of human energy suffered by the Parisian Sections in 1793. In the Section des Piques, which had 3,540 voters aged 21 and over in the Year II, 233 volunteers enrolled for the Vendée from 3 to 17 May 1793 alone—mainly sans-culottes in the prime of life. The lists of citizens capable of carrying arms drawn up by the Sections underlines this sapping of the armed strength of the Sections: men of over 50 and, occasionally, of 60 years of age represent a large proportion of the companies formed. Out of the 3,231 men in the Section de Quatre-Vingt-Douze, 767 (23·7 per cent.) were over 50 years of age. In the Section des Arcis, the companies totalled 2,986 men 'of whom, a quarter would have to be subtracted' of men aged over 60.[1] The popular movement grew old as a result of these successive enrolments: the inevitable effect on the revolutionary enthusiasm and combative keenness of the Parisian masses can readily be appreciated.

[1] *A.N.*, AA 15, d. 783. Lists by Section of citizens capable of carrying arms.

Finally, the dialectical effect of success led to a gradual disintegration of the framework of the popular movement. Many of the sectionary militants, even if they were not motivated by ambition alone, regarded an official position as the legitimate reward for their militant activity. The stability of the popular movement largely depended upon the satisfaction of these personal interests which happened to coincide with the need for purging the various committees. But, in such cases, success breeds a new conformity, as the example of the *commissaires révolutionnaires* illustrates. At first, their revolutionary ardour had distinguished them from the other members of the political organizations of the Sections. But since they had been recruited chiefly from the lowest social ranks of the sans-culotterie, it became necessary, even for the success of the Revolution, for them to be paid a salary. The fear of losing their position, just as much as the strengthening of the Revolutionary Government, soon turned them into willing instruments of the central power. Throughout the Year II, many of the militants were transformed into salaried civil servants as a result of this process, which was not only a necessary outcome of the internal evolution of the sans-culotterie, but also of the intensification of the class struggle within France and on her frontiers. The really politically-minded elements of the sans-culotterie became part of the administrative machinery of the State; the sectionary organizations suffered a corresponding loss of political activity, allowance having been made for the accumulated demands of national defence. At the same time, the democratic ideal was being weakened in the Sections, the process of bureaucratization gradually paralysing the critical spirit and activity of the masses. The eventual outcome was a relaxation of the control exercised by the popular movement over the Revolutionary Government which became increasingly authoritarian in character. This bureaucratic encroachment deprived the sans-culottes of many of the channels through which the popular movement had operated.

These various considerations—which have a far wider application than to the events of the Year II—account for the weakening of the popular movement, and clearly precipitated its collapse.

It would be wrong, however, to draw up a purely negative balance sheet of the popular movement in the Year II. Doubtless it was impossible for it to attain its particular objective—the egalitarian and popular republic towards which the sans-culottes were moving without any clearly defined programme—prevailing circumstances as well as its own contradictions raised far too many obstacles. Nevertheless, the popular movement has still contributed towards historical progress by its decisive intervention in support of the bourgeois revolution.

Without the Parisian sans-culotterie, the bourgeoisie could not have triumphed in so radical a fashion. From 1789 to the Year II, the sans-culottes were used as an effective weapon of revolutionary combat and national defence. In 1793, the popular movement made possible the installation of the Revolutionary Government and, consequently, the defeat of the counter-revolution in France and the allied coalition in Europe. It was the Thermidoreans who really benefited from this victory; and if they failed to use their advantage to secure peace, it was because the decision to abandon a controlled economy, added to the demoralization of the troops totally deprived of supplies, paralysed the army and gave the enemy the necessary time to prepare new campaigns. This contrast helps us to appreciate the work of the Revolutionary Government as well as the importance of the popular movement of the Year II.

If we widen the perspective, its intervention in the course of history does not appear to be less significant. The success of the popular movement during the summer of 1793 led to the organization of the Terror which struck such an irreparable blow to the old social order. The upper bourgeoisie of the *ancien régime*, founded on commercial capital and linked in some ways with the old social and political system of the feudal aristocracy, failed to survive the upheaval. In the Year II, the shopkeeper and craftsman element of the sans-culotterie, its leading members drawn from the ranks of the small independent producers (this is proved by the analysis of the Parisian *comités révolutionnaires*), became the most effective weapon in the struggle for the destruction of outmoded methods of production and the social relationships founded upon them. Thermidor was, in fact, the signal for an economic as well as a political reaction; for, by this time, the Terror had cleared the way for the introduction of new relationships of production. In the capitalist society born of the Revolution, industry was destined to dominate commerce: the function of commercial capital, against which the sans-culottes had fought so bitterly in the Year II, would be subordinated henceforth to the sole productive form of capital—industrial capital.

As for the sans-culottes themselves, the economic evolution would eventually lead to a new division of their ranks. Of the small and fairly substantial producers and merchants who had filled the leading positions in the popular movement from 1793–4, some would succeed and become industrial capitalists, others would be eliminated to swell the ranks of the wage-earners. Many would retain their interest in the workshop and the store. Economic freedom accelerated the concentration of small concerns, transforming the material conditions of social life, but altering, at the same time, the structure of the so-called 'popular' classes. Craftsmen and *compagnons* had a dim awareness of the fate which awaited them (for one craftsman who would succeed in industry, how many were destined to fail?), the latter realizing that mechanization would increase the risks of unemployment; the former that capitalist concentration would lead to the closing down of their workshops and transform them into wage-earners. Throughout the nineteenth century, both craftsmen and shop-keepers defended themselves desperately against this threat. It would be interesting to know, in this respect, the part played by the proletariat—in the accepted meaning of the word—from the *journées* of 1848 to the Commune of 1871, and that played by the popular classes of the traditional type. This information would enable us to measure the disintegration of the latter faced with the triumph of industrial capitalism and to emphasize by so doing one of the causes for the failure of revolutionary attempts in the nineteenth century.

Thus, as we are reminded of the dramatic character of class struggles in the Year II by an examination of their ultimate consequences, so we are able to distinguish more clearly the original characteristics of the national history of contemporary France.

APPENDIX I

Historical Table of the Parisian Sections from
21 May 1790–19 Vendémiaire Year IV

1. *Section des Tuileries* (1790–Year IV).
2. *Section des Champs-Elysées* (1790–Year IV).
3. *Section du Roule* (1790–October 1792), *de la République* (October 1792–30 Prairial Year III), *du Roule* (30 Prairial Year III–Year IV).
4. *Section du Palais-Royal* (1790–August 1792), *de la Butte-des-Moulins* (August 1792–August 1793), *de la Montagne* (August 1793–21 Frimaire Year III), *de la Butte-des-Moulins* (21 Frimaire Year III–Year IV).
5. *Section de la Place-Vendôme* (1790–September 1792), *des Piques* (September 1792–5 Prairial Year III), *de la Place-Vendôme* (5 Prairial Year III–Year IV).
6. *Section de la Bibliothèque* (1790–September 1792), *de Quatre-Vingt-Douze* (September 1792–October 1793), *Lepeletier* (October 1793–Year IV).
7. *Section de la Grange-Batelière* (1790–August 1792), *Mirabeau* (August–December 1792), *du Mont-Blanc* (December 1792–Year IV).
8. *Section du Louvre* (1790–6 May 1793), *du Muséum* (6 May 1793–Year IV).
9. *Section de l'Oratoire* (1790–September 1792), *des Gardes-Françaises* (September 1792–Year IV).
10. *Section de la Halle-au-Blé* (1790–Year IV).
11. *Section des Postes* (1790–18 August 1792), *du Contrat-Social* (18 August 1792–Year IV).
12. *Section de la Place-Louis XIV* (1790–August 1792), *du Mail* (August 1792–September 1793), *de Guillaume-Tell* (September 1793–Messidor Year III), *du Mail* (Messidor Year III–Year IV).
13. *Section de la Fontaine-Montmorency* (1790–October 1792), *de Molière-et-Lafontaine* (October 1792–12 September 1793), *de Brutus* (12 September 1793–Year IV).

14. *Section de Bonne-Nouvelle* (1790–Year IV).
15. *Section du Ponceau* (1790–September 1792) *des Amis-de-la-Patrie* (September 1792–Year IV).
16. *Section de Mauconseil* (1790–August 1792), *de Bon-Conseil* (August 1792–Year IV).
17. *Section du Marché-des-Innocents* (1790–September 1792), *des Halles* (September 1792–May 1793), *des Marchés* (May 1793–Year IV).
18. *Section des Lombards* (1790–Year IV).
19. *Section des Arcis* (1790–Year IV).
20. *Section du Faubourg-Montmartre* (1790–Year IV).
21. *Section Poissonnière* (1790–Year IV).
22. *Section de Bondy* (1790–Year IV).
23. *Section du Temple* (1790–Year IV).
24. *Section de Popincourt* (1790–Year IV).
25. *Section de Montreuil* (1790–Year IV).
26. *Section des Quinze-Vingts* (1790–Year IV).
27. *Section des Gravilliers* (1790–Year IV).
28. *Section du Faubourg-Saint-Denis* (1790–January 1793), *du Faubourg-du-Nord* (January 1793–Year IV).
29. *Section de Beaubourg* (1790–September 1792), *de la Réunion* (September 1792–Year IV).
30. *Section des Enfants-Rouges* (1790–September 1792), *du Marais* (September 1792–June 1793), *de l'Homme-Armé* (June 1793–Year IV).
31. *Section du Roi-de-Sicile* (1790–August 1792), *des Droits-de-l'Homme* (August 1792–Year IV).
32. *Section de l'Hôtel-de-Ville* (1790–21 August 1792), *de la Maison-Commune* (21 August 1792–Fructidor Year II), *de la Fidélité* (Fructidor Year II–Year IV).
33. *Section de la Place-Royale* (1790–August 1792), *des Fédérés* (August 1792–4 July 1793), *de l'Indivisibilité* (4 July 1793–Year IV).
34. *Section de l'Arsenal* (1790–Year IV).
35. *Section de l'Ile-Saint-Louis* (1790–November 1792), *de la Fraternité* (November 1792–Year IV).
36. *Section Notre-Dame* or *de l'Ile* (1790–August 1792), *de la Cité* (August 1792–21 Brumaire Year II), *de la Raison* (21–25 Brumaire Year II), *de la Cité* (25 Brumaire Year II–Year IV).
37. *Section Henri IV* (1790–14 August 1792), *du Pont-Neuf* (14

August 1792–7 September 1793), *Révolutionnaire* (7 September 1793–10 Frimaire Year III), *du Pont-Neuf* (10 Frimaire Year III–Year IV).

38. *Section des Invalides* (1790–Year IV).

39. *Section de la Fontaine-de-Grenelle* (1790–Year IV).

40. *Section des Quatre-Nations* (1790–April 1793), *de l'Unité* (April 1793–Year IV).

41. *Section du Théâtre-Français* (1790–August 1792), *de Marseille* (August 1792–August 1793), *de Marseille-et-Marat* (August 1792–Pluviôse Year II), *de Marat* (Pluviôse Year II–22 Pluviôse Year III), *du Théâtre-Français* (22 Pluviôse Year III–Year IV).

42. *Section de la Croix-Rouge* (1790–3 October 1793), *du Bonnet-Rouge* (3 October 1793–Germinal Year III), *du Bonnet-de-la-Liberté* (Germinal–Prairial Year III), *de l'Ouest* (Prairial Year III–Year IV).

43. *Section du Luxembourg* (1790–Brumaire Year II), *de Mutius-Scaevola* (Brumaire Year II–Prairial Year III), *du Luxembourg* (Prairial Year III–Year IV).

44. *Section des Thermes-de-Julien* (1790–8 September 1792), *de Beaurepaire* (8 September 1792–20 Pluviôse Year II), *Chalier* (20 Pluviôse Year II–Pluviôse Year III), *des Thermes-de-Julien* (Pluviôse Year III–Year IV).

45. *Section de Sainte-Geneviève* (1790–August 1792), *du Panthéon-Français* (August 1792–Year IV).

46. *Section de l'Observatoire* (1790–Year IV).

47. *Section du Jardin-des-Plantes* (1790–August 1792), *des Sans-Culottes* (August 1792–10 Ventôse Year III), *du Jardin-des-Plantes* (10 Ventôse Year III–Year IV).

48. *Section des Gobelins* (1790–August 1792), *du Finistère* (August 1792–Year IV).

APPENDIX II

Abridged Table of the Relationship between the Republican and Gregorian Calendars

YEAR II

Vendémiaire	*Brumaire*	*Frimaire*
1–22 September 1793	1–22 October	1–21 November
9–30 ,, ,,	10–31 ,,	10–30 ,,
10– 1st October	11– 1st November	11– 1st December.
20–11 ,,	20–10 ,,	20–10 ,,
30–21 ,,	30–20 ,,	30–20 ,,

Nivôse	*Pluviôse*	*Ventôse*
1–21 December	1–20 January	1–19 February
11–31 ,,	12–31 ,,	10–28 ,,
12– 1st January 1794	13– 1st February	11– 1st March
20– 9 ,, ,,	20– 8 ,,	20–10 ,,
30–19 ,, ,,	30–18 ,,	30–20 ,,

Germinal	*Floréal*	*Prairial*
1–21 March	1–20 April	1–20 May
11–31 ,,	11–30 ,,	12–31 ,,
12– 1st April	12– 1st May	13– 1st June
20– 9 ,,	20– 9 ,,	20– 8 ,,
30–19 ,,	30–19 ,,	30–18 ,,

Messidor	*Thermidor*	*Fructidor*
1–19 June	1–19 July	1–18 August
12–30 ,,	13–31 ,,	14–31 ,,
13– 1st July	14– 1st August	15– 1st September
20– 8 ,,	20– 7 ,,	20– 6 ,,
30–18 ,,	30–17 ,,	30–16 ,,

17, 18, 19, 20, 21 September 1794—1st, 2nd, 3rd, 4th, 5th *jours complémentaires* Year II.

YEAR III

Vendémiaire	*Brumaire*	*Frimaire*
1–22 September 1794	1– 22 October	1–21 November
9–30 ,, ,,	10–31 ,,	10–30 ,,
10– 1st October	11– 1st November	11– 1st December
20–11 ,,	20–10 ,,	20–10 ,,
30–21 ,,	30–20 ,,	30–20 ,,

Nivôse	*Pluviôse*	*Ventôse*
1–21 December	1–20 January	1–19 February
11–31 ,,	12–31 ,,	10–28 ,,
12– 1st January 1795	13– 1st February	11– 1st March
20– 9 ,, ,,	20– 8 ,,	20–10 ,,
30–19 ,, ,,	30–18 ,,	30–20 ,,

Germinal	Floréal	Prairial
1–21 March	1–20 April	1–20 May
11–31 ,,	11–30 ,,	12–31 ,,
12– 1st April	12– 1st May	13– 1st June
20– 9 ,,	20– 9 ,,	20– 8 ,,
30–19 ,,	30–19 ,,	30–18 ,,
Messidor	Thermidor	Fructidor
1–19 June	1–19 July	1–18 August
12–30 ,,	13–31 ,,	14–31 ,,
13– 1st July	14– 1st August	15– 1st September
20– 8 ,,	20– 7 ,,	20– 6 ,,
30–18 ,,	30–17 ,,	30–16 ,,

17, 18, 19, 20, 21, 22 September 1795—1st, 2nd, 3rd, 4th, 5th, and 6th *jours complémentaires* Year III.

GLOSSARY

arrondissement—unit of local administration which may be compared to an electoral ward.

bas-de-soie—literally, wearers of silk hosiery, but more broadly used by the sans-culottes to denote the well-to-do.

buveurs de sang—'bloodthirsty militants', frequently applied to describe all the political personnel of the Sections in the Year II.

canaille—term of abuse directed at the lower ranks of society, the 'mob' or 'rabble'.

certificat de civisme—documentary evidence testifying to the political orthodoxy and civic responsibility of citizens.

commissaire aux accaparements—official appointed to deal with problems relating to food-supplies such as hoarding.

commission des salpêtres—committees concerned with the collection of saltpetre, indispensable for the war-effort.

compagnons—workers attached to a particular trade who had completed the customary tour of France gaining experience.

culottes dorées—literally, wearers of fancy trousers or breeches, but again more generally used for the well-to-do.

décade—the ten-day week created in accordance with the new Republican Calendar introduced in the autumn of 1793—each tenth day of the week being the *décadi*.

enragés—a term denoting the followers of Jaques Roux and Varlet who preached the doctrine of the *loi agraire*, violently denouncing monopolists and speculators.

hommes aux quarante sols—citizens who received forty *sous* for attending each meeting of the general assembly of the Section in which they lived as compensation for the loss of working time involved.

honnêtes gens—ironic and derogatory term adopted by the sans-culottes to denigrate the more affluent or cultured members of society.

indigents secourus—destitute citizens receiving assistance from the authorities.

insouciants—thoughtless or politically indifferent citizens.

journées—days marked by popular riots or insurrections such as 5 October 1789 or 10 August 1792.

loi agraire—a term used to describe the forced subdivision of large agricultural estates in favour of the small independent producer.

meneurs—leading militant figures in the Sections.

métayage—the leasing of farms on condition that the owner received an agreed portion of the crops.

muscadins—elegantly dressed citizens, also somewhat foppish in their behaviour.

Père Duchesne—popular newspaper edited by Hébert, effective exponent of literary demagogy.

possédants—not to be identified with any precise social class, but 'property-owners' of any kind.

représentants en mission—deputies chosen by the Government to fulfil certain assignments in the provinces or with the armies.

sociétés sectionnaires—popular societies of the Sections created to circumvent the law suppressing the meetings of the general assemblies in September 1793.

Droit à l'existence and *l'égalité des jouissances*, see p. 55.

comités civils, pp. 188–92.

comités révolutionnaires, pp. 180–4.

INDEX OF NAMES

INDEX OF SUBJECTS

POPULAR SOCIETIES

Amis-de-la-Liberte-et-de-l'Egalité (*société des*) (Section de l'Indivisibilité), 218.

Amis-de-la-Liberté, de l'Egalité-et-de-l'Humanité (*société des,* sometimes referred to as société de-la-rue-du-Vert-Bois) (Section des Gravilliers), 195–6, 215.

Amis-de-la-République-Française (*société populaire des*) (Section des Piques), 197, 198, 202.

Amis-de-la-Patrie (*société populaire et fraternelle des*) (Section des Amis-de-la-Patrie), 195, 197–203, 224, 239.

Amis-de-la-République-une-et-indivisible (*société des*) (Section du Contrat-Social), 108, 201.

Amis-de-la-section-de-la-Bibliothèque (*société des,* then *société patriotique de la*), 215, 219.

Amis-de-l'Egalité (*société populaire des*) (Section de la Réunion), 208, 213, 218.

Amis-des-Droits-de-l'Homme, Ennemis-du-Despotisme (*société fraternelle des*) (Section de Montreuil), 196, 198.

Arcis (*société populaire, fraternelle et républicaine des*) (Section des Arcis), 215, 218.

Bon-Conseil (*société republicaine de*) (Section de Bon-Conseil), 218.

Bonne-Nouvelle (*société populaire de*) (Section de Bonne-Nouvelle), 30, 90.

Brutus (*société populaire de*) (Section de Brutus), 209, 211, 213.

Butte-des-Moulins (*société patriotique de la*) (Section de la Montagne), 201, 218.

Club électoral or *Club central des Electeurs du département de Paris* or *Club de l'Evêché,* 196, 206.

Comité central des sociétés populaires, occasionally, *Club central,* 205–6.

Contrat-Social (*société populaire du*) (Section du Contrat-Social), 195.

Défenseurs-de-la-République-une-et-indivisible (*société des*), 154, 196, 218.

Défenseurs des Droits de l'Homme (*société populaire des*) (Section de la Maison-Commune), 196.

Droits de l'Homme (*société populaire de la section des*), 208, 218.

Gardes-Françaises (*société populaire des*) (Section des Gardes-Françaises), 196, 198.

Gravilliers (*société populaire des*) (Section des Gravilliers), 196.

Halle-au-Blé (*société populaire de la section de la*), 198, 200, 201.

Homme-Armé (*société fraternelle* or *club républicain de la section de l'*), 201, 204, 213.

Hommes-Libres (*société populaire des*) (Section Révolutionnaire), 87, 140, 197, 200, 204, 208, 209, 214–17, 219, 220.

Hommes-du-14-Juillet, formerly *Gardes-Françaises* (*société des*), 196.

Hommes-Révolutionnaires-du-10-Aout (*société des*), 196.

Lazowski (*société fraternelle de*) (Section du Finistère), 50, 94.

SECTIONS